Advance Praise for *Religicide*

"This is a timely and richly informed reminder of the central place that religious and cultural conflict has in our contemporary world. It is also a reminder of how religion can be misused to attack the liberal secularism upon which we depend to protect our human rights."

—**Sir Simon Schama**, University Professor of History and Art History at Columbia University

"Naming something gives us the power to fight it. That's what White and Bennett do in their call to name the violence against religious groups like Yazidis, Uyghurs and Rohingya. And you'll see why protecting religion is a moral imperative for the most secular of global power brokers."

—**Erin Burnett**, News Anchor, *Outfront, CNN*

"*Religicide* offers a visionary and pragmatic road-map to curb religiously motivated violence. The authors transcend conventional foreign policy wisdom by proposing unprecedented engagement of religious leaders and civil society to cultivate peace, justice, and healing for the communities most at risk."

—**Queen Noor of Jordan** Author, *Leap of Faith*

"This timely book offers an opportunity for policymakers, activists, and diverse religious leaders to dive deeper into the underlying causes of anti-religious violence. Georgette Bennett and Jerry White call for dynamic, cross-border, cross-sector collaboration to put an end to religicide—heretofore unrecognized as a distinct crime under international law."

—**Zeid Ra'ad al Hussein**, Former UN High Commissioner for Human Rights

"How can our conflicted, crisis-plagued world, where over 80 percent of people identify with some religion, have a healthier, more peaceful future that respects our pluralist reality? The global achievements of Georgette Bennett and Jerry White in both religious and secular spheres give their answer unique credibility and weight. They not only offer a prophetic, realistic, and well-researched response to the ways in which religions are being horrendously and increasingly persecuted today; they also propose a practical solution that they themselves have begun to realize. Their vision of how a Global Covenant of Religions can in practice mobilize towards a better global future is the wisdom our century most needs."

—**David F. Ford OBE**, Regius Professor of Divinity Emeritus University of Cambridge

"As a lawyer and diplomat who has had to navigate myriad global violations of religious freedom, I deeply appreciate Bennett and White's well-grounded book, which courageously tackles the alarmingly growing form of violence: Religicide. This sophisticated analysis identifies the gaps in human rights law and provides realistic correctives for those gaps. As has been the case time and again in these authors' distinguished careers, *Religicide* pulls no punches in revealing the limits of the UN and other international bodies on which we depend for security. But its prescription for derailing anti-religious violence goes far beyond officialdom to tap the economic, political, and social resources, local and national, that can be mobilized in a comprehensive covenant to protect oppressed religious groups. *Religicide* is a must-read for diplomats, policy makers, religious leaders, scholars, and anyone who cares about human rights and religious freedom."

—**Rabbi David Saperstein**, former U.S. Ambassador-at-Large for International Religious Freedom and Director Emeritus, Religion Action Center of Reform Judaism

"Religicide is a new word for an old problem. Nevertheless, we are witnessing acts of violence perpetrated against religious minorities at a scale not seen in centuries. The authors of this indispensable volume have not only documented these crimes, they have given the victims a voice and offered some measure of hope for the world's most vulnerable religious communities. This is a timely and invaluable treatise."

—**Reza Aslan**, author of *No god but God* and *Zealot: The Life and Times of Jesus of Nazareth*

RELIGICIDE

RELIGICIDE

Confronting the Roots
of Anti-Religious Violence

GEORGETTE F. BENNETT
AND JERRY WHITE

A POST HILL PRESS BOOK
ISBN: 978-1-63758-101-8
ISBN (eBook): 978-1-63758-102-5

Religicide:
Confronting the Roots of Anti-Religious Violence
© 2022 by Georgette F. Bennett and Jerry White
All Rights Reserved

Cover design by Tiffani Shea

Post Hill Press
New York • Nashville
posthillpress.com

Published in the United States of America
1 2 3 4 5 6 7 8 9 10

TABLE OF CONTENTS

We dedicate this book to survivors of religicide worldwide.

We bow to our ancestors and to our wise spouses,

Leonard Selwyn Polonsky and Kelly Gammon White.

We bless and pray for the rising generation.

FOREWORD BY ZEID RA'AD AL HUSSEIN

Zeid Ra'ad Al Hussein served as the United Nations High Commissioner for Human Rights (2014-2018) and as Jordan's Ambassador to the United Nations (2000-2007, 2010-2014) and the United States (2007-2010). He represented Jordan before the International Court of Justice and played a key role in the establishment of the International Criminal Court (ICC). He currently serves as President of the International Peace Institute (IPI) and a Professor of Practice of Law and Human Rights at the University of Pennsylvania.

This book focuses on protecting a particular set of rights: those associated with religion—our freedom to believe what we believe and our responsibility to protect religious groups and Indigenous minorities who face existential threats. This is an urgent matter for attention and action.

There were historic negotiations in the 1960s to establish a UN Convention on the Elimination of All Forms of Religious Intolerance, but they failed to materialize. To this day, those negotiations remain the most ambitious UN attempt to make religion a subject of international law. In 1960, the stage had been set for the development of a convention with the negotiation of the

International Covenant on Civil and Political Rights to end religious intolerance. Article 18 of this covenant is specifically worded to protect freedom of religion and belief worldwide:

1. Everyone shall have the right to freedom of thought, conscience, and religion. This right shall include freedom to have or to adopt a religion or belief of his choice, and freedom, either individually or in community with others and in public or private, to manifest his religion or belief in worship, observance, practice, and teaching.

2. No one shall be subject to coercion which would impair his freedom to have or to adopt a religion or belief of his choice.

3. Freedom to manifest one's religion or beliefs may be subject only to such limitations as are prescribed by law and are necessary to protect public safety, order, health, or morals or the fundamental rights and freedoms of others.

The authors believe this remains insufficient and argue that there ideally ought to be a new international legal instrument with a new Global Covenant devoted to the protection of religious minorities and their sacred heritage. After all, the earlier and unsuccessful draft convention against religious discrimination endeavored to reach much further than the International Covenant on Civil and Political Rights. For example, it proposed *the freedom to learn about religions*; in other words, the freedom to recognize that other narratives also exist.

When I first was asked to consider "religicide" as a category of threat—the intentional murder of a religion, its followers, and their heritage—I was less than three months away from taking up my assignment as UN High Commissioner for Human Rights. I believed that this issue merited discussion and have therefore welcomed this timely contribution by Jerry White and Georgette Bennett, whom I've known for nearly four decades combined. While I may not agree with them on every point, I fully recognize the extent to which these two authors are formidable advocates for interreligious engagement, humanitarian action, and social justice. Both have led game-changing initiatives to prevent violence and promote human rights.

I first met Jerry White in 1998 when he led the Landmine Survivors Network. Jerry proved himself a persuasive advocate with an irreverent sense of humor. Jerry shares in the 1997 Nobel Peace Prize, awarded to the International Campaign to Ban Landmines. An amputee landmine survivor himself, he joined forces with Princess Diana during the last year of her life, escorting her on what was to be her last humanitarian mission to Bosnia and Herzegovina, a heavily mine-affected country, just three weeks before she tragically died in Paris. Inspired by her gift of courageous compassion, the landmine movement proved a remarkable success in terms of impact after her death, with tens of thousands of victims receiving care, tens of millions of mines cleared and destroyed in national stockpiles, and more than 160 countries joining the historic 1997 Mine Ban Treaty. Jerry and I later collaborated on other high-impact campaigns, such as the UN Convention on the Rights of Persons with Disabilities. How many people can say they were in the room where it happened— privileged to cocreate historic treaties that affected hundreds of millions of lives? Jerry White has been in rooms where a lot gets done.

He was appointed US deputy assistant secretary of state under President Barack Obama and used the levers of government to launch a new Bureau of Conflict and Stabilization Operations. In government service, he wasted no time to enact innovative reforms. Within three years, his team of data-driven diplomats became super-forecasters who outperformed several US intelligence agencies that participated in government competitions to predict with high accuracy fast-breaking global events.

Georgette Bennett, like Jerry, is friendly and fierce. Her work as a criminologist, human rights activist, and peacebuilder has garnered international recognition, including the OLAM–Society for International Development Israel Branch Global Impact Award, *Forbes* 50 Over 50, and the prestigious AARP Purpose Prize, known as the genius prize for those over fifty. Upon completing her PhD, Georgette embarked on a career that had nothing to do with religion and everything to do with crime. She expanded the role of women in law enforcement, did pioneering work in community policing—which is now practiced in countries around the world, including Jordan—successfully lobbied for the first sex crimes unit in the United States, and helped launch the victims' rights movement with the idea for the first federally funded crime victim service center.

As a criminologist, she became interested in the link between religion and violence. Her late husband, Rabbi Marc Tanenbaum, was a driving force in the interreligious reconciliation movement and a renowned human rights activist. After he died in 1992, Georgette founded the Tanenbaum Center for Interreligious Understanding, an organization that works to combat religious prejudice and violence.

In 2013, Georgette became immersed in addressing the Syrian humanitarian crisis and wanted to focus her efforts on aiding Syrian refugees in Jordan. I advised Georgette to consider an interreligious approach to the crisis, and I provided a private briefing to a group of select organizations gathering to launch the Multifaith Alliance for Syrian Refugees (MFA) in 2013. Today, the Alliance is made up of more than one hundred partner organizations delivering aid to more than 2.3 million displaced Syrians. Georgette revealed the unlikely story of the partnerships she fostered and the geopolitical obstacles she overcame in her book, *Thou Shalt Not Stand Idly By: How One Woman Confronted the Greatest Humanitarian Crisis of Our Time.*

With these two authors joining forces to focus on how to end what they call religicide, we are well-advised to listen to their urgent call to action. Killing in the name of religion—or being killed because of your religion—continues unabated. There are warning signs everywhere that anti-religious violence is a fast-spreading threat to humanity.

This timely book offers an opportunity for policymakers, activists, and diverse religious leaders to dive deeper into the underlying causes of anti-religious violence. Georgette Bennett and Jerry White call for dynamic, cross-border, cross-sector collaboration to put an end to religicide—heretofore unrecognized as a distinct crime under international law. I know from decades of professional experience how difficult it will be to expand categories of international law that cover a range of intersectional crimes, from genocide (well-defined), ecocide (recently proposed), and what they call "factocide" (defined as a battle for truth).

Their findings will no doubt challenge governments, civil society, and business leaders who have started to think more seriously about human rights and the role of religion in economics. Building a coalition across sectors—working with faith leaders, civil societies, policymakers, and corporations—will help raise the stakes for collective efforts to prevent the proliferation of religion-related violence. This is an ambitious and hopeful proposal to mobilize a truly concerted effort appropriately led by Indigenous survivors of religicide. It will take several years to build a movement to enact the hoped-for Global Covenant of Religions to reverse current trends. That said, this timely push, including its attention to climate crises, might just deliver the sort of creative shock therapy needed to confront the systemic roots of religiously motivated violence.

Defining religicide is only one of the daunting challenges we face. Then comes the hard part: how to admit our collective failings and work toward systemic reform. It is all easier said than done. Specifically, we can protect our diverse neighbors by learning how to respect those who believe and look differently than we do. We need to expand and extend protections for ethno-religious groups denied equal rights and citizenship. We need to be more than bystanders or legal analysts. We must commit to interrupting violence, not just observing it. To start, perhaps our hearts must be broken open with compassion as we watch as members of our human family—our brothers and sister—are violated through no fault of their own. Now is the time for us to stand with courage, dignity, and respect for human rights and join in solidarity to interrupt the emergence of new strains of anti-religious violence accelerated by advanced technology and artificial intelligence in the world today.

Chapter One

A PROBLEM WITH NO NAME

*I was wandering alone among the crumbling barracks
of Birkenau, part of the Auschwitz complex outside
Krakow, Poland. It is a gray day. With no other person
in sight, I am free to weep and to rage. It is here that
my maternal grandparents literally went up in smoke
before I was born. Their ashes are somewhere beneath
me, layered with decades of topsoil. I felt helpless to do
anything but say Kaddish—the life-affirming Jewish
prayer for the dead. Twenty years later, when I started
working on this book, I began to explore whether my
grandparents had been victims of religicide.*

—Georgette Bennett

Looking at a map of the world, one can stick pins in at least
sixty countries where there are active armed conflicts.
Contemporary violence has killed more than six million people
and displaced more than eighty million, including twenty-six million refugees.

Behind each number is a person whose rights are being violated. Hear some of their voices:

Rahim is a Rohingya high schoolteacher in Myanmar. "I knew
I was dead if I got caught. They were hunting me. They knew that

I would always speak out for the people. They wanted to destroy us, because they knew that without us, they could do whatever they wanted to the rest of the Rohingya."[1]

A Rohingya farmer from Rakhine State, in the westernmost part of Myanmar, lost two sons and two daughters. We must protect his name because he's still under threat. "At midnight, the military come [sic] in my house and burnt the house. But first they raped...shot my two daughters in front of me. I have no words to express how it was for me to suffer, to look at my daughters being raped and killed in front of me. My two sons were also killed by the government. I was not able to get the dead bodies of my daughters. It is a great sorrow for me."[2]

Shireen, a young Yazidi girl from Rambusi village on the south side of Mount Shingal (also known as Sinjar), was forced into sex slavery. She told of being herded to a wedding hall near Shingal town with many other Yazidi families. When everybody was unloaded from trucks, ISIS "sold me to someone in Raqqa city in Syria. In Syria I was tortured. I was sold and bought as a cheap commodity for more than five times.... There were hundreds and thousands of Yazidi girls there being sold as sex slaves."[3]

In 2019, the *New York Times* reported on 150 pages of leaked directives on how the Chinese Communist Party (CCP) planned to control its Uyghur population.[4] These included students returning from university to find that their parents were gone, sent to a "training school set up by the government." Although they weren't criminals, the parents weren't allowed to leave these "schools" because they "had been 'infected' by the 'virus' of Islamic radicalism and must be quarantined and cured."

A Tibetan monk living in Drepung Monastery recalls how members of the Communist Party "burst in, breaking the doors and gates of the colleges and dormitories. The soldiers were armed and equipped with hatchets and hammers, as well as torches, handcuffs, and wire ropes.... They would first ask for phones, which were systematically confiscated."[5]

Steven Charleston, a member of the Choctaw Nation, laments: "In historic memory, we have seen our reality come crashing down as invaders destroyed our homeland. We have lived through genocide, concentration camps, religious persecution, and every human rights abuse imaginable."[6]

These testimonies of inhumane cruelty are not uncommon. Today, there are entire populations and cultures at risk of being wiped out because of their religion. This is modern-day extinction. While violence between states has declined steadily since World War II, there is one insidious strand of violence resurging in the twenty-first century—attacks against people who believe in a god. This violence is either committed in the name of religion itself or in the name of a state or ideology aimed at eradicating a religion. Surprisingly, there is no unique law for this kind of violence. But in order to respond to or prevent a crime, we must first name it.

We call it religicide.

Absent a name, and absent appropriate laws and methods for dealing with religicide, it continues unabated, unrecognized, and unprosecuted.

In 2015, Jordan tried to address these gaps, working with several faith leaders and religious scholars to identify significant fractures in the protection of religion and sacred heritage targeted for eradication.

When the Islamic State (ISIS) emerged in 2012, countries worldwide witnessed modern religicide on fast forward. ISIS targeted all other religions, condemning them to destruction and death. In response, Jordan drafted a UN resolution that defined religicide as a systematic policy of causing "unwanted immigration or displacement of a religious group, sect, or community" or divestment "of its identity based on religious or sectarian motives, even if not committed in relation to an armed conflict." Jordan asserted two primary criminal acts that would comprise religicide:[7]

- Intimidating or threatening religious communities or groups and subjecting them to a humiliating treatment, including making them practice acts contrary to their religious faiths; and
- Confiscating, destroying, or displacing the tangible religious heritage of a religious community or group or otherwise depriving them thereof.[8]

The Jordanian initiative quickly came up against a Western human rights bias that favors a focus on individual rather than group rights. This first attempt to criminalize religicide also faced a perception of legal redundancy. An argument was made that this crime was already covered by international law (specifically, as crimes against humanity as defined in Article 7 of the Rome Statute of the International Criminal Court, discussed in detail later in the book). US State Department lawyers concurred that elements of religicide were already covered by international laws that dealt with religious discrimination and atrocity. Both the United States and United Kingdom are permanent members of the UN Security Council and are mostly loath to recognize group rights, including social and economic rights. They did not see a need for additional legal protections, despite the growing threat of religiously motivated violence proliferating worldwide. In the end, the Jordanian draft resolution against religicide was never sent to the UN Security Council for deliberation.

Consequently, the laws that address human rights violations continue to have significant gaps that allow crimes of religicide to slip through the cracks. Even those laws that could be invoked go unenforced. It is critically important to find new laws and new methods to prevent and respond to this form of fast-growing violence, which threatens billions of believers around the world.

The United Nations, with its 193 member states, recognizes four distinct types of atrocities: war crimes, genocide, crimes against humanity, and ethnic cleansing. None of these is mutually exclusive. The concept of religicide has evolved from and incorporates these other forms of human rights violations. But it has two additional hallmarks—ecocide and factocide.

Ecocide is the destruction of the natural habitat, property, and homes to drive people off their land or make it impossible for them to return or survive in place. In the case of the Islamic State and Abu Bakr Naji's *The Management of Savagery*, the scorched-earth policy fits this criterion. We see systematic destruction of the environment, including poisoned water wells and deforestation of food sources.

Factocide is the deliberate and chronic distortion of truth and dissemination of falsehoods in media and education to dehumanize and incite violence against a religious group. In the modern era, religicide is accelerated through calls for mass slaughter issued through online media channels constructed for, and dedicated to, driving false narratives that incite dominant groups to kill a religious group as a "service" to humanity.

In the chapters that follow, we will parse the difference between religicide and other forms of atrocities and explain the urgency of creating a new category of collective cruelty. We will examine the nightmare of regimes that torture individuals and punish groups for simply believing differently. We will explore several ongoing religicides—criminal cases in which the world can still intervene before it's too late. And we will offer a set of policies and strategies for doing so, including a new covenantal approach that taps the wisdom of Indigenous peoples who align with nature in order to reduce violent conflict and promote the collective healing of survivors.

Conventional wisdom in the West holds that the world is becoming increasingly secular. However, more than 80 percent of the world's people affiliate with a religion. That is more than six billion individuals believing in something bigger than themselves, associating with religious institutions, practicing faith, and professing spiritual beliefs. Religion is not going anywhere soon. On the contrary, the number of religious adherents is growing globally.

The Pew Research Center projects that the world's proportion of the non-religious will shrink from 17 percent today to 13 percent by 2050.[9] This is despite the growing number of "nones" in the United States—now at nearly 30 percent of the population.

Many of us in the United States take our religious freedom for granted—including the right to be free of religion. But consider how might you react to someone forcing their beliefs upon you, let alone punishing you for believing differently? Today, we are witnessing families and communities struggling to simply worship their god and practice their traditions without punishment, persecution, and discrimination.

Religicide is the systematic attempt to eradicate a religion and its followers through forms of persecution that destroy their heritage, culture, and hope. Religicide is designed to wipe out an entire religious community. In the face of such persecution and despair, many in a target group seek to end their own lives. Suicide becomes a form of religicide in slow motion, with rising rates of collective traumatic stress, depression, and existential despair.

Chapter Two

ATROCITIES AND
HUMAN RIGHTS LAW

We believe the existing international instruments are insufficient to combat religicide. Religicide warrants its own category of law that will integrate and build upon previous laws and declarations in order to protect people who believe differently. But one must first understand the existing statutes.

The concept of war crimes dates back more than one hundred years. At that time, international humanitarian law was codified in the Hague Conventions of 1899 and 1907. These early conventions prohibited certain actions between warring parties. Later treaties, such as the Geneva Conventions of 1864, 1949, and 1977, focused on mistreatment of prisoners of war and direct attacks on civilians. In international armed conflicts, the conventions protect those who are not actively taking part in fighting: those who have laid down their arms by virtue of illness, wounds, imprisonment, and other reasons; as well as medics, clergy, humanitarian workers, and civil defense staff. In short, war crimes can be committed against combatants or non-combatants. But the protections are specific to actions between hostile parties during a state of war.

The Syrian war is an obvious and egregious example of war crimes committed against civilian populations and was perpetrated not by one party, but at least three: the Syrian regime,

Russia, and Iran. Iran is managing the ground war. Russia is running the air war. The regime of Bashar al-Assad is driving the domestic terror campaign. As victims of all three, Syrian civilians have been bombed, tortured, starved, raped, and displaced with impunity.

Attacks on medical workers and facilities have been an ongoing feature of Syrian war crimes. Dr. Osman al-Haj Osman, a senior doctor and emergency room physician at Dar al-Shifa hospital in Aleppo, treated civilians who had been wounded in the illegal bombardments. He attested that the Syrian government bombed the hospital six times between August and November 2012, claiming it was a "terrorist hideout." The military gave no warning before the attacks, so there was no opportunity to evacuate patients and save civilian staff.

Essentially, the war in Syria has become a proxy war among competing powers: the United States and Saudi Arabia against Russia and Iran. It does have a religious element, in that the majority Sunni population has revolted against the minority Alawite ruling group. But this does not meet the criteria for religicide.

In contrast to war crimes, genocide is directed at an entire ethnic or racial group—generally civilians. The first genocide of the twentieth century took place during World War I, initiated by Turkey against ethnic Armenians. At that time, there was no name for the mass murder and displacement that later created the model for Hitler's war against the Jews. The Young Turks, committed to creating a racially pure Turkic state, deported and resettled Armenian Christians. More than one million Armenians were murdered and falsely branded as traitors who "collaborated with the enemy." With this justification, Armenians were systematically "driven into the desert where they were raped, shot, starved, poisoned, suffocated, or burned to death."[10]

The unthinkable was made even more awful because Turkish doctors played a central role in organizing the systematic extermination of ethnic Armenians. Defining them as "dangerous microbes," Dr. Mehmed Reshid, the governor as executioner, declared: "Isn't it the duty of a doctor to destroy these microbes?"[11] Destroy them, they did. Foreshadowing the infamous Nazi doctor, Josef Mengele, Turkish physicians sacrificed medical ethics to nationalism by committing medical murder and other atrocities. Physicians had Armenians drowned at sea, butchered them, and subjected to medical experiments.[12]

The Ottomans had suffered defeat after defeat in World War I and needed to find an explanation. They convinced themselves that an enemy within—the "treacherous" Armenians—was collaborating with the Entente countries (France, Britain, Russia, Italy, Japan, and the United States). As such, their annihilation was justified as a military necessity and a proportional response to alleged perfidy. But the brutality of the Ottomans needs to be understood in the context of Turkey's alliance with Germany.

German military advisers and personnel had long been embedded in Turkey and been part of the Ottoman army. Aspects of German military culture had thereby been transferred to Turkey. From the start of the war, the German government was fixated on the possibility of mass civilian resistance. When Germany invaded Belgium, which it viewed as a "reservoir of potential guerrilla fighters," it circulated false stories about atrocities committed against German soldiers. Viewing civilians as legitimate targets of war, Germany pursued a policy of collective punishment against all Belgians.[13] But an even more lethal aspect of German military culture was the equating of victory with annihilation. Lines were blurred between the military and civilians and between normal conduct of war and atrocities.[14]

While the Armenian genocide was not specifically about religion, the mechanisms through which it was carried out are typical of religicide. In religicide, attacks are geared to destroy the presence, heritage, and members of a particular religion inside a country. In the case of Armenians, the primary target was an *ethnic* group, not their orthodox brand of Christianity. Germany, a Christian country itself, was fully aware and complicit in this war against fellow Christians.[15] That war was consistent with its racialist policies.

Germany's silence on the Armenian genocide was one means of solidifying its needed alliance with the Ottoman Empire.

The wholesale slaughter and displacement of Armenians predated the Holocaust by decades. But it was only in the wake of the Holocaust that the world began to grapple with the meaning of "atrocity" in novel ways—ways not contemplated in the earlier war crimes statutes. Two new international offenses entered the vocabulary: genocide and crimes against humanity. Genocide focused on crimes against groups, while the other concept focused on violations of individual rights.

Raphael Lemkin was the first to give voice to the concept of genocide. Lemkin, a Polish Jewish lawyer who lost nearly fifty family members in the Holocaust, led the campaign for genocide to be recognized as a crime under international law. He was supportive of individual rights, but he believed a sole focus on the individual ignored a basic fact: Members of one group often turn against members of another precisely because they are members of a particular group and not because of their individual qualities.

The infamous Nuremberg laws operationalized this idea by specifically targeting *Jews as a race.*

The systemic war against the Jews "officially" began with Kristallnacht on November 9, 1938—a pogrom in which synagogues were torched and Jewish homes and businesses were vandalized throughout Germany. More than ninety Jews were killed by paramilitary forces and civilians while authorities looked on without intervening. The aftermath signaled the beginning of the roundup of Jews. Seven years later, the war ended with two-thirds of Europe's 9.5 million Jews slaughtered and 250,000 of the surviving remnants living in displaced person camps. However, the foundation for Kristallnacht had long existed in the deeply embedded anti-Semitism of Christian Europe.

Although the Holocaust attempted to annihilate Jews and was anti-Judaic, it was not initially an all-out war against Judaism itself. But over time, the Nazi threat became more obvious.

A vast trove of ritual objects and Torah scrolls were preserved in Prague for the purpose of creating a museum of the extinct Jewish race. In discussing religicide, this is an important distinction: was the Holocaust an attack on Judaism or an ill-fated attempt to eliminate the Jewish people as a race? Race versus religion became conflated in the case of the Holocaust. Without Jews, there is no Judaism. Without Judaism, there are no Jews.

The Holocaust was, at its root, a Darwinian, pseudo-scientific race war in which religion was supplanted by a quasi-religious, secular, messianic ideology. It started with blaming Jews for Germany's humiliating defeat in World War I. But it was updated in 1939 when Chaim Weizmann, president of the World Zionist Organization, sent a letter to British Prime Minister Neville Chamberlain affirming that Jews stood with Great Britain and would fight on the side of democracies. But the Zionism that Weizmann espoused was a political Zionism, not a religious Zionism. And the early Zionists were largely secular socialists. Twisting the meaning for their own propaganda purposes, Nazis proclaimed that Jews had declared war on Germany and were backed by an international Jewish conspiracy. Thus, the Nazis justified the Holocaust as self-defense, with Aryans to be seen as the real victims.

The Nazis branded Jews as traitors, making them victims of what we call factocide. They were demonized daily in sophisticated multimedia propaganda campaigns. They became seen as the anti-Christ: children of darkness who had to be defeated by the children of light—racially pure Aryans—in an apocalyptic struggle that would usher in the Thousand-Year Reich. The Führer became the stand-in for the Messiah, intent on eliminating the satanic forces (read: Jews) undermining the Fatherland. As such, he set out to make Germany *judenrein* (free of Jews).

The Jews were just the first of the "inferior races" and "undesirables" that Nazism intentionally targeted for destruction. Slavs, blacks, Roma (and nomadic Indo-Aryan ethnic groups living mostly in Europe), homosexuals, and people with physical and mental disabilities. In her book, *Caste: The Origins of Our Discontents*, Isabel Wilkerson writes at length about Hitler's fascination with US racial practices and the lengths to which we went to segregate whites and African Americans. The dehumanizing racial slur, *Untermensch* (sub-human), came to the Nazis from an American geneticist who wrote about white supremacy and sat in on Nazi sterilization trials.[16] Hitler admired the near genocide against Native Americans and the banishing of survivors to reservations.[17] The Nazis borrowed their miscegenation laws banning intermarriage and intercourse between Jews and Germans from the "association clause" in Texas's and North Carolina's marriage bans.[18]

Beyond race, Hitler planned on the elimination of entire political systems, such as communism, socialism, capitalism, and democracy. Even the clergy and institutions of Christianity were on the list of those to be crushed as the racially pure Aryan master race marched toward world domination and ethno-nationalism overwhelmed the movement of the Confessing Church.[19] Hence, exterminating the Jews was not an end in itself, but a means to the end of subjugating other nations.[20]

Even as the Nazis were losing the war, they stepped up the killing of Jews. This was nowhere more evident than in Hungary, the country of Georgette's birth. Under the supervision of Adolf Eichmann, more than half of Hungary's 825,000 Jews were deported in less than two months in 1944. Most were sent to Auschwitz, where four-fifths were gassed upon arrival—Georgette's grandparents among them.

The genocide flourished and was enabled by the bedrock of centuries-long anti-Semitism. Under Nazi rule, Jews were forbidden to observe their holidays or teach their children about Judaism, a form of cultural genocide with the hallmarks of religicide. German churches, still immersed in the pre-Vatican Council II teaching of contempt for the Jews, were complicit in eliminating all traces of Judaism. After all, wasn't it the Jews who killed Christ? (Short answer: No, it wasn't. It was the Romans.)

The unique attempt to eradicate both a race and its religion included desecration of cemeteries, destruction of synagogues, burning of holy books, and attempts to destroy Jewish heritage and rituals. "The attacks on libraries and archives...were a cultural assault in its broadest sense; it was not merely the religion of the Jews that the Nazi machine sought to eradicate but all aspects of Jewish existence: from living beings to the gravestones of their ancestors," Richard Ovenden wrote in *Burning the Books*.[21]

Most historians and scholars would agree that the twentieth century Shoah combined the desire to annihilate the Jewish people along with all traces of their religion and culture. As such, the Holocaust may be a bridge between the concept of genocide and the broader concept of religicide—and may be considered the first modern religicide.

The Nuremberg trials overturned the idea that sovereign states could act with impunity in committing atrocities—confiscation, pillage, torture, terror, enslavement, persecution, imprisonment, and mass murder—against their own people. In such a case, the international community has a legal basis for responding because these acts violate international law and are "not mere matters of domestic concern."[22]

After Nuremberg, the UN General Assembly adopted Resolution 95, which dealt with crimes against humanity. Resolution 96 came in 1948, affirming genocide—denying the right of existence of entire human groups—as a crime under international law.[23] Article II of the Genocide Convention describes the components of this crime as follows:

- Killing members of the group
- Causing serious bodily or mental harm to members of the group
- Deliberately inflicting conditions of life on the group calculated to bring about its physical destruction in whole or in part

- Imposing measures intended to prevent births within the group
- Forcibly transferring children of the group to another group.

All these elements are also evident in cases of religicide. In both instances, it's a challenge to prosecute these cases because they require proof of intent by the perpetrators to destroy a group in whole or in part. The term "genocide," with its focus on the group, tends to heighten the sense of "them" and "us," burnishing feelings of group identity, giving rise to the very conditions it seeks to address because it pits one group against another. This makes reconciliation unlikely.[24] Religicide is faced with the same challenge but goes further. It needs to demonstrate and prove intentional attacks against sacred heritage and culture, and the removal of a right for individuals and groups to practice their particular religion.

Genocide, however, isn't solely about eradicating an entire religious or ethnic group. It's about clashes between cultures, castes, race, and ethnicity.

In 1994, a genocide took place in the East African country of Rwanda. It was the most compressed genocide of the last century. In a mere one hundred days, eight hundred thousand Tutsis were savagely murdered by the Hutu ethnic majority. Ethnic tensions were rooted in the colonial period when Belgium showed favoritism to the Tutsi minority, sowing deep resentment among the Hutu. A Hutu revolution in 1959 led to the displacement of three hundred thousand Tutsis, and by 1961, the Tutsi monarch was overthrown. In 1990, many of those refugees joined the Rwanda Patriotic Front (RPF) and invaded Rwanda from Uganda. As in the Armenian genocide, the Hutu ruler accused Rwanda's Tutsi residents of being accomplices to the invaders. Government officials ordered massacres, but a ceasefire was declared in 1992 when they reached an agreement to form a power-sharing government that would include Tutsis. But in 1994, a plane carrying the Hutu president was shot down over Kigali, the capital of Rwanda. Within hours, the slaughter of Tutsis began.

Hate-filled radio broadcasts by Radio Rwanda, the official government-owned radio station, and Radio Télévision Libre des Mille Collines (RTLM) incited Hutus to go from house to house, where they butchered Tutsis—people of a different cultural classification. Referring to Tutsis as *inyenzi*, or "cockroaches," and as *inzoka*, or "snakes," the radio stations broadcasted anti-Tutsi disinformation that spread fear of a Tutsi genocide against Hutus and identified specific Tutsi targets. Just a month before the genocide, RTLM's Noël Hitimana gave the first hint over the radio:

> On the day when people rise up and don't want
> you Tutsi anymore, when they hate you as one
> and from the bottom of their hearts...I wonder
> how you will escape.[25]

Claver Irakoze, a Tutsi survivor of the genocide recalls: "I remember RTLM broadcasting songs conveying hatred and demonizing the Tutsi. The songs would openly call for our extermination. Political slogans were translated into song and young people were mobilized into youth movements. These youth movements were the key to executing the genocide."[26] One of these songs was the frequently played "Nanga Abahutu (I Hate Tutsis)," by the popular Hutu singer-songwriter, Simon Bikindi. The International Criminal Tribunal for Rwanda (ICTR) charged

Bikindi with conspiracy to commit genocide and crimes against humanity. Bikindi was tried and convicted for incitement to genocide by the ICTR in 2008. He died in 2018.[27]

Incited by the likes of Bikindi, the Hutus attacked mostly with machetes, hacking men, women, and children to death. Others were buried or burned alive, or clubbed to death. Shockingly, in a country that is 90 percent Christian, Rwanda's churches were the main killing fields. The slaughter was often abetted by clergy who enabled the belief that the Hutus were doing God's will. Death squads were known to attend mass prior to embarking on their grisly work in the name of God. Indeed, some interrupted that work to pray at the altar.[28] That said, the conflict was not driven by religion, nor was it an attempt to wipe out a religion. But its methods and the world's slow response are common in contemporary religicides.

Tutsis and Hutus shared the same religion, but Tutsis enjoyed more privilege. Timothy Longman, in a prescient article on church politics and the Rwandan genocide, points out that religious affiliation is an insignificant determinant of identity in that country. He cites ethnicity and region as far more important. That's where the churches come in. Historically, Christian churches played a significant role in defining ethnic identity in Rwanda and in doling out the status and riches that came with it. As such, they essentially functioned as political institutions. According to Longman, "Christians could kill without obvious qualms of conscience, even in the church, because Christianity as they had always known it had been a religion defined by struggles for power, and ethnicity had always been at the base of those struggles."[29] In the end, eight hundred thousand Tutsis and moderate Hutus were brutally slaughtered by rampaging Hutu extremists over the course of only one hundred days in 1994. The churches stood by silently as the final solution for the Tutsis unfolded, but neither their passivity nor their participation fall under the umbrella of religicide. Why? Because religion was not the driver of the Rwandan genocide. This, in no way, diminishes the atrocities that were committed, but these are already covered by international law, while religicide is not. That said, Rwanda is an example of how politicization of religion can drive the kind of atrocities that lead to religicide.

In July 1998, following the genocides in Bosnia and Rwanda, 150 states signed on to the Rome Statute that set up the International Criminal Court (ICC). The court investigates and, where warranted, tries individuals charged with the gravest crimes of concern to the international community: genocide, war crimes, crimes against humanity, and crimes of aggression. Under the ICC, the meaning of "atrocity" became even more finely parsed. Ethnic cleansing was added to our vocabulary of horrors.

The term "ethnic cleansing" is the literal translation of a Serbo-Croatian term describing a terror tactic used during the Bosnian genocide in the 1990s. Ethnic cleansing is not recognized as an independent crime under international law, but it has been referenced in the actions of the ICC.

Ethnic cleansing has been defined as the attempt to create ethnically homogeneous geographic areas through the deportation or forcible displacement of persons belonging to particular ethnic groups. The geographic element sometimes involves "the removal of all physical vestiges of the targeted group through the destruction of monuments, cemeteries, and houses of worship."[30] Ethnic cleansing is another element of religicide, given that it attacks religious heritage and removes religious groups from their sacred spaces.

In Bosnia, ethnic cleansing took the form of blowing up houses, appropriating property, looting, beatings, systematic rape, concentration camps, and starvation—all focused on killing and displacing so many Muslims that diverse Bosnians could never coexist again. The Serbs, who were the main perpetrators of the slaughter, had learned savage lessons from the Nazi's genocide against the Jews. The systematic spewing of hate, raised to a fever pitch, abruptly transformed neighbors into enemies. The conflict between Bosnian Muslims and Serbians was rooted in historic and political rivalry and clashes that translated into attacks on religious groups.

The media can play an active role in justifying "preventive genocide." By labeling the ethnic others as "enemies," the media put forth the notion that "If we don't kill them, they will kill us." With complete nationalist control of the airwaves, opposing voices were labeled as "traitors" or "foreign mercenaries." Media editors and journalists boosted their patriotic credentials by admitting they were "proud to lie for the homeland."[31] These lies included completely fabricated stories. Examples of this propaganda against Bosnian Muslims were listed in a 2010 symposium paper by Bosnian journalist Kemal Kurspahic:

- *Politika* report of the "Ustasha killing of 41 Serb children in Vukovar"
- Bosnian Serb TV report on "Serb children being fed to the lions in Sarajevo Zoo"
- Croatian daily *Vjesnik* report of "35 Croats hanged [by Bosnian Muslims] in front of the Catholic church in Zenica"

- Belgrade daily *Vecernje Novosti* presenting a 115-year-old painting, exhibited in the Belgrade National Museum, claiming that it was a photograph of a Serb orphan boy whose parents had been killed by Bosnian Muslims.

These made-up stories had one purpose: to instill fear and incite violence against other ethnic groups. This being the early 1990s, there was no internet with which to challenge these stories, nor were there any independent media.[32]

Ironically, in the Nazi era, the Croat Ustashe, a fascist organization with many Muslims members, were the perpetrators and the Serb Chetniks were the victims. Bosnia was attacked by the Axis powers, Germany and Italy, in 1941. During the Nazi era in this region, Serbs were singled out as an enemy race, and Croatia became independent under the rule of the fascist Ustashe. Believing that they had German roots, Ustashe members bought into Nazi theories of racial superiority. The Ustashe, which included a Muslim division of the SS, slaughtered four hundred thousand Croats along with tens of thousands of Jews, Roma, and Communist Partisans. In that era, it was the Serb Chetniks who were the heroes that resisted the Nazis. Of the one million former Yugoslavians who perished during the war, most were Serbs.[33]

With Bosnia's national media cheering on ethnic cleansing and other atrocities, the 1990s brought a gruesome role reversal. Abetted by the media, in 1987, Slobodan Milosevic revived that Serbian memory of collective persecution and death when he whipped the Serbs into a frenzy of nationalism. Serbian newspapers began to feature articles and photos about the Ustashe concentration camps of World War II. Croats were referred to as criminals who wore necklaces made with the fingers of Serbian children. The media warned of an imminent Ustashe genocide against Serbs. War criminals were celebrated as national heroes.[34]

The impact of the relentless propaganda is evident in the story of Elvedin Pasic, a survivor who testified at the International Criminal Tribunal and was featured in a *Frontline* documentary. While celebrating Eid al-Adha (the "Feast of Sacrifice" that celebrates Ibrahim's willingness to demonstrate his faith in Allah by sacrificing his son Ishmael) in 1992, Pasic's village was bombed by Serb forces. He and his family had to run for their lives. Months later, they returned home and found their village burned to the ground. Those who were too old and weak to escape had been burned alive. The family dog had been shot. The Pasic family went back into hiding in a tunnel with scores of other Muslims. After five months, they were caught by Serb soldiers. The villagers were told to form three lines and lay down on the ground. Women and children were instructed to get up. Pasic was only fourteen years old at the time and didn't want to leave his father and uncle. But his father urged him to go with his other siblings. He never saw his father and uncle again. Their bodies were never found.[35]

Many Serbs saw the slaughter of Muslims not as a war against Islam, but as payback for Serbian losses in World War II and even earlier losses to Ottomans nearly six hundred years ago. Perceived historic injuries are often cited by the perpetrators as justification for atrocities such as ethnic cleansing.

Nor is the Syrian war, which began in 2011, a war against Islam. But it does have an element of ethnic cleansing, as the Syrian government has made the return of displaced families and refugees nearly impossible. The Syrian regime has invoked Assad's "Law 10" to seize and redevelop land that belonged to families that were forced to flee—especially Sunnis. Law 10 requires that, if a property owner does not appear on official documents, he or she has one year to provide proof of ownership after being notified that their property is designated for reconstruction. For displaced families and refugees who have fled for their lives without papers and other vital possessions, it is almost impossible to provide that kind of proof remotely. As a result, those displaced persons are unable to reclaim and return to their homes. According to the Washington Institute for Near East Policy, Law 10 provides a patina of legitimacy to upending the ethnic mix in Syria by preventing Sunnis from returning to their homes.[36] Here again, we have a form of ethnic cleansing imposed by a minority ruling sect against a majority Sunni population. In this case, the regime isn't trying to eradicate a sect of Islam as a religion. However, it echoes a key element of religicide in that it attempts to make it impossible for its victims to return home.

In 2020, in Ethiopia, the Tigray region became the site of another ethnic cleansing. War had broken out between the Tigray People's National Liberation Front (TPLF) and the Ethiopian National Defense Force (ENDF).

The ENDF was abetted by the Ethiopian Federal Police, forces from the neighboring Amhara and Afar Regions, along with Eritrean Defense Forces. Tigrayans, who make up about 6 percent of Ethiopia's population, suffered discrimination under Ethiopian dictators for much of the twentieth century—especially during times of famine that decimated their numbers. After fighting the dictators that ruled Ethiopia in the 1970s and 1980s, the Tigray People's National Liberation Front swept into power in 1991. During that time, ethnic Eritreans were deported and Amharans were expelled from the Oromia Region and discriminated against in the Harari Region.

The overwhelming majority of Tigrayans—roughly 90 percent—are Eastern Orthodox, as is over 40 percent of Ethiopia. This conflict is not about pitting Muslims against Christians or wiping out an entire religion. It is more about targeting a particular ethnic group for discrimination and removing its rights to participate with dignity and equality in Ethiopia.

When Prime Minister Abiy Ahmed was elected in 2018, he restructured the government. He upended the TPLF's ethnic federalism and merged the ethnic and region-based political parties into one Prosperity Party. The TPLF refused to join the new party and declared the new prime minister an illegitimate leader. The TPLF held its own elections in defiance of the federal government. In turn, the Ethiopian government deemed the Tigray Region election illegitimate.

Fighting began on November 4, 2020, when the TPLF attacked the ENDF headquarters in the capital, Mekele. Amnesty International documented massive war crimes committed by both sides, including ethnic cleansing.

An article from *Vice World News* published in February 2021 featured a farmer from central Tigray whose crops had been set on fire and whose home was burned. To protect him from reprisals, Vice gave him the name Gebru Habtom. Habtom said, "They said they'd burn me next, so I fled for my life."[37] He was right. Soon after, Eritrean soldiers raided Habtom's village, killing, looting, and burning homes. "They shot at everyone. They even killed priests who were hiding in the church."[38]

For context, ethnic profiling against Tigrayans had been taking place for several years. Starting in 2017, the Ethiopian Satellite Television and Radio network (ESAT) aired genocidal messages targeting Tigrayans for extermination. In 2020, Ethiopia enacted its own version of the Nazi Nuremberg laws. Tigrayan passengers were refused permission to board Ethiopian Airlines. Ethnic Tigrayan pilots and other employees of Ethiopian Airlines were put on indefinite leave. Foreign travel was forbidden. All ethnic Tigrayans in government agencies and NGOs had to be identified and registered. Their homes were searched, and bank accounts suspended. Tigrayan soldiers on a peacekeeping mission had their weapons removed. We see similar methods being employed in full-blown religicides.

A series of massacres took place: some at the hands of the TPLF and its sympathizers, and some at the hands of the ENDF and its allies. Dual ethnic cleansing, targeting both Amhara and Tigrayans, caused more than two million to flee their homes. Widespread pillaging and looting, including prized cultural and religious artifacts, have been reported.

In mid-2020, the Tigrayan fighters recaptured their region's capital along with a wide swath of territory in their region. They drove out the Ethiopian army, imprisoning 6,600 and claiming to kill three times that number, according to the *New York Times*.[39] As of this writing, the Tigrayan leader, Getachew Reda, is planning a referendum on Tigrayan independence.

As these examples demonstrate, the atrocities of ethnic cleansing, war crimes, and genocide still need to be addressed more carefully and holistically. But we are adding a pressing, further category: that of religicide. This type of abuse needs to be added to this list of atrocities which we internationally recognize, condemn, and work to prevent. The Armenian genocide, Holocaust, Rwanda genocide, Bosnian war, and Tigrayan conflict amply illustrate other forms of mass atrocities. While religicide incorporates all their features, additional conditions must be met to qualify as religicide.

One of the dangers of religicide in the modern era is forcing everyone to be the same or renounce their religious beliefs. This impossible demand—to conform or die—is where religicide begins.

Religicide includes, but is distinct from, other crimes covered so far. It has deep historical antecedents. The Spanish Inquisition targeted Jews who had converted to Christianity but were suspected of having lapsed in their beliefs. The Catholics thought that the rebels of the Protestant Reformation were in thrall to the devil. Killing them was deemed an act of mercy—an example of what the late Rabbi Jonathan Sacks called "altruistic evil."

Once a conflict becomes "holy" and violence is unleashed, it is more difficult to tamp down. That's because all the combatants are convinced God is on their side.

Although the conflicts in this chapter aren't all religicides, they lay the human rights framework for this new concept. With that background, it becomes easier to understand the conflicts that do qualify as religicide.

Perhaps the most obvious and recent example is the Islamic State's (ISIS) campaign to eradicate Yazidis and Yazidism. Yazidism holds a monotheistic view of divinity, as well as a particular reverence for the sun. Most Yazidis speak Kurmanji, a dialect of the Kurdish language. Yazidis worship God and honor Malek Taus and other angels. Based on their oral traditions, Yazidis believe that, after creating Malek Taus and six other angels, God created humans and asked the angels to venerate this new species. Six of the angels agreed, but Malek Taus refused to worship anyone other than God. According to Yazidism, God praised this angel for his wisdom, designating him as the leader of all other angels. Nevertheless, ISIS fighters believe that Yazidis have to be eradicated, or else they would have to answer to their own God.

Their intentions are evident in their playbook, *The Management of Savagery*. This hate-filled tract, written by Abu Bakr Naji, an extremist Sunni polemicist and first leader of ISIS, outlines the stages and methods of conquest, including the surveillance and infiltration necessary to establish a new caliphate.

The first stage is to create vexation: disruption and distraction to exhaust and weaken the enemy state and create favorable propaganda for *mujahideen*, a term for Islamic guerrillas who engage in jihad (a fight on behalf of the faith or Muslim community). The second stage involves providing food, services, security, and establishing Sharia justice (religious regulations governing the lives of Muslims) to ensure the loyalty and compliance of the population. The third stage is the establishment of an Islamic caliphate (the reign of a caliph or chief Muslim ruler) and its relentlessly harsh form of governance.

The Management of Savagery emphasizes the virtue of jihadi fighters and the corruption of the *taghut* (anyone not deemed righteous Muslims), crusaders (i.e., Christians), and infidels. More to the point of religicide, this manual for jihad liberally quotes from the Qur'an to justify violence in the name of God. "Our battle is a battle of *tawhid* (unification) against unbelief and faith against polytheism and it is not an economic, political, or social battle," writes Abu Bakr. And that battle must be a bloody one in which violence is strategically employed. Explaining that "our troops are not afraid of blood and death; rather they seek it out," the manual instructs:

- "Violence...spreads hopelessness in the heart of the enemy."
- "We must make this battle very violent" so that opposing groups "will realize that entering this battle will frequently lead to death."
- "There is nothing preventing us from spilling [the enemy's] blood; rather we see this as one of the most important obligations since they do not repent, undertake prayer, and give alms."
- "We must burn the earth under the feet of the tyrants so that it will not be suitable for them to live in."

The justification for such extreme violence is the fervent desire for certain and absolute victory of their beliefs. That means the utter eradication of the enemy—its religion, heritage, traditions, sacred space, and cemeteries—with no mercy whatsoever. It's a how-to manual, detailing instructions to eliminate all traces of a religious minority, past, present, and future.

We will delve deeper into the case of the Islamic State vs. Yazidism, but the parameters are very clear: Leave no survivors. Poison wells. Destroy homes. Rape and enslave women to birth Muslim children. Kill all Yazidi men, the elderly, and persons with disabilities. Burn all evidence of their existence.

Per Abu Bakr, "Missionary activities...relapse and fall to pieces if there are not those who nourish it with blood and build it with skulls and corpses" and "Killing in the path of God...is easily done through jihad." The Islamic State's leader scapegoats and blames the victims for their own victimization. "As everyone can see, [the enemy] are clearly destroying everything. They are even extracting the cost of their murder and destruction from us."[40]

None of this is new. In the seventeenth century, for example, the proposed solution to self-righteous, religion-related slaughter was the 1648 Peace of Westphalia, which ended the Eighty Years' and Thirty Years' Wars in Europe. These long-running conflicts were primarily religious wars. Westphalia, for the first time, subordinated religion to citizenship and heralded the rise of the sovereign state. With religion having been privatized and replaced with secular nationalism, any foreigner was regarded "as fair game for exploitation and mass slaughter, especially if he belonged to a different ethnic group."[41]

War crimes, genocide, crimes against humanity, and ethnic cleansing can include attacking the enemy's religion. But religicide has two further signatures: destroying cultural and natural heritage (ecocide) and propagating false narratives (factocide).

One of the most effective ways to destroy both narrative and heritage is to erase memory by prohibiting Indigenous language instruction and destroying the evidence of culture contained in libraries and books. Lucien Polastron offers many examples in his 2004 book, *Books on Fire*.

When China claimed to "liberate" Tibet, eighty-seven thousand Tibetans were killed, and more than six thousand monasteries were eliminated. Chinese forces destroyed their libraries on the spot. In greater China, Mao burned Buddhist scripture, and a two hundred thousand-volume Jesuit library was pillaged.[42]

In Stalin's Russia, reading was systematically suppressed.

In Hitler's Germany, instructions were sent to student associations to rid the land of "Judeo-Asiatic poison." On May 10, 1933, a human chain of those students tossed truckloads of books into a gigantic bonfire on Berlin's Opera Square.[43]

In Cambodia, the Khmer Rouge destroyed the books in the national library and seven hundred thousand documents in the Buddhist institute were reduced to ashes.[44]

In Bosnia, the national library, with its two million books, periodicals, and rare manuscripts, burned for three days during the siege of Sarajevo. Ovenden observes: "These provided the recorded memory not just of a nation but the culture of an entire region, one that had a significant Muslim population."[45] The Serbs systematically strove to destroy the book collections in the land they intended to "cleanse."[46]

In Afghanistan, the Taliban sacked the public library in Kabul in 1996. Along with libraries, it destroyed the Buddhas of Bamiyan, the artworks of the Hakim Center, and the treasures of the Kabul Museum.[47]

In his 1823 drama, *Almansor: A Tragedy*, Heinrich Heine presciently intoned, "Where they burn books, they will also burn people." Once people begin to burn, literally and figuratively; once they are displaced and their institutions dismantled; then displaced communities and migrant families are more easily massacred.

Today, many religious minorities are facing existential threat: the Yazidis, the Rohingya, the Uyghurs, and Tibetan Buddhists. Each will be given a case-by-case analysis in later chapters where we will also explore the past systemic and religicidal slaughters of Indigenous people. As noted earlier, religion-related violence is the fastest-growing type of violence worldwide, and one of the greatest threats to humanity.

So, what can be done to interrupt cycles of religion-related violence and prevent an all-out religicide? Any concerted effort to stop systemic violence will require innovative strategies that engage diverse religious actors, policy makers, civil society, women, and youth. It will require a new way of thinking that we call "covenantalism." But first we must understand what can drive and possess one group of humans to commit mass atrocities against another.

Chapter Three

THE ROOTS OF RELIGICIDE

We indiscriminately shot at everybody. We shot the Muslim men in the foreheads and kicked the bodies into the hole.

—**Private Myo Win Tun**, Myanmar
Army, September 8, 2020[48]

We've examined what religicide is and what it is not. To understand religicide fundamentally, we need to explore what drives individuals to commit and permit mass murder. What leads groups to demonize and eradicate a religion, annihilate its followers, and destroy its cultural heritage? Why would anyone want to kill off a whole religion?

The drivers include a deadly mix of group narcissism, scapegoating, hate speech, the human need to belong, and fear-based "apocalyptic thinking" that fuels false conspiracy fantasies. In modern times, all of this is accelerated by technology and amplified by social media to incite hatred and violence against a religious group and deny its right to exist.

Group narcissism is the belief that one's own group holds a monopoly on truth. It functions as a dividing force between believers and nonbelievers—those who agree and those who don't.[49] Group identity is natural and not a bad thing in and of itself. We have evolved and survived in groups. We have defined and defended our identities in relation to other groups. Social grouping builds resilience and psychosocial health. But too often, we view those who are different from us as a threat. "They" become the problem and "they" are responsible for what is wrong with the world.

Collective narcissism is linked to group aggression. According to sociologist Agnieszka Golec De Zavala, one of the outcomes of group narcissism is a strongly perceived threat—whether real or not—from out-groups. Narcissism reinforces the group's sense of exceptionalism—feeling chosen, set apart, and pure. This is one of the reasons such groups are attracted to military aggression, authoritarianism, and blind patriotism.

History is full of examples of collective narcissism embodied in authoritarian regimes that created enemies and perpetrated violence against them, from Nazism and Stalinism to Kim Jong-Un's rule of North Korea. However disastrous, these do not amount to religicide, because they did not set out to eradicate religion. The medieval Christian Crusades offer a better example of religicide. The eleventh century Crusaders left a path of blood and ashes on their march to conquer Jerusalem and to remove Islamic "infidels" from the Holy Land.

Derogation of an out-group and an emotional investment in a glorified, unrealistic belief in the in-group's superiority and exceptionalism hold victimized out-groups responsible for the in-group's aggression against them, otherwise known as "blaming the victim." Blaming and scapegoating are always prominent in a religicidal campaign. The scapegoated victims in the out-group are reduced to "others" with their individual humanity obliterated.

Apocalyptic thinking taps into our fear of displacement, fear of the stranger, fear of status and economic loss, and even fear of modernity. Fear is part of our evolutionary survival instincts. But in modern times, most of us don't encounter grizzly bears on the attack or poisonous vipers on the street. Today, fear is manipulated to induce anxiety and project evil intent onto those who appear different. What begins with fueling false fears often ends with atrocity.

Philosophical and religious traditions exhibit different versions of apocalyptic and binary thinking embedded in good versus evil:

- In Judaism: The war of Gog and Magog in Megiddo. As prophesied in the Hebrew scriptures, Gog and Magog are the enemies who will invade Israel. It is against them that God wages a final war against evil. Their defeat brings on the messianic age. Gog and Magog make their appearance in the New Testament and in the Qur'an as well.

- In Christianity: Armageddon. In the New Testament, the book of Revelations pinpoints Armageddon as the location in which the final battle between God and the forces of evil will take place. (Armageddon is the translation from the Hebrew Megiddo.) Earthly kings worldwide make their last stand against the triumph of the Kingdom of God.

- In Islam: The Qur'an contains a rich trove of revelations that begin with "God's cosmic undoing of the 'old world' followed by the last judgment and creation of a 'new world' of everlasting paradise and hell."[50] Dajjal, the anti-Christ, comes from the East bringing temptation followed by destruction. One of the signs that "the Hour" of the end times has come is the descent of Jesus from Heaven to save Muslims in their time of need.[51]

- In Hinduism: Vishnu returns to battle evil on a white horse. Kali Yuga is the worst of four cycling world ages—a period of strife associated with the demon Kali. Vishnu is the second of a triumvirate of gods responsible for creation, maintenance, and destruction in the world. His role is to come to earth during contentious times and restore the balance of good and evil and usher in the age of truth.
- In Buddhism: Shambhala appears in some Buddhist prophesies as the equivalent of Armageddon. It is how good triumphs over evil. But unlike Armageddon, the world is restored rather than destroyed. In Tibetan Buddhism, for example, it is prophesied that when the world descends into greed and war, a great army will rise to vanquish the forces of evil and bring in a worldwide golden age.

Binary thinking and dualism are common in history, making groups feel comfortable with a simple reductionist choice, never having to wrestle with complexity. Good versus Evil. Us versus Them. Once we identify and dehumanize the outsider group as an enemy, we can alienate and scapegoat them too. Any treatment toward them can be harsh, aggressive, and, well, justified, simply because *they* are different, and *they* are against us, and *they* are to blame for all our problems. The practice of scapegoating has been around since the dawn of time. It justifies classifying others as evil.

"Azazel" is the biblical Hebrew word for scapegoat. It first appears in Leviticus 16:8-10. For the ancient Israelites, the scapegoat represented the removal of the people's sins by literally casting a goat into the desert. As such, the scapegoat played an honored role in the rituals of the Day of Atonement—Yom Kippur. Over time, that ritual symbol of atonement and purification was perverted into a vehicle for human othering and blaming. Projecting negativity onto others and blaming them for all that has gone wrong is a human tendency seen from sibling dynamics to schoolyards to historic and sociopathic violence. Scapegoating is always a part of religicide—blaming a religion and its followers for what is wrong in society while laying the groundwork for committing crimes against targeted out-groups.

Rigid in-group and out-group classification breeds apocalyptic thinking that divides the world into the children of light and the children of darkness. This creates what the late rabbi and scholar Jonathan Sacks described as pathological dualism. It does three things: first, dehumanize and demonize your enemies; second, portray yourself as the victim; and third, commit altruistic evil, which is killing others as a perceived favor to humanity. Dehumanization is what destroys our human empathy, thwarting basic emotions that would normally prevent us from inflicting suffering on others. Playing the victim allows us to try to deflect our moral responsibility. "Altruistic evil recruits good people to a bad cause," wrote Sacks, "It turns ordinary human beings into murderers in the name of high ideals."[52]

Words and narratives matter. There is a powerful link between verbal violence and physical violence. It starts with dehumanizing the "other" with labels: infidel, *taghut* (Arabic), *takfir* (Arabic) *banda* (Amharic), *judenschwein* (German), vermin, kike, nigger, towel head, parasite, fag. Words like these empty individuals of their humanity, reducing them to contemptible caricatures. It's then a short step to swing a hate-filled misrepresentation from a lynching tree, shove him or her into the fires of a Nazi oven, shoot them while at prayer in a New Zealand mosque, or decapitate them on a video gone viral. This intentional process of dehumanization is a necessary step toward religicidal thinking and messaging.

As stated earlier, four-fifths of the world's population affiliates with faith and religious institutions. The core precepts of each of the great religions are rooted in love, peace, respect, mercy, and caring for the stranger. In 2001, the Durban Declaration enacted at the 2001 World Conference against Racism optimistically declared: "Religion, spirituality, and belief may and can contribute to the promotion of the inherent dignity and worth of the human person and to the eradication of racism, racial discrimination, xenophobia and related intolerance." Ironically, the participants in the Durban Conference used that opportunity to equate Zionism with racism. (Apparently, Jews were not regarded as worthy of protection, even at a conference to engender religious harmony.)

So why do people hate people who look different and believe differently? Because people bond with people who look and think like them. And they fear others who differ in their beliefs, rituals, and social behavior.

Yes, religion can be a source of healing and peace-building. But too often, religion is used as a weapon to hurt and divide. In religion at its worst, one can find the roots of group narcissism and hate speech.

Hate speech is legally different from incitement to violence. Hate speech is the *prelude* to incitement, and incitement is the intermediate step to atrocity. One of the most common red flags of impending violence is an increase in hate speech. For it to result in violence, the United Nations cites several preconditions: a context conducive to violence, an influential speaker, wide dissemination, a receptive audience, and a target.[53]

America is not immune to these tendencies. Our history is replete with linkages between moral fervor expressed in hate speech and incitements to violence. From the pious Puritans who burned their witches in Salem to the Ku Klux Klan (KKK) who lynched innocent Black people, to neo-Nazis who marched in Charlottesville chanting "Jews will not replace us" or those who later shot up a synagogue in Pennsylvania.

White supremacist members of the Ku Klux Klan used scripture to justify their hatred—even praying fervently before going on night rides to lynch and terrorize the Black communities the KKK blamed for "polluting" America. The 2016 Anti-Defamation League (ADL) report, *Tattered Robes*, quoted the website of the Elders Blood-N-Blood Out Knights (EBBOK), a new Klan group: "We are a Christian hate group.... We accept all Nazis and skinheads 'cause we have the same beliefs." In the name of being "one-hundred percent American," Klansmen also targeted immigrants, Catholics, Jews, and organized labor. They participated in scapegoating, hate speech, and altruistic evil—turning their vigilante violence against anyone deemed outside the pale of their "purity."

World history is replete with many more examples. One need only look at the roots of the genocides in Bosnia and Rwanda—genocides that began with leaders spewing hate speech. The use of broadcast media to incite violence against Tigrayans in Ethiopia. The cultural, if not physical, genocide of Uyghurs in China. Even the conspiracy theories about Asians, Muslims, and Jews spawned by the COVID-19 pandemic.

An Oxford University survey regarding the pandemic revealed that nearly 20 percent of respondents agreed that either Jews or Muslims were responsible for spreading the virus. Almost half endorsed, to some degree, the unproved idea that "[COVID-19] is a bioweapon developed by China to destroy the West." One fifth endorsed the false idea that "Jews have created the virus to collapse the economy for financial gain." Nearly 20 percent agreed with the false narrative that "Muslims are spreading the virus as an attack on Western values."[54]

Then there's the politics of the extreme right in the United States and Western Europe, with the anti-immigrant and anti-refugee rhetoric that pervades public policy. Leaders use such words as: "infestation," "cockroach," "invasion," "vermin," and "rapists." In an earlier era, the more vociferous hate speech came from the Left. In the 1960s, police were "pigs" and fair game for assassination.

How do we bring ourselves to think such thoughts? Religious historian Karen Armstrong described the atrocity mindset: "We envelop the effort in a mythology—often a 'religious' mythology—that puts distance between us and the enemy. We exaggerate his differences, be they racial, religious, or ideological. We develop narratives to convince ourselves that he is not really human but monstrous, the antithesis of order and goodness.... We tell ourselves that we are fighting for God and country."[55] Armstrong's analysis evokes echoes of the Armenian genocide as well as the Holocaust but can also be linked to the religicides on our watch today.

The Holocaust spawned an entire literature that explored how it was possible for Germany, one of the most civilized nations on earth, to get caught up in such brutality. Germany's humiliating defeat in World War I and the ravaged economy it engendered left its citizenry ripe for a demagogue who could restore national pride and deflect blame for the country's troubles onto a scapegoat: the Jews. The anti-Semitic image of the hook-nosed, horned, conspiratorial "international Jew" who controlled banks and the media provided the shamed Germans with someone to hate. A messianic, charismatic, narcissistic Führer gave them someone to follow. And the Thousand-Year Reich offered a vision with meaning—the mirage of a powerful state to which they could belong.

In his seminal book, *Escape from Freedom*, Erich Fromm puts forth a theory of personality based on two primary human needs—freedom and belonging. As societies become increasingly individualistic and atomized, many people lose their sense of connection. We feel isolated, powerless, and insignificant. Absent love or productive work, those feelings can lead us to relinquish our independence to an external authority to regain a sense of connection.

This mechanism is evident in the appeal of ISIS to Americans who joined its ranks. "ISIS and the Lonely Young American," a 2015 story in the *New York Times*, detailed the recruitment of "Alex," a socially isolated young woman living with her grandmother in a rural community. Her addict mother had lost custody of Alex, and Alex suffered from fetal alcohol syndrome. Step-by-step, she was lured into a manufactured sense of community by ISIS recruiters through unrelenting online interaction. She was enticed to convert from Christianity to Islam with a gift certificate for an Islamic bookstore and gift packages of a prayer rug, hijab, bars of Lindt chocolate, and pizza money. She was surrounded by a sympathetic online community that appeared to treat her confusion with seriousness and respect. She was ripe to "escape from freedom" and cede her identity to ISIS.

Fromm observes, "Freedom has a twofold meaning for modern man: that he has been freed from traditional authorities and has become an 'individual,' but that at the same time he has become isolated, powerless, and an instrument of purposes outside of himself, alienated from himself and others." Excessive individualism can alienate us from the common good.[56] And the feeling of separation makes us more susceptible to joining groups, particularly ones that provide an intense mission where we can define ourselves against the rest of the world. ISIS fit the bill for Alex. This state of separation undermines one's sense of self, which weakens and frightens an individual like Alex, making her ready to submit to new kinds of bondage.[57] That bondage may be to authoritarianism or hyper-conformity. As purpose-seeking creatures, we human beings need to belong and affiliate, even if that means joining causes that may appear extremist or violent to others. The intensity and passion of being an insider who believes in a calling fosters an alluring sense of community belonging. That's what ISIS gave Alex. So far as we know, she hasn't committed any acts of terror.

However, a feeling of isolation, powerlessness, and alienation absolutely drove Tamerlan Tsarnaev, and his hapless brother, to commit a shocking act of domestic terrorism: the Boston Marathon bombing of 2013. Living in near poverty with his wife and daughter, Tamerlan returned for a visit to his last family home in the Dagestan region of Russia. There, he was drawn to "The Union of the Just," an Islamist group that advocates for Sharia law. He spent hours in cafés with his newfound friends, debating the Qur'an. Tamerlan felt he was taken seriously. He felt important.

He felt at home. He felt accepted. Then, he returned to the US and was nobody again. As Masha Gessen, author of *The Brothers* observes, "the thing about international Islamic terrorism...it's an opportunity for somebody who doesn't belong to engage and claim greatness.... And you can engage with a great power like the United States simply by throwing a bomb.... So someone like Tamerlan, who feels small and insignificant, can suddenly claim a sense of belonging to a great, big effort—and a place in history."[58]

Once we cede ourselves to external authority, as Tamerlan Tsarnaev did, our destructiveness is easily unleashed on command, even by very religious people among us. Emotions that were once activated by religion are now triggered by nationalism and war are called "'*ekstasis:*' a sense of liberation, freedom, equanimity, community, and a profound relationship with other human beings," observes Karen Armstrong.[59] This is what happens when religion becomes politicized and intermingled with nationalism and violence—people are motivated by an intense and ecstatic feeling of belonging to a cause greater than themselves and are willing to sacrifice lives.

These same social tendencies and feelings sow the seeds for religicide today. It takes group narcissism, scapegoating outsiders, hate speech, and demonizing anyone who appears different or threatening—whether it's Yazidis in Iraq, Rohingya in Myanmar, or Uyghurs and Tibetans in China.

Totalitarian movements often depend on the sheer force of numbers to replace the agency of the individual with a collective buy-in to some mass delusion. "This common-sense disinclination to believe the monstrous is constantly strengthened by the totalitarian ruler himself."[60] Again, as per Hannah Arendt, the ideal target for totalitarian rule is gullible people who can no longer distinguish fantasy from reality. We see this lack of critical thinking play out today with adherents to QAnon. Big lies and outrageous conspiracy theories are wrapped in concern for children allegedly being abused in a preposterous web of stories of pizza parlor sex trafficking. But these outlandish lies find their willing, believing, susceptible audience. Jitarth Jadeja, a former QAnon adherent explains: "I wanted to believe that the good guys were fighting the good fight and [for] a better future. Q makes you feel important and gives you meaning and self-esteem. You are saving the world when you're in Q, [it's] the highest way you can view yourself."[61] The fact that Q makes up demonstrably false "truths" seems to matter not at all to its followers.

If one can induce a significant minority to believe a blatant falsehood—even 5 to 10 percent of a community—the media can magnify the false narrative quickly, tapping into people's uncertainty and fear, as well as their need for acceptance by their peers. Such movements fill a psychological need for us to believe and belong.

These concepts are not new. In 1952, Eric Hoffer wrote his pivotal work, *The True Believer*, analyzing the nature of fanaticism and the psychological appeal of mass movements. Like Fromm and Arendt, he explored why true believers surrender the self to a fanatical or authoritarian movement or figure.

Hoffer rejected the notion that fanaticism is ideological or simply a matter of identity politics. Rather, fanaticism has its roots in alienation. "Passionate hatred can give meaning and purpose to an empty life," Hoffer wrote, "People haunted by the purposelessness of their lives try to find a new content not only by dedicating themselves to a holy cause but also by nursing a fanatical grievance. A mass movement offers them unlimited opportunities for both."[62] When he says "them," he means us.

All of this is evident in today's white supremacy movement, in which identity, ideology, and alienation get easily intertwined. Ideology is a system of ideas focused on bringing about changes in the world. Identity is about who and what one believes they are—and that is most often defined by the groups to which one belongs. A former skinhead explained how his identity became melded with the ideology of hate groups: "I felt power where I felt powerless. I felt a sense of belonging where I felt invisible."[63]

Sociologist Emile Durkheim researched how rapid social change and upheaval loosen ties to the broader community and can induce a state of "normlessness." The absence of rules and clarity induces feelings of purposelessness, futility, emptiness, and despair. This was manifest in Robert Bauer, one of those criminally charged for the 2021 Capitol insurrection. He explained to the FBI, "People in the crowd were angry about pedophiles, the news cycle, and losing their businesses during the lockdown."[64] Under these conditions, collective consciousness becomes weakened and normal constraints on behavior are removed. A person becomes vulnerable to join a mass movement and participate in some form of extremism.

Religious fundamentalism is one type of mass movement that lends itself to extremism, in part because it tries to offer easy answers to complex questions. We seek to make sense of the struggle between good and evil by making "us" good and "them" evil—children of light versus children of darkness. According to Hoffer, extreme violence cannot spread without belief in a devil. Religious fervor combines with the traits that attract a person to authoritarian ideologies. This is a combustible mixture.

The ISIS religicide against Yazidis was driven by a fervent belief that Yazidis were devil worshippers worthy of death. Actually, Yazidis are members of a distinctive religious and cultural group. They have lived in present-day Turkey, Syria, Iran, and Northern Iraq for centuries and maintain that the roots of modern Yazidism are pre-Abrahamic.

The late scholar Jonathan Sacks, former chief rabbi of the United Kingdom, used to say, "When religion turns men into murderers, God weeps."[65] Mass murder becomes possible because of the psychic numbing induced by the dehumanization of the "other" via weaponized language and hate speech.

Dr. Robert Jay Lifton wondered how physicians could evolve from healers to mass murderers in Nazi Germany. He gives his answer in *The Nazi Doctors: Medical Killing and the Psychology of Genocide*. There, he identifies "doubling" as a mechanism that enabled good Christians (in Germany and Poland) to commit atrocities. (His findings apply equally to good Muslim doctors in Turkey.) Through doubling, the genocide doctors could divide the self into two functioning wholes: the past self, guided by the Hippocratic oath to prioritize their patients' well-being; and the present self, guided only by duty and loyalty to the state. By eroding the boundary between healing and killing, the genocide doctors could avoid guilt and convince themselves that they were helping mankind by removing something harmful.[66] Whether the victims are Armenians, Jews, Uyghurs, or Rohingya, it is an altruistic evil—religicide—that drives their destruction.

The impact of dehumanization is increasingly evident in the United States. The FBI reports that in 2020 there were 8,052 single-bias hate crime incidents that affected 11,126 victims.[67] Of these crimes, 61.8 percent of the victims were targeted based on race, ethnicity, or ancestry, 20 percent were victimized due to the offenders' sexual orientation bias, and 12.3 percent were motivated by the offenders' religious bias.[68]

Jews remain the group most easily and often singled out for hate crimes. The Kantor Center for the Study of Contemporary European Jewry at Tel Aviv University found that anti-Semitic violence increased by nearly 20 percent worldwide just between 2018 and 2019. According to Anti-Defamation League surveys, more than one billion people harbored anti-Semitic sentiments, with 75 percent of those being in the Middle East and 24 percent (the second highest number) being in Europe.[69]

If one can go after Jews with impunity, that constitutes social permission to target any minority group for scapegoating and violent persecution. Anti-Semitism is the quintessential example of chronic scapegoating, wrapped in big lies and conspiracy theories that falsely blame and punish Jews for nearly anything. Hate crimes against Jews normally increase in lockstep with rising social unrest and conflict. Whenever there is a growing power struggle between, among, or within countries, there you will find a rise in anti-Semitism. Political leaders and their followers find their convenient scapegoat in a religious minority—the Jewish people—and then fan the flames of hate speech and persecution.

But how can we respond meaningfully to hate speech to end anti-Semitism and crimes against other minorities? International and US laws do not prohibit hate speech. They only forbid "incitement" that deliberately triggers violence and discrimination. The criminal justice system can only deal with the consequences of hate speech and react *after* it turns into a hate crime or mass atrocity. As of this writing, thirty-three countries (plus the forty-seven countries of the Council of Europe) have enacted hate crime legislation. Most of what is ruled illegal in these countries would be considered protected free speech under the First Amendment of the US Constitution. However, incitement to violence is excluded from that protection. Although the United States has no national hate speech statutes, forty-seven out of our fifty US states have enacted hate crimes legislation.[70] The three holdouts are Arkansas, South Carolina, and Wyoming.

The gaps in criminal law mean that religious leaders and other cultural influencers have a special responsibility for calling out hate speech when it happens, cutting it off at the source. Further, people of faith must address and contextualize the hate and violence-inciting language that appears in the sacred scriptures and oral traditions of most religions.

Chapter Four

DEFUSING TOXIC SCRIPTURES

*In the towns of the peoples that the Lord your God
is giving you as a heritage, you shall not let a soul
remain alive. No, you must annihilate them...as the
LORD your God has commanded you.*
(Deuteronomy 2:16-17)[71]

*Peter said to [Sapphira], "How is it that you [and your
husband] have agreed together to test the Spirit of the
Lord?..." Immediately, she fell down at his feet and
breathed her last.* (Acts 5:9-10)[72]

*Wherever you encounter the idolaters, kill them, seize
them, besiege them, wait for them at every lookout post.*
(Qur'an 9:5)[73]

Religions and their scriptures are susceptible to misinterpretation, and the link between religious texts and actual violent acts remains unclear. There are many factors that influence how religious texts are used. Extremist groups weaponize scripture. But there are plentiful religious texts that pave the way for empathy and peace building.

Because religion is such a charged issue, governments, philanthropies, and human rights groups tend to treat it as a third rail, avoiding the religious dimension in addressing conflict or bringing about social change. But we would do better to co-opt religion as part of the solution, not just part of the problem. The religious lens is important, even in a largely secular West.

It bears repeating that more than 80 percent of the world's population identifies with a religion. And yet, today 70 percent of the globe's population is living in countries that restrict them from practicing their faith freely. There is an inverse correlation between freedom of religion and the likelihood of violence.[74]

Religious institutions and faith leaders have a critical role to play in interpreting the scripture that can lead to atrocity. It's their job to provide context and defuse the incitement inherent in some ancient texts. Responsible faith leaders bring assets to the table that equip them to influence others because of their

- moral authority,
- constituencies and communication networks,
- convening power,
- deep understanding of their communities, and
- emotional and social intelligence—capacity for understanding others.

ISIS offers one example of how scriptural language is used to incite violence and manipulate thousands of followers. *The Management of Savagery* manual cites violent battles that lead to death as a powerful motive for Muslims "to fight in the ranks of the people of truth...One of the two opposing groups is in Paradise and the other is in Hell." By offering jihad as "the greatest medicine for one with many sins," ISIS offers purification for souls—a compelling appeal for those who have not found meaning in life. And when "exposing oneself to death is one of the most important elements for advancement" within the movement, the glorification of violence is self-evident. But it directly contravenes the core precepts of Islam focused on compassion, justice, and mercy.

In the *Open Letter to Abu Bakr Al-Baghdadi* directed to the late leader of ISIS, more than 120 Islamic scholars resoundingly rebutted the ideology and actions he espoused in the playbook he authored under his birth name, Ibrahim Awad Ibrahim al-Badri.

ISIS often invokes the text: "God bless Prophet Muhammad who was sent with the sword as a mercy to all worlds." But in referring to the Prophet, the holy Qur'an states: "We did not send you, except as a mercy to all the worlds." (Al-Anbiya', 21:107).[75] The phrase "sent with the sword" is part of a Hadith (collection of traditions containing sayings of the Prophet Muhammad), and Islam forbids the mixing of Qur'an and Hadith in this way. The *Open Letter* further points out that ISIS perverts the meaning of that verse to imply that mercy is dependent on the sword, which is untrue. This document challenges ISIS's harsh reign of terror, saying that severity should be avoided, as should the idea that severity is the measure of piety. "Indulge [people] with forgiveness, and enjoin kindness, and turn away from the ignorant." (Al-A'raf, 7:199).[76]

It condemns as *haraam* (forbidden) the slaying of any soul and reviles the Islamic leader al-Baghdadi for ordering the killing of innocents "who were neither combatants nor armed," just because they disagreed with ISIS ideology.[77] The same censure applies to the murder of emissaries, such as journalists and humanitarian aid workers.

Perhaps most damning is al-Baghdadi's distorted invocation of jihad, and his declaration of July 2014: "There is no life without jihad."[78] The *Open Letter* avers that jihad is conditional upon the consent of one's parents and that "the greater jihad" is against the ego and involves the purification of the soul. It is a means "to peace, safety, and security, and not an end in itself." Nor is jihad to be invoked against anyone who is not fighting or transgressing against Muslims. Jihad without a legitimate cause, goals, and purpose "is not jihad at all, but rather, warmongering and criminality." But if one must wage war, "do not be severe, do not be treacherous, do not mutilate or kill children...Those retreating are not to be killed."[79] The Qur'an explicitly prohibits killing prisoners, the elderly and disabled, and women and children, along with the destruction of buildings, livestock, and trees (without good cause). Nor is slavery condoned. ISIS clearly violates all these prohibitions. And all are hallmarks of religicide.

The *Open Letter* is one example of how religious leaders can respond to the misuse of texts to justify violence. The Tanenbaum Center for Interreligious Understanding offers more examples through its Peacemakers in Action Network. One of those is Sakena Yacoobi, founder of the Afghan Institute of Learning. During the first reign of the Taliban in Afghanistan, she secretly taught literacy to women through reading the Qur'an. In so doing, she compared how the actual Qur'anic texts differed from the Taliban's practices and demonstrated how their debasement of women's rights was a debasement of Islam. With the Taliban in control again, it remains to be seen whether these lessons will hold.

Similarly, another Afghan Tanenbaum Peacemaker practitioner, Jamila Afghani, mobilized Imams from large local mosques and conducted trainings on Muslim women's rights of inheritance, ownership, and property, patriarchal violence associated with marriage, and women's political and social participation. Among the authorities cited—national laws and international human rights instruments—was the Qur'an itself and the distorted interpretations that were used to justify attacks on women.

Azhar Hussain, another Muslim Peacemaker practitioner, tackled madrassa reform in Pakistan. Bringing together the leaders of all five of Pakistan's Muslim sects, he secured their support in broadening the sweep of madrassa education to include Qur'anic concepts of religious tolerance, human rights, and conflict resolution.

But the obligation to interpret religious texts in positive ways applies not only to Muslim religious leaders. All religious leaders have a responsibility to contextualize passages that have the potential to be weaponized. The words they use and the way they frame their teachings can accelerate or defuse the spread of hatred and the use of force.[80]

In the Hebrew scriptures, the book of Joshua and Deuteronomy contain what appear to be genocidal instructions from God to wipe out every living thing in the Promised Land that Joshua is ordered to conquer. The rhetoric is about mass killing. But a closer reading reveals that the focus is more on expulsion than killing—an expulsion that will be conducted by God, not Joshua.

Knowing of God's plan to displace the Canaanites, their kings dispatch their armies to strike the first blow against the Israelites. Therefore, lethal actions are focused primarily against rulers and cities in the context of regular warfare. Further contradicting the genocide interpretation, Joshua must meet two preconditions before being allowed to lead the Israelites to occupy Canaan: one is to stipulate that no Israelites will intermarry with Canaanites (Deuteronomy 7:2-5). How can there be any Canaanites to marry if the intention is to wipe them out? The other is to destroy all the Canaanites' cultic objects so that the Israelites are not tempted to engage in idolatrous worship. God is more concerned with keeping the Israelites separated from Canaan's native inhabitants than killing them. Nevertheless, the superficial genocidal reading had long reach. Oliver Cromwell, for example, cited Joshua and the Battle of Jericho to justify mass killing of Catholics when he invaded Ireland in 1649.

Prior to entering the Promised Land, the Hebrews were slaves in the land of Egypt. In Exodus, we find Pharoah who both fears and has contempt for his Hebrew slaves. He repeatedly defies God's command, conveyed through Moses, to "let my people go." (Exodus 9:1) (NIV)[81] It is not until God exercises raw power by drowning Pharoah's pursuing army in the Red Sea that the Hebrews are finally free to embark on their forty-year trek through the desert to find the Promised Land. What is the lesson here? Is it really that raw power is the answer to freeing a people? No. One must read the drama that unfolds in the desert and ends with the delivery of the Ten Commandments that became the underpinning of Judeo-Christian civilization.

By the time we move from Exodus, the second book of the Torah, to Deuteronomy, the fifth book of the Torah, there is a dramatic shift in tone: "Justice, justice alone shall you pursue." (Deuteronomy 16:20) (NABRE)[82] A later book, Isaiah, offers a vision of positive peace: "The fruit of justice will be peace; the effect of righteousness will be quietness and confidence forever. My people will live in peaceful dwelling places, in secure homes, in undisturbed places of rest." (Isaiah 32:17-18)[83] "They shall beat their swords into plowshares, and their spears into pruning hooks; nation shall not lift up sword against nation, neither shall they learn war anymore." (Isaiah 2:4) (ESV)[84]

Hatred of Jews may have its seeds in Pharoah, but its real biblical rationale derives from the Gospel of Matthew 27:25. That Gospel narrates the trial of Jesus before Pontius Pilate. After the verdict "Crucify him!" is pronounced, the people attending the trial say the fateful words: *"His blood is on us and on our children!"* [85] That one line has long been cited as the justification for the collective punishment of Jews, for all time, as a cursed people. But there are less destructive and more accurate interpretations of that sentence. For example, the "blood" that is mentioned is the purifying blood of Jesus, which signifies eternal redemption and forgiveness of sins. When Jesus prayed from the cross, "Father, forgive them, for they know not what they do," (Luke 23:34), (ESV)[86] his prayer included the Romans who executed him as well as the limited number of Jews who were present at his trial and called for his crucifixion. Jesus did not pray for the eternal damnation of his oppressors.

Other statements attributed to Jesus have been weaponized as a call to arms for Christians. "I have come to bring not peace but the sword." (Matthew 10:34) (NABRE)[87] Beginning with the reign of Constantine and his adoption of Christianity as the state religion of the Roman Empire, violence was expected and even embraced by most adherents. As practiced, Christianity became a religion of conquest, conversion, and persecution like the early Christians had endured—but now inflicted on others. Later still,

Christian terrorists cited biblical scripture to justify violence to induce the end times prophesied in the New Testament. The symbol of the cross in Christianity was distorted by hate groups. In the twentieth century, the Ku Klux Klan's burning of crosses to instill terror perverted the symbol from a source of comfort and protection to an emblem of fear.

The violent Christianity of Emperor Constantine introduced the concept of "just war," which allows combatants to retake what was perceived as wrongly taken and punish evil. The "just war" theory is the underpinning of international law, which allows for retaliation. More on that later.

Today, Christians are on the receiving end of violent persecution in Arab countries. But one must distinguish the actual threats to Christian survival—in places like Sudan and other countries controlled by Muslim extremists—from perceived threats in the United States. In the first case, churches are being burned down. Christians are being slaughtered by the hundreds. By contrast, many Christians in the United States view attempts to accept multicultural diversity as a war against Christianity. Witness the many cases in which business owners insist that making wedding cakes for gay couples, allowing medical insurance to cover contraception, or keeping crèches out of the workplace during the December holidays violate their beliefs and discriminate against them as Christians.[88]

Like Christianity, Hinduism is generally thought to be a peaceable belief system. But Hinduism also contains the seeds for the same dualisms as other religions. On the one hand, it eschews doing harm to any living thing and strongly promotes peace and nonviolence. Mohandas Gandhi is perhaps the best-known example of this philosophy. On the other hand, while condemning war and violence, Hinduism endorses it as a duty. "Hindus lived by war and worshiped gods of war, and Hinduism unquestioningly sanctioned and assisted war."[89] The *Rig Veda* text 1-39:2 justifies the use of force in self-defense: "May your weapons be strong to drive away the attackers, may your arms be powerful enough to check the foes, let your army be glorious, not the evil-doer."[90]

Killing in an impersonal way, uncontaminated with anger or selfishness, is ennobled. Warriors are taught that their personal feelings should not interfere with killing because violence only affects the body and cannot harm the soul. At the same time, Hinduism lays down rules of war similar to those of Islam: Do not poison the tip of your arrow. Do not attack the sick or old. Do not attack a child or a woman. Do not attack from behind. Any warrior who violates these precepts is doomed to hell. Yet, in *Rig Veda* 6-75:16, the warrior is told: "Go to the foemen, strike them home, and let not one be left alive."[91]

When such scripture combines with nationalism and patriotism, militant extremism can easily follow. One need only look at growing Hindu aggression against Muslims in modern-day India. Like the case of Myanmar, hate speech and demonization of Muslims are being driven by extremist clergy, with Yati Narsinghanand, chief priest at the Dasna Devi Temple, being among the most vocal. Like the Serbs in the Bosnian war, he is amplifying a sense of historic injury.

In the case of India, it dates back to the end of British rule in 1947 and the partition of India and Pakistan. The establishment of modern India as a secular rather than a Hindu state was perceived as a deep offense to hard-liners and ultimately led to the assassination of Gandhi for his nonviolent methods and perceived appeasement of Muslims. Gandhi's assassin was shaped by a fringe movement that has now moved into the mainstream. Invoking fear that Muslims will take over India, hardline right-wing monks are calling for a religious war to kill them. Their chief priest invokes the Taliban and ISIS as role models. Some, in the government, are attempting to ban conversion by marriage and to change the citizenship status of Muslims. These actions are shades of the Rohingya statelessness in Myanmar and the Nuremberg laws in Germany. In India, we may be witnessing religicide in the making.

The meaning of the Hindu symbol for the sun, prosperity, and well-being—"swastika" in Sanskrit—was upended when it was appropriated by the Nazis as the symbol for the Thousand-Year Reich. It seems to have been lost on the Nazis that they had adopted the symbol of a race that they surely deemed inferior. And, like the Christian cross, when connected with atrocity, the swastika became an enduring symbol of mass violence and threat.

Buddhism is generally viewed as the zenith of a nonaggressive pacifistic religion largely due to the influence of His Holiness the 14th Dalai Lama, known as Gyalwa Rinpoche to the Tibetan people. But Buddhism has a long history of religion-inspired violence, including its history of violent religious competition in modern times.[92] In a *New York Times* op-ed, Dan Arnold and Alicia Turner wrote: "Even the history of the Dalai Lama's own sect of Tibetan Buddhism includes events like the razing of rival monasteries, and recent decades have seen a controversy centering on a wrathful protector deity believed by some of the Dalai Lama's fellow religionists to heap destruction on the false teachers of rival sects." Buddhist violence has also been evident in Sri Lanka's long civil war between the Tamil Hindus and Sinhalese Buddhist majority. Going back even further, the op-ed cited a "martial complicity of Buddhist institutions in World War II-era Japanese nationalism."[93]

The military regime in Myanmar in the late 1980s and early 2000s pushed for conversion of ethnic minorities and advanced Burmese Buddhist nationalism to legitimize itself in the face of pro-democracy forces. Much of the aggression and repression was goaded by the hardline nationalist 969 Movement of Buddhist monks. 969 stoked fears that Myanmar would be overrun by Muslims fixated on destroying Buddhist communities. The reality is that only 4 percent of the population was Muslim, and that percent has nearly been cut in half in recent years (according to Myanmar's census, which may in fact undercount the actual Muslim population). Disenfranchised and persecuted, by mid-2012, tens of thousands of Rohingyas had been displaced and hundreds killed. This oppression has continued to this day and is one of the case studies discussed in chapter 8. "Buddhism's lack of worldly attachments may render it more susceptible to nationalism: while Hinduism and Islam...have their own primary loyalties (Hinduism to caste, Islam to the caliphate), Buddhism has none."[94]

Buddhism justifies violence if the motivating intentions are compassionate—e.g., *yisha duosheng*: killing the few to save the many.[95] *Arya-Satyakaparivarta* says that warfare can be deemed meritorious when "the action [is] conjoined with intentions of compassion and not abandoning."[96] The *Milinda Panha* goes further by arguing that punitive violence is the outcome of one's own karma. The *Arya-Satyakaparivarta* makes allowances for compassionate torture—so long as there is no permanent physical damage—because of its potential salutary influence on the victim.[97]

As in the cases of India, Myanmar, and Ethiopia, nationalism can breed xenophobic attitudes toward outsiders.[98] But religion often provides the justification. Author Jonathan Sacks puts it succinctly: "Religion leads to violence when it consecrates hate."[99] This is how religious texts can lead to religious-sanctioned violence.

Our dogmatic beliefs can separate us, but shared values can bring us together. Shared values require that we be outward facing, not insular. In the case of Judaism, those outward-facing values include the notion that every human being is made in the sacred image of God and is, therefore, intrinsically worthy of dignity and respect. This, Judaism's greatest contribution to civilization, is the foundation of all human rights. Leviticus 19:16, "Do not stand by while your neighbor's blood is shed," (CEB)[100] obliges us to act in the face of suffering. The idea that besmirching a person's reputation is akin to murder is a powerful repudiation of hate speech. Finally, there is a core value of Judaism: *tikkun olam*—the call to repair the world.

In *Scripture and Violence*, Daniel Weiss observes, "Rather than encouraging human propensities for violence, the rabbinic framework...sharply restricts the possibility of using 'God said' as a justification for violence."[101] But how many religious leaders are teaching or using this framework?

Renowned Cambridge theologian David Ford applies Christianity's outward-facing values to counter religiously motivated violence. Ford describes the resurrection of Jesus as "God's verdict on torture, violence, evil, and death." When Jesus displays the stigmata on his body from the nails with which he was crucified and the spear thrust into his side by a Roman soldier, Ford interprets these as signs of solidarity with those who suffer and die. That solidarity is echoed when Jesus sends his disciples to emulate his life and asks us to do the same. As he breathes his Spirit on his disciples, he is inspiring them to face the ugly realities of the world with God's love. That same love reverberates throughout Jesus's beatitudes in the Sermon on the Mount. Among these: "Blessed are you when people revile you and persecute you and utter all kinds of evil against you falsely on my account." Jesus cites Isaiah: "He has sent me to proclaim release to the captives...to let the oppressed go free..." When combined with the beatitudes, Christianity commands its followers to eschew religicide and care for our neighbors—however remote and unfamiliar they may be. Ford concludes by noting, "The face of Jesus is especially turned toward those who are suffering, humiliated, vulnerable and marginal, among them the victims of religion-related violence and those at risk of it."[102]

Buddhism also espouses powerful values that offset violence. On mercy and compassion, Sutta Nipata 149-150 calls on Buddhists to love others with the same boundless love and protection that a mother feels toward her child—even at the risk of her own life. On nonviolence, Dhammapada 256-57 decries the use of violence to settle conflict. "Whoever settles a matter by violence is not just."[103] On religious freedom, Sutta Nipata 918 eschews group narcissism by proclaiming the equality of belief systems and Sutta Nipata 798 says: "To be attached to a certain view and to look down upon others' views as inferior—this the wise men call a 'fetter'—a chain or manacle used to restrain a prisoner, typically placed around the ankles."[104] And against hate speech, Dhammapada 133 admonishes: "Do not speak harshly to anybody; those who are spoken to will answer thee in the same way. Angry speech is painful, blows for blows will touch thee."[105]

These universal values notwithstanding, influential leaders often cherry-pick scripture and misuse religious symbols to justify violence to support their political ambitions. The *UN Plan of Action for Religious Leaders and Actors to Prevent Incitement to Violence that Could Lead to Atrocity Crimes* provides some antidotes to these tendencies: rapid response, promoting respect for cultural diversity, repealing blasphemy laws, training religious leaders in de-escalation techniques, literacy about religious diversity, and collaboration with media in communicating respect for others, among many other elements. The report further recommends establishing networks of religious leaders around a common goal of preventing and countering any incitement to violence. Ehrenkranz and Coppola, in *Religion and Violence and Peace,* underscore the point: "One task of religious leaders is to consciously teach and preach the scriptures in their entire context and moral framework, thus deterring oversimplified and impatient interpretation that could lead to violence."[106]

Rabbi Jonathan Sacks wrote, "There are times when only one thing has the power to defeat dualism and the division of the world into two, namely role reversal. To be cured of potential violence toward the Other, I must be able to imagine myself as the Other."[107] The case studies of religicide that follow demonstrate the failure of empathy that happens when group narcissism overtakes compassion.

Chapter Five

RELIGION KILLING RELIGION: ISIS AGAINST THE YAZIDIS

The 3rd of August 2014 is a dark day in the history of the Yazidis.... Men were killed, women and girls were enslaved, while children died from thirst and hunger on the slopes of Mount Sinjar.... They blew up our shrines, temples, and everything sacred to the Yazidis.... I remember that when all this happened, I thought within myself, "I wish I had not seen this day in my life, I wish I had died before I saw what happened to our people."[108]

—Baba Sheikh Khurto Ismail,
The late spiritual head of Yazidism

In 2014, the Islamic State (ISIS) began its religicidal assault on the Yazidis living in Northern Iraq. Many smaller attacks occurred in the years that followed, but the next major attack was the devastating blow caused by ISIS on August 3, 2014. A UN report describes the attack:

> In the early hours of 3 August 2014, ISIS fighters attacked Sinjar from Mosul and Tel Afar in

Iraq, and Al-Shaddadi and the Tel Hamis region (Hasakah) in Syria. The attack was well organised with hundreds of ISIS fighters acting in concert with each other as they seized towns and villages on all sides of Mount Sinjar.[109]

A girl captured at the age of sixteen described that day:

> After we were captured, ISIS forced us to watch them beheading some of our Yazidi men. They made the men kneel in a line in the street, with their hands tied behind their backs. The ISIS fighters took knives and cut their throats.[110]

A Yazidi religious authority sums it up: "When ISIS attacked Sinjar, they came to destroy."[111] This attempt to eradicate the Yazidi people, religion, heritage, and right to exist in Iraq was formally recognized as a genocide by the United Nations. Rightly so, as the tactics used against Yazidis certainly illustrated genocidal intent. But we classify this attack as religicidal because it combines the features of genocide, ecocide, and factocide, as well as the sexual enslavement of women and their ensuing suicides.

What were the religious motivations and methods used by the Islamic State? Why and how did ISIS attack the Yazidi people? And what circumstances made it possible for ISIS to attack them with such force? Finally, what is required for Yazidis and Yazidism to recover from such an all-encompassing attack, and how can we prevent such atrocities in the future?

Yazidism is fundamentally a very humane religion. Yazidis are not allowed to insult others. Traditionally, they are taught to pray for all other people and religions before presenting their personal requests to God. They do this with their arms folded across their chests while facing the sun. Some other tenets of Yazidism include:

- A taboo on saying the name of the evil one.
- All Wednesdays and the month of April are considered holy because, according to Yazidi tradition, God created the world on a Wednesday in the month of April.
- Yazidis are not permitted to marry outside their own order.

There are many other daily customs that carry an element of the sacred for Yazidis. For instance, they do not cut bread. They tear it because all bread is holy. Many Yazidis wear white undergarments and refrain from wearing blue in public. Yazidis consider white to be a color of purity and blue to be a color of divinity. This reflects their deep respect for their creator.

Though distinctive, Yazidism shares much in common with other religions of the Middle East. Like the Abrahamic religions—Judaism, Christianity, and Islam—Yazidis believe in one creator God. Many of the figures who appear in the Hebrew Bible and Christian New Testament, such as Adam, Eve, Moses, Mary, and Jesus, are also mentioned in Yazidism. Baptism and male circumcision are practiced as well. One major distinction is that, in Yazidism, there is no concept of hell, no trace of the biblical fall of man, and no practice of sacrifice comparable to Judaism or Christianity. Instead, Yazidis share a spirituality of blessing in which the giver and receiver participate in the blessing with equal measure and dignity. Yazidism is strictly nondualist.

Although they have strong connections with other religions and cultural groups, a basic identifying feature is the belief that

Yazidism has existed as a religion—and Yazidis as a people—since the creation of the world. Yazidis inherited their identity, faith, culture, and tradition from their ancestors through endogamy, meaning the only way to become Yazidi is to be born from two Yazidi parents. Ethnic belonging and adherence to the Yazidi faith, Yazidism, are inextricably linked. One cannot be Yazidi without believing in Yazidism; and one cannot adhere to Yazidism without being born Yazidi.[112]

Until ISIS attacked, most Yazidis lived in Nineveh—the historic region in present-day Iraq known from the Hebrew Bible in the Book of Jonah. For centuries they coexisted—albeit not without tension at times—with Sunni Arabs, Shia Turkmen, Shabaks, Christians, and other minority communities. Yazidis also live clustered around Lalish in present-day Iraqi Kurdistan. Lalish is the holiest place for the Yazidi pilgrimage. They believe Lalish is where God created humanity through the work of Taus Malek, who is symbolized by the peacock that was believed to act on behalf of God as the custodian of the universe.

In the eleventh century, the Sufi mystic, Sheikh Adi, lived in Lalish and influenced the evolution of Yazidi social norms, including rituals such as baptism in the Lalish holy spring. Because of its religious significance to Yazidis, Lalish is their central place of gathering. Yazidis who live in the region try to visit Lalish every year, especially in the month of October when they gather for Jemaya, their most important religious holiday. Although the main highlight is the shrine to Taus Malek, the valley of Lalish is also home to many other shrines dedicated to prominent religious figures. Notably, nearly all the shrines built in the valley of Lalish had counterparts on the sacred Mount Shingal over two hundred kilometers away. These shrines and the Jemaya, funerals, and other events that took place in Shingal prior to the ISIS attack, are part of what make the mountain sacred to Yazidis.

Yazidis claim they once formed the majority population in Kurdistan, but since the advent of the Ottoman Empire in the seventh century, they have been subject to dozens of attacks, many of which would now be considered genocidal. During the Armenian genocide (1915-1917), Yazidis were targeted by Turkish Muslims as a religious minority worthy of eradication. Many fled to the Shingal region, where they and roughly twenty thousand Christians were received hospitably by the Yazidi communities already residing there. After World War I toppled the Ottoman Empire, Kurdistan was carved up by government treaties among Iran, Iraq, Syria, and Turkey.

Yazidis once made up a large minority of the Turkish population, but Turkey has only a few hundred Yazidis at present. Most fled persecution there before the 1980s, resettling mostly in Iraq, Armenia, and Germany. More recently, Syria also had a flourishing Yazidi population. However, after a decade of war, the community is largely gone.

Iraq is the last major space where Yazidis live in their traditional manner. Although they still number some five hundred thousand people, the community has been placed under increasing pressure in recent decades. Saddam Hussein worked to strip Yazidis of their ethnic identity, along with other minorities. In the 1970s, Yazidis were forced to leave the security of their mountainside homes to live in collective villages in the plains below. There, they were separated from their ancestral land, holy places, and natural water sources, as well as their earlier means of employment. Saddam Hussein's Arabization policy (forcing religious minorities to leave their homeland) reached its peak in 1987-88 during the Anfal campaign. Tens of thousands of Kurdish Muslims, Yazidis, and Assyrian Christians were killed and displaced for not being Sunni Muslims.[113]

After the fall of Saddam Hussein in 2003, Iraqi Kurds worked to expand the boundaries of what eventually became the autonomous region of Kurdistan. Although Yazidis around Lalish, who lived in this newly formed autonomous state, were integrated with few problems, those in and around Shingal faced the challenge of being pressured to identify as Kurdish. This was intended to inflate the numbers of Kurdish citizens inhabiting a territory disputed by Iraq and Kurdistan, and to improve the Kurdish case for governing that region.

Once the power vacuum developed in 2003, radical groups became increasingly powerful. One of the most potent tools used by extremist groups has been religion. Over time, more and more fundamentalist Imams used the sermon during the Friday prayers to promote a pure Islamic society, denouncing other religions, including Yazidism. Since then, Yazidi villages and their community shrines have been targeted for destruction just for being different.

One of the worst attacks occurred August 14, 2007, when an Islamic terrorist group detonated four truck bombs in the Shingali villages of Tal Azeer and Seba Sheikh Kheder. An estimated eight hundred people were killed, and more than 1,500 wounded. No perpetrators were charged. There have been no consequences in Iraq for ongoing and systemic violence against the Yazidis.

Members of the group targeted for attack or sexual slavery often internalize pain and despair. Melancholy suicide often "appears with the dissolution of the traditional society."[114] Egoistic suicide results when an individual no longer finds any basis for his or her existence. Altruistic suicide is more about serving or sacrificing your individual life for some larger group.[115] Some, who are deeply religious, choose martyrdom—death over shame or conversion. All these forms of suicide are evident among the Yazidis and other victims of religicide.

GENOCIDE

ISIS overtly used religious language when declaring their reasons for murdering Yazidis. After taking over Shingal, they published an article in their English-speaking magazine which celebrated the return of slavery as a shift back to the original form of Islam. There they set out the stakes of not killing Yazidis:

> Upon conquering the region of Sinjar in Wilāyat
> Nīnawā, the Islamic State faced a population
> of Yazidis, a pagan minority existent for ages
> in regions of Iraq and Shām. Their continual
> existence to this day is a matter that Muslims
> should question as they will be asked about it on
> Judgment Day.[116]

The major grievance the Islamic State had with the Yazidis was their religious practice of honoring the angel known as Malek Taus. To Yazidis, the angel's decision to eschew worship of humans is a demonstration of his wisdom that God alone should be worshipped—something for which God praised him. But ISIS followed a long tradition of Yazidi detractors by claiming that Taus Malek was disobedient to God and that this act led him to become the devil himself:

> The Yazidis present-day creed...entails the wor-
> ship of Iblīs whom they consider to be a fallen
> but forgiven angel amongst the angels who were
> ordered to prostrate to Ādam! He alone refused
> to prostrate himself to Ādam, and they consider
> this arrogant disobedience of Allah to be his
> noblest deed!... So, they have made Iblīs—who is
> the biggest tāghūt—the symbolic head of enlight-
> enment and piety! What arrogant kufr can be
> greater than this?[117]

Because of this, and because Yazidism is not a "religion of the book," the Islamic State dealt with this group as the majority of *fuqahā* have indicated how *mushrikīn* should be dealt with. Unlike the Jews and Christians, there was no room for *jizyah* payment. Also, their women could be enslaved unlike female apostates who the majority of the *fuqahā* say cannot be enslaved and can only be given an ultimatum to repent or face the sword.[118]

This reasoning is distorted and divergent from most Muslim ideology. But it is impossible to ignore the religious terminology and motivation for killing Yazidis. This is religion killing religion: an extremely violent sect of Islam seeking overtly to destroy a religious minority. What ISIS did in the name of Islam represented a return to a seventh century mindset and legal environment. Their believers passionately wanted to bring about a final apocalypse, as prophesied in the Qur'an.

The only way to make sense of ISIS killing five thousand Yazidi men and older women, enslaving six thousand young boys, girls, and women, and displacing some four hundred thousand Yazidis, is that they were convinced of their moral and religious duty to do so. This pathological religious conviction led to a devastating conformity in the implementation of their lethal monopolistic doctrine.

One family who fell victim to this dogma was that of Mahmoud Khero. They lived on a farm along the road between the villages of Tal Azeer and Jidale. Approximately 150 members of the family gathered there because they believed it was safer than Tal Azeer. They remained because they wanted to assist the many Yazidis who stopped at their house to get water from their well as they fled to the mountain. Shortly after the original attacks, ISIS arrived at the farm in twelve cars. Within half an hour, they killed twelve family members—eleven men and one woman—and abducted twenty-eight boys, girls, and young women. A further fifty were separated but spared because the ISIS soldiers were called away for an emergency.[119]

One of these survivors reports that the ISIS fighters asked the men to identify their religion. When the men confirmed that they were Yazidis, the ISIS fighters said that they were infidels and that killing them was halal, considered lawful and permissible. After being made to hand over their keys, telephones, and money, the men were asked if they wanted to convert. When they refused to do so, they were executed on the spot.[120]

Such accounts are numerous. Men and older boys were killed because it was thought they would pose a physical threat if they were kept alive. Older men and women were killed because they were not seen as being valuable enough to enslave.

Six thousand young boys, girls, and younger women were treated very differently. Taken into captivity, they were integrated into the Islamic State's oppressive system. Boys who were later released—few ran away—report that they underwent a strenuous military training as well as religious indoctrination. Some who returned to their original families continue to insist that their Yazidi relatives are unclean and should be killed and that they, themselves, would like to return to their new "families" in ISIS. Others who resisted ISIS ideology are now unwilling or unable to go to school after returning from captivity—not only because of their physical trauma, but also because they had forgotten how to speak Kurmanji after years of only speaking Arabic.[121]

Women and girls faced a different type of horror. They were forced to convert to Islam and sold as sex slaves. Many were coerced to enter "marriages" with their captors. ISIS justified this practice explicitly in religious terms:

> One should remember that enslaving the families of the *kuffār* and taking their women as concubines is a firmly established aspect of the Sharī'ah that if one were to deny or mock, he would be denying or mocking the verses of the Qur'ān and the narrations of the Prophet (*sallallāhu 'alayhi wa sallam*), and thereby apostatizing from Islam.[122]

ISIS maintained that reinstating slavery and the practice of having concubines enabled ISIS fighters to remain sexually pure since:

> The desertion of slavery had led to an increase in *fāhishah* (adultery, fornication, etc.), because the shar'ī alternative to marriage is not available, so a man who cannot afford marriage to a free woman finds himself surrounded by temptation towards sin.[123]

Reading ISIS' sexist and racist justifications for modern-day slavery and rape is made more horrifying when hearing about the actual violence experienced by Yazidi women and girls. In her book, *The Last Girl: My Story of Captivity and My Fight Against the Islamic State*, Nadia Murad, who was enslaved by ISIS and later became co-laureate of the 2018 Nobel Peace Prize, explains:

> Taking girls to use as sex slaves wasn't a spontaneous decision made on the battlefield by a greedy soldier. The Islamic State planned it all: how they would come into our homes, what made a girl more or less valuable, which militants deserved a *sabaya* [sex slave] as incentive and which should pay.[124]

Accounts from testimonies to the US Congress in 2015 described markets where ISIS traded young women "like cattle, or even rented them to each other. Those crimes were condoned, even celebrated, by ISIS's official publications."[125]

Rape has long been used as a weapon of war. However, it is important to emphasize that ISIS went even further than this. They used rape to wipe out religious identity and solidify their homogeneous caliphate. With Muslim fathers, the children born of these rapes could not be considered Yazidi under the laws of endogamy. Enslaving young boys and youths and training them as militants also served a purpose far beyond that of strengthening ISIS fighting forces; it made Yazidi children a lethal threat to their own community. The very act of enslaving part of the population traumatized the whole community, who knew that their loves ones were almost certainly enduring unimaginable horrors. All of this was done to weaken Yazidis and Yazidism. It also served to strengthen the arguments of ISIS "scholars," who claimed that by enslaving Yazidis, Islam was in the process of returning to its roots and fulfilling prophecies related to the final days.

The multifarious consequences of the ISIS attack were immediately clear to many Yazidis. A young woman shared how, when stranded on Mount Shingal and uncertain of whether ISIS would find them, she and the other women and girls in her family begged their male relatives to kill them. They explained that if ISIS found them, they would simply put the men to death. The women and girls, however, would face a long and agonizing fate far worse than death. In the end, the men talked them out of this, and the family survived to tell their story, but psychological scars remain.[126] Many women who survived know their friends and sisters did not.

ISIS hoped that enslaving and raping Yazidi women would destroy the social "purity" of Yazidism. There was good reason to believe so. Over the course of centuries, both Muslim and Yazidi women who lost their virginity outside of marriage were not accepted back into their communities—whether they had had sex voluntarily or were victims of rape. Likewise, Yazidis who converted to another religion had no chance of return. ISIS understood that converting to another religion, even under duress, was long considered an unpardonable sin in the Yazidi religion.[127] Forcing unmarried Yazidi women and girls to convert to Islam and then raping them would mean these women would have no way back into their community, thus ending their acceptance as Yazidis.

The reason this strategy failed is that Yazidis responded differently than ISIS predicted. They prioritized the safety of the women. Khidhir Domle, a Yazidi activist, explains that when women in captivity would call him every day asking fearfully about what would happen to them, his advice was: "Don't worry, convert to Islam, just keep yourself safe." Khurto Ismail (deceased 2020), who was then Baba Sheikh, the religious head of Yazidism, understood the gravity of the situation. He issued a decree declaring that, upon return, these women and girls would be allowed to undergo a simple purification ritual after which they would be reinstated into Yazidism.[128]

Unfortunately, many of these women became pregnant during their enslavement, creating an even greater dilemma for the Yazidi community. Based on the women's understanding of family and communal structures, accepting children who were born of non-Yazidis—men who wanted to annihilate their people—would be tantamount to accepting ISIS itself into the community. Yazidis are aware that the children themselves are innocent and that their mothers are not to blame. But most Yazidis, including the Yazidi Spiritual Council, have rejected the idea that such children should be able to join their mothers and integrate into the Yazidi community.

This may seem harsh. However, accepting these children not only goes against the endogamous basis of Yazidi society, but it is also illegal in Iraq, where life is regulated by social and religious norms that are rarely questioned publicly. "Based on Iraqi legislation, a child with an unknown identity must be considered Muslim and the Iraqi government does not allow such children to join Yazidis."[129] As Murad Ismael, director of Yazda, a multinational Yazidi organization, explains, "The magnitude of ISIS crimes makes it extremely difficult for many people to accept raising children linked to ISIS."[130]

This leaves the women, as well as the community, in an impossible quandary. Women who are prepared to be separated from their children can rejoin the Yazidi community in Iraq without legal repercussions or being marginalized—an unprecedented step. But women who are not prepared to give up their children risk the legal repercussions of having a child fathered by a Muslim and the societal repercussions of raising an ISIS child within the Yazidi community. Most Yazidis believe that the best solution is for these women to leave Iraq and move to the West with their children. In a *New York Times* article, Ali Elias Haji Nasir, who was elected Baba Sheikh in 2020, shows the level of harm done by ISIS as he describes why he, the Spiritual Council, and the Yazidi community could not welcome these "orphans": "Yazidis are all orphans. No one is taking care of us."[131]

This is exactly what ISIS wanted.

Even today, Yazidis are dying. Those who have returned to Shingal face the dangers of landmines and other unexploded ordnance that have not yet been cleared. Most Yazidis in both Kurdistan and Shingal suffer harsh living conditions in tents or poorly build structures with little access to medical care. Some Yazidis lost their relatives in mass executions. Nearly all Yazidis lost friends and family, and most remain displaced from their homeland or separated from their loved ones. Anyone who has been enslaved, witnessed atrocity, or experienced genocide will suffer from a range of post-traumatic stress disorders, understandably including higher rates of depression. Yazidi women have been kidnapped, raped, and serially abused in the thousands. Tens of thousands of Yazidis have been displaced for years and despair of a better future. As such, they exhibit a significantly higher rate of suicide—one of the hallmarks and effects of religicide.

SUICIDE

Given the multiple and historic pain points, the effects of religicide continue, reaching across generations. The ISIS achievement of religicide through mass slaughter continues through rising rates of mental illness and suicide, which the international organization, Doctors Without Borders (MSF), has dubbed a suicide epidemic.[132]

Between April 1 and July 29 of 2019, when the medical charity began counting, it noted the suicide of twenty young Yazidis (ages thirteen to thirty), including women setting themselves on fire. Doctors Without Borders assessors, who were clinical psychologists, evaluated over four hundred Yazidi women and girls in internally displaced persons' (IDP) camps. Some of their tests showed that "all formerly enslaved and 97.2% of non-enslaved participants fulfilled the DSM-5 criteria for a PTSD diagnosis." Essentially the entire group had experienced severe trauma.[133] It is fair to ask whether the current situation can be considered "post-traumatic" as the trauma is ongoing.

Put yourself in the shoes of a Yazidi who lived through this genocide and ecocide. Every time there is some hopeful news of one Yazidi escaping or being released from captivity, Yazidis can't help but wonder: what has happened to all the others? Daughters, sons, and relatives have all gone missing. Every time a sporadic fire breaks out in a displacement camp, Yazidis are faced with the reality that their people still live in thin, dry tents that were supplied more than seven years ago and easily catch fire. Every time a mass grave is discovered, or a Yazidi unjustly taken into custody, Yazidis are reminded that their ISIS neighbors continue to show signs of aggression against them. Not to mention the stress inflicted as Turkey repeatedly bombs their holy Mount Shingal, trying to attack nearby members of the PKK (Kurdistan Workers' Party).

Every day is infused with triggers and trauma, rekindled and real.

And yet, ISIS is not the only source of this chronic trauma and danger. Yazidis suffered moral injury and social trauma from Kurdish forces, as well. The Peshmerga troops left their posts in Shingal on the morning of August 3, 2014, leaving Yazidis unprotected and exposed. They gave no warning and left no arms with which Yazidis could defend themselves. To this day, it is unclear why they departed, leaving the Yazidis completely exposed.

An equally painful betrayal came from their Arab neighbors. When ISIS arrived, many of these former friends arrived with them, pointing out where Yazidis could be found. The trust that had developed over decades and centuries was largely destroyed.

This is not to say that no one cared. On August 3, 2014, the sole Yazidi parliamentarian in Iraq, Vian Dakhil, cried out for help to her fellow politicians and citizens in Baghdad.[134] Yazidis living in Texas and Nebraska joined together, hoping that they could persuade the United States to intervene. What came was too little and too late.

Recovery had barely begun. Then the COVID-19 pandemic made things exponentially worse.

The pandemic hit Yazidis particularly hard. Not only do they fear getting sick, especially given the severe lack of medical care, but the organizations on which they had come to rely cut much of their support to focus on the Covid crisis. In the spring of 2020, there was a complete lockdown in Kurdistan. Yazidis living outside of camps and working hand to mouth as day laborers had their income wiped out. The rest were confined to their tents with no certainty and no prospects—this in a population where an estimated 97.2 percent of the population was demonstrating symptoms of PTSD.

The mental health crisis among Yazidis is severe because their conditions remain traumatic. But it is exacerbated by the fact that there are few mental health resources. In Iraq, there are only eighty psychologists for a population of forty million—roughly one psychiatrist per 250,000 residents. (By comparison, in the United States, there is one psychiatrist for every twelve thousand residents.) Not even one of these psychiatrists or psychologists are Yazidi. Doctors Without Borders, reporting on mental health in Iraq, observed that:

> The combination of psychological trauma from ISIS captivity and limited access to basic psychological services, due to the stigma around mental health in Iraq, has unfortunately led many Yazidi people, primarily women, to search for suicide as an answer to their suffering.[135]

The only way for Yazidis to recover from their trauma is to be given security and protection. This includes, but goes well beyond, physical protection from ISIS. Yazidi community structures, farmland, houses, shrines, and infrastructure must be restored in Shingal and developed in the regions where they have since found refuge. Dangerous misinformation about Yazidism must be refuted and authentic Yazidi voices must be amplified. In short, religicide must be recognized and actively fought.

ECOCIDE

As if killing and enslaving Yazidis weren't harmful enough, ISIS displaced approximately four hundred thousand Yazidis—nearly the entire population of Shingal. Tens of thousands of Yazidis who tried to flee to safety in August 2014 were surrounded by ISIS fighters on Mount Shingal. They remained stranded there for more than a week, exposed to extreme heat with little water or food. Those who escaped were forced to leave their weaker relatives behind, knowing they would be killed. The intention was for them to die on the mountain. Hundreds did. Those who were eventually rescued were taken to internally displaced people (IDP) camps. Some went on to find refuge or asylum abroad, especially in Germany. The majority stayed.

Although the northern villages of Shingal were freed in 2015, it was impossible for Yazidis to return immediately, since ISIS placed explosive devices and landmines in fields and houses throughout the region. The southern villages, which were not freed until the summer of 2017, fared even worse.

Roughly one hundred thousand Yazidis live in the region today. Some minefields have been cleared and a small number of Yazidis have begun to farm, especially in North Shingal, which was not as heavily destroyed as the South. Most Yazidis describe the ghost towns as a frontier. They live as pioneers trying to reclaim their land and their way of life in the face of an array of dangers. Anyone who dares to return must be able to dig a well for water, build shelter, and support themselves in a harsh climate. The region has almost no work opportunities, as it is run in large part by competing militia groups supported by Turkey, Iran, Iraq, and Kurdistan.

True to its playbook, *The Management of Savagery*, the Islamic State boasted about its scorched-earth policies. According to an engineer describing the devastation to Amnesty International, "Wells and boreholes were blocked by all sorts of foreign items pushed into them: oil and bits of metal but also clothes, garbage, old pumping equipment, pieces of old pipe...."[136] By signaling its ability to control and deliver basic resources, ISIS used water as an effective means to assert power. Even as the Islamic State began losing territory, its fighters eviscerated the landscape by indiscriminately sabotaging and poisoning wells as well as destroying the pumps and stealing cables, generators, and transformers. A 2017 assessment documented that 400 of 450 irrigation wells around Shingal were completely inoperable.[137]

ISIS also scorched and chopped down Yazidi orchards. Majdal, a Yazidi farmer in his mid-fifties from Solakh, a Yazidi village on the south side of Mount Shingal, laments:

> There is nothing left. Now the house is destroyed, and all the trees burned down. We had 100 olive trees, but when I went, I didn't see a single tree in any direction. They were chopped down and burnt....They wanted us to lose everything. They didn't want us to be able to come back to our land.[138]

ISIS ecocide also included the slaughter of animals. One Yazidi who managed to escape after spending more than a week on Mount Shingal shares how he still has nightmares about what happened to their farm.

We not only had many chickens, but we also kept hundreds of doves as well as several peacocks. When I was on Mount Shingal, I kept thinking about them, hoping that the doves would somehow manage to fly away. Later on, someone who had been in the area reported back to us. ISIS burnt them alive in their barn.[139]

This was not a singular event. One assessment of the damage to Shingal city in November 2015 estimated that 70 percent of livestock and 70 percent of crops and agricultural machinery had been looted.[140] In Sinune, one of the sub-districts of Shingal, the UN Food and Agriculture Organization (FAO) reported that the pre-ISIS population of 120,000 sheep and goats declined to 35,000, while all 500 cows and 1,000 beehives were lost.[141]

When Dakhil and his Yazidi family returned, he felt sadness. "We have come back to dead land. It's as if we never worked here at all."[142] Crops, sheep, and chickens were gone. The two buildings the family had owned for farming chickens were without roofing and all the feeding devices were missing. ISIS had blocked the farm's well.

Hadi, a farmer in his mid-forties from a small village south of Sinjar Mountain, testifies:

I had a well—220 meters deep—as well as a generator and an irrigation pipe system. They threw rubble in my well and filled it to the top. My trees were chopped down—I could see the marks from chopping with a chainsaw. The irrigation system—from the pump to the pipes—was stolen.

They did this to send a message: that you have nothing to return to, so if you survive don't even think of coming back.[143]

"Talking about his reasons for remaining in Dohuk, Hadi told Amnesty International, 'Our lives depend on agriculture. I don't have anything now: no salary, no savings, just land which I cannot use.'"[144]

Eylo, a farmer in his mid-thirties from a village north of Sinjar Mountain, recounts, "When I first came back [my farm] was a disaster, it was destroyed. Before IS [Islamic State] I had 400 olive trees, now I have 250 because a lot were burnt down. They were burnt before this area was liberated."[145]

Kamal, a former farmer in his early thirties from near Daquq, says he had to flee with his family to live in Kirkuk city, fifty kilometers to the north, where he found some work selling onions and tomatoes by the side of the road. When Kamal returned briefly to visit his farm, he found it contaminated with mines. He tells Amnesty International, "This is no kind of life [in Kirkuk] but I can't go back. The explosives are still all there."[146]

Farmland was not the only target of ISIS ecocide. They went after Yazidi shrines and temples. The chief Yazidi spiritual leader Baba Sheikh assesses the situation:

> They blew up our shrines, temples, and every-
> thing sacred to the Yazidis. They did all this,
> thinking that Sinjar would become theirs.
> They even told the boys and women that they
> had exterminated all Yazidis... ISIS blew up
> the Amadin shrine on the southern side of the
> Sinjar mountains and, as I have been told, they

imprisoned a man in the shrine and blew him up along with it.[147]

The United Nations reports a full-on massacre at the Sheikh Mand shrine:

> Eyewitnesses have confirmed that on 24 or 25 August, ISIL executed by gunfire 14 elderly Yezidi men in Sheikh Mand Shrine, Jidala village, western Sinjar. The elderly could not flee when ISIL took over the village on 24 August. ISIL later destroyed the shrine.[148]

When combined, ecocide with genocide, are a strong indicator of religicide.

FACTOCIDE

Another key element of religicide is factocide. The Islamic State nearly perfected the art of propaganda. In addition to sermons by extremist Imams and statements from Baghdadi and other leaders, multiple online sources amplified propaganda to radicalize recruits.

ISIS ideology is not accepted by the vast majority of Muslims. The belief and practices of the movement are rooted in an archaic version of Muslim ideology based on seventh century practices described in the Qur'an. Most Muslims today would acknowledge that the Prophet Muhammad's conquests and prescriptions for war were born of the turbulent and violent times in which he lived. Even so, this reliance on tradition means that in some respects the fighters of the Islamic State must be seen as authentic throwbacks to early Islam, who are faithfully reproducing its norms of war, adhering strictly to the prophecy and example of Muhammad given more than 1,500 years ago. Yes, nearly all Muslims have rejected the Islamic State. But we can't pretend ISIS is not actually a religious group with its own theology. Its tenets must be understood to be countered effectively.

Preaching sermons and posting online were not the full extent of their work. Repetition and practice hammered home their message. ISIS followers continually spouted propaganda, recording videos that repeated their doctrines and practices with pride, including justifications to massacre others in the name of Allah.

In the case of the Yazidis, ISIS continually claimed they worshipped the devil. The relentless charge that Yazidis are devil worshippers seems archaic, absurd, and easily disproved. Yet, this was, without question, the primary disinformation ISIS used to justify and mobilize support to implement the slaughter and enslavement of Yazidis. Not everyone goes as far as ISIS, but nearly all Yazidis have had the experience of Muslims refusing to eat food that they prepared for them because many Muslims consider Yazidi food and its Yazidi preparers to be "unclean." The consequences of disinformation and related prejudice, whether extreme or more nuanced, are ongoing.

The danger caused to Yazidi youths who were recruited by ISIS must also be considered factocide. ISIS not only made these Yazidi boys attend religious classes, but indoctrination went so far that even word problems in mathematics were focused on killing infidels, destroying military opponents, and the like. ISIS indoctrination filled every corner of its members' daily lives. As a 2019 report from Yale University makes plain:

Propaganda videos, and the firsthand account of released Yazidi child soldiers have also evidenced that, after kidnapping, forcibly conscripting and brainwashing children, ISIS trained them to kill their 'infidel' parents, and to be suicide bombers. These acts continue to have long-term consequences for the Yazidi community: freed children are viewed as a source of risk and future insurrection—'ticking time bombs.'[149]

This description of Yazidi children who were trained by ISIS demonstrated how the organization used factocide as part of their strategy to promote their religious ideology and destroy Yazidism, causing deep psychological strain in the Yazidi community.

As one Yazidi religicide survivor from Shingal told us in October 2020, "Our house is destroyed and there are many dangers here. Sometimes it is hard to hope, and the task of rebuilding is daunting because we have to start over from scratch."[150]

WHAT CAN BE DONE

The religicide against Yazidism was accomplished primarily by murder, enslavement, destruction of ancestral lands, false information, and the ongoing trauma triggered by this violence. The only way to reverse the effects of religicide is to take seriously the religion-against-religion roots of the violence done against Yazidis, ensure that Yazidis have an increased political role in decision-making, and take practical steps to care for the dead, the enslaved, and the displaced. The response must tap into cultural and religious resources for community building and social support, relying on both the historic resilience of Yazidism and the fierce hope that many Yazidis hold for the future.

One priority must be finding mass graves, identifying the dead, burying them in a dignified way and performing these actions in a space and manner where loved ones can remember, mourn, and celebrate them in accordance with Yazidi customs. This must also be done in a way that allows the ISIS perpetrators of these crimes to be brought to justice.

Iraqi and international units should prioritize the release and rescue of Yazidis who were sold into slavery. This is made more challenging by the reticence of most governments to exchange money with a terrorist group such as ISIS. Even so, it is more reasonable for governments with elite military and peacekeeping forces to rescue enslaved women and children than to expect Yazidis to heal and rebuild trust when thousands of members of their community remain enslaved.

The Iraqi and international community must ensure that Yazidis have the freedom and resources to leave temporary, dangerous, and impoverished displacement camps. They should be able to choose between living in safety elsewhere or rebuilding their ancestral homeland and communities in a dignified and secure way.

In all these initiatives, steps must be taken to ensure that Yazidis are given the sovereignty to shape their own recovery and rehabilitation plans organically and authentically. Likewise, they must be given a meaningful voice in Kurdish and Iraqi politics.

Political

To protect the safety and security of the Yazidis in their ancestral home, political actions must be taken to ensure their safety and livelihood both now and in the future.

On an international level, the United Nations Office of the High Commissioner for Human Rights (OHCHR) is key for helping ensure Yazidi rights are protected and respected. Several UN treaties, such as the Universal Declaration of Human Rights (UDHR), the International Covenant on Civil and Political Rights (ICCPR), the Declaration on the Rights of Persons Belonging to National or Ethnic, Religious and Linguistic Minorities, and the Convention on the Prevention and Punishment of the Crime of Genocide (UNCG) can be employed at the very least. These treaties and declarations guarantee the right of groups and individuals to various forms of protection that are enforceable by law.

The international court system can draw upon these treaties to demand and secure justice and safety. An important start has already been made by a German court that, for the first time, handed down a "conviction for religious and gender-based persecution."[151] This is a victory for women, survivors, and victim rights advocates who demand a reappraisal of the atrocities committed by ISIS in regard to the gender and religious dimensions of their crimes.

Germany has invoked universal jurisdiction to try and convict a Syrian accused of overseeing the torture of thousands of his countrymen during the years of the Arab Spring uprising there. It should likewise be invoked to try ISIS perpetrators. Universal jurisdiction applies when a crime is so egregious that it transcends borders and allows individuals to be tried, regardless of where the alleged crime was committed.

In addition to availing themselves of UN resources, both Iraq and Kurdistan should look to modify their parliamentary systems in a way that emphasizes both equity and equality. Inclusion is critical—revising the system in such a way that it gives Yazidis and other small minorities a stronger political voice is essential.

Importantly, the Yazidis are not alone as religious minorities in Iraq. Other minorities include Christians, Sabean-Mandean, Baha'i, Yarsani, and the remnants of the Jewish community. If multi-religion coalitions were formed, the Yazidis and other minorities could secure regional safety and prevent a recurrence of the abandonment of the Yazidis in 2014 by regional partners. These regional coalitions would provide Yazidis and other minorities with political support in the Iraqi and Kurdish government legislatures. But such coalitions cannot form absent an understanding of each other's religions. In cases where religion is misconstrued, someone on the ground must be designated to stop violence before it ignites.

The most daunting and essential point of action for the Iraqi and Kurdish governments is to finally come to an arrangement on Article 140 of the Sinjar agreement in the Iraqi Constitution and build on it in a way that involves Yazidis in the planning and implementation of recovery and rehabilitation programs in their homeland.[152] This should include an agreement between the Iraqi government, Baba Sheikh, and the Yazidi Spiritual Council to set out practical ways of helping Yazidis who are especially at risk: women with children born of ISIS, women and children who have not yet been rescued from ISIS, and children who were brainwashed by ISIS and now pose a threat to their own community.

All of this will certainly require substantial support and accountability from the international community, especially from the United States, France, Germany, Jordan, and Egypt. Although such partnerships take time to develop, a June 2020 meeting between the Egyptian, Jordanian, and Iraqi heads of state was an important step in this direction. In the wake of the 2021 Taliban takeover in Afghanistan, the urgency of maintaining stability in Iraq became even more obvious. Regional and world leaders are clearly aware of this. President Emmanuel Macron of France and several Middle Eastern heads of state held a meeting on August 29, 2021. On that occasion, Macron promised to "do whatever we can, shoulder to shoulder, with the governments of the region and with the Iraqi government to fight against this terrorism" as well as rebuild schools, shrines and provide "economic opportunity."[153] This statement recognizes the work that must be done for Yazidis and others affected by ISIS. The remaining question is how the United States will engage in this process, especially as they move toward a military withdrawal from Iraq.

The international community needs to officially and publicly recognize the genocide committed against Yazidis. France, Belgium, and the Netherlands have already done so. A petition to the Bundestag in Germany passed in September 2021. It is likely that the Yazidi genocide will be formally recognized there as well. Statements like these are important. But recognition of the genocide will only be useful if words are transformed into action, including offering protection to Yazidi survivors. To that end, countries that welcome Yazidis must work with them to develop best practices for integration. As well, they must create mechanisms by which these survivors can help their families and other community members in Iraq and worldwide.

In addition to offering practical aid that allows Yazidis to return to Shingal or leave Iraq, it is important to set the historic record straight. The story of the violence and disenfranchisement of the Yazidis must be heard. It should go without saying, but we'll say it anyway: future negotiations must be more inclusive and respect the dignity, rights, and participation of Yazidis, who are critical for any effective implementation. Yazidi women could play a more substantial leadership role to help their communities adapt to contemporary circumstances. All initiatives must incorporate gender considerations, promoting women as crucial actors in future climate, peace, and security discussions.[154]

Economic

The economic situation in Iraq is important for understanding the underlying issues and ways to address them. Oil sales constitute nearly 90 percent of government revenue. Any drop in price per barrel threatens the government's ability to pay workers and provide basic services, such as water and electricity, to its citizens. Iraq now faces a massive budgetary crisis due to the pandemic and overdependence on declining oil revenues. Recovery solutions for Shingal and Iraq must broadly be more diverse, ecologically sound, and financially sustainable than those proposed to date.

If only the Shingal region is developed, resentment elsewhere in the country could lead to more violence. Therefore, Iraq's overall economy must be made more stable and revenue sources more diversified. The International Monetary Fund (IMF) and the World Bank suggest that Iraq's economic issues can be remedied by rebuilding the labor force through skills training. This especially applies to youths, who have high unemployment rates.

All recovery and rehabilitation initiatives must be based on regenerative practices that start with the soil and go all the way up to the highest political relationships. Solar and other renewable energy sources that exist in abundance in a warm country like Iraq must be preferentially tapped for investment. In addition to being environmentally sound, this would increase regional and national sovereignty, decreasing or eliminating Iraq's dependence on Iranian gas—a perpetual source of conflict.

Yazidis can be important contributors to these goals. Shingal Mountain must be replanted with trees to counter the alarming desertification of the region. Yazidis can return to their agrarian economy and increase the fertility of the soil in a way that is financially sustainable and productive. A new initiative in Kurdistan is indication of openness to this.[155] The Greening the Desert Project in Jordan provides an economically profitable model for combining regenerative farming with education and tourism. Israeli expertise in desert agriculture should also be tapped, especially since such humanitarian organizations as IsraAID have a track record working with Yazidis.

New sources of income, including access to broadband, will enable work that can be done remotely and online. This will allow Yazidis to remain in their ancestral community. This would be a huge advancement over Yazidis working as poorly paid day laborers in Kurdistan.

Support from USAID, the World Bank, the Islamic Development Bank, and others can help pull Yazidis out of poverty. However, money alone is never enough. Partnerships with universities and fair-trade organizations, as well as training sessions with experts, can teach the skills that are necessary for sustainable development.

Loans and grants of all sizes, whether for small enterprises or medium-sized farming and construction companies, are essential for securing Yazidi sovereignty and financial security, especially if Shingal becomes a heritage site and tourism is increased. But sustainability takes priority over tourism. For thousands of years, Yazidis were farmers. The World Bank and IMF suggest—for Iraq as a whole—that farming needs to be developed both for food security and future export goods such as olive oil.

Cultural

Physical structures are an important facet of Yazidism. They are traditional gathering places of communities as well as historical artifacts. With UNESCO status for Shingal, the Yazidis could have more funding to rebuild and restore their shrines. These renewed shrines open the possibility of tourism in the future and, more importantly, would provide a sense of healing to Yazidis who have worshipped in these spaces for thousands of years.

Locally in Sinjar, as well as in key places throughout Iraq and the diaspora, educational and research centers (both academic and popular) need to be developed that promote awareness of the Yazidi religion and culture.

Social

Iraq lags behind other Middle East countries in indicators such as child mortality rates, life expectancy, and years of schooling. Compounding these issues is the exodus of skilled workers triggered by the 2003 Iraq War. They have yet to return. Many conflicts in the intervening years have left 1.4 million internally displaced peopled (IDPs) scattered throughout the country.[156]

If Yazidis are to recover, community structures must be rebuilt and strengthened. Yazidis themselves must shape this process. Women, including and extending far beyond the courageous

Nadia Murad, have played a crucial role in doing this from the start and should be encouraged to expand their role.

The collective trauma of the Yazidis must be addressed in ways that are healing and ultimately empowering. Religion will necessarily play a role in this, both in terms of collective healing and individual treatment of trauma. People heal in different ways, but the bonds of community that have held the Yazidis together for thousands of years are their greatest resource.

The number of psychiatrists in Iraq and Kurmanji and Arabic-speaking psychiatrists worldwide needs to be increased, and remote online counseling services could supplement services on the ground. Above all, Yazidis should be trusted to rely on their own cultural and religious resources to respond to their trauma.

Our experience working with Yazidi partners in Iraq shows that if provided with tools to recover their land, rebuild their towns, and develop meaningful connections with local and international allies, Yazidis can and will regenerate their land, culture, religion, and economy. But they need the support of international partners who respect the distinct contributions and qualities of this little known, but resilient community.

As Iraq continues to shape its future and recover from the war against the Islamic State, restoring the mosaic of ethnic and religious diversity—including supporting the Yazidis, who previously existed in Shingal and the Nineveh governorate—is crucial to promote a healthy and stable civil society within Iraq. It's perhaps the best defense against future religicide.

In late 2021, a Yazidi, who was participating in the rebuilding of Shingal, reported proudly:

> Last week, our family hosted Baba Sheikh, when
> he visited our village. Hundreds of Yazidis came.

Things have not returned to normal; what is that even? But we were able to come together. Just imagine! And we are about to plant onions and potatoes. Other families keep telling us that they want to join us, but there is still no housing for them. We will work toward that, though. We will not give up.[157]

Chapter Six

STATE KILLING RELIGION: CHINA AGAINST THE UYGHURS

I was abused, persecuted, and tortured in my own homeland.... My courage to speak out comes from my faith and hope, and my aspiration for freedom and liberty for my oppressed people who are left behind.[158]

—**Mihrigul Tursun**, Uyghur survivor of religicide

Mihrigul Tursun is a Uyghur mother, wife, and daughter who returned to China from Egypt in 2015 with her three newborn triplets to introduce them to their proud and eager grandparents. When she arrived in Xinjiang, the nightmare began. Because she is Uyghur, Tursun was detained at the airport and separated from her children. She was held in prison until she was granted parole to care for her traumatized children. One of her triplets died in state custody after undergoing an unapproved medical treatment.

Tursun was detained for a third time in January 2018, repeatedly interrogated for details regarding her Uyghur relatives, friends, and associates in China and Egypt, where she has citizenship. She was imprisoned in an underground cell whose population increased during her incarceration from forty women to more than sixty. She watched nine of her cellmates die without receiving proper medical attention. When she was finally released, Tursun brought her two surviving children back to Egypt. She says that Chinese authorities continued their efforts to coerce her, across borders, to return to China by threatening the safety of her relatives still living in Xinjiang. Tursun does not know the whereabouts of her parents but knows her sister was detained and her brother-in-law sentenced to sixteen years in prison. She refuses to keep silent.[159]

Religicide is about individuals like Tursun, but it's also collective. China has locked up hundreds of thousands of Uyghurs over the past four years as part of its so-called war against terror. By labeling Uyghurs "terrorists," China can act with impunity to persecute those who practice Islam. Religicide is deeply embedded in the Chinese Communist Party culture with its renunciation of religion itself and zero tolerance for dissent and criticism. As such, religious groups in China typically face systemic persecution.

Its ideological atheism notwithstanding, five religions are officially recognized in China: Buddhism, Catholicism, Taoism, Islam, and Protestantism. Despite its stated policy, modern China is largely intolerant of religion. The Chinese government is systematically eradicating religious adherence among tens of millions of Chinese who derive strength and meaning from their faith and culture. These include the 16 percent of China's population who identify as Buddhist, 7.4 percent who are Christian, and 1.8 percent who are Muslim.[160]

Under special threat are 1.5 million Kazakhs, 200,000 Kyrgyz, 50,000 Tajiks, 10,000 Uzbeks, 10 million Uyghurs, and 3.5 million

Tibetans, whose practice of religion is interpreted by the Chinese government as separatist terrorism.[161]

Uyghurs are Muslims, and Tibetans are mostly Buddhists. In theory, their religions are legitimate in China. Yet we are witnessing an accelerating religicide conducted by one of the world's most powerful and populous nations against its two largest minorities: Uyghur Muslims and Tibetan Buddhists. The two cases are inextricably linked, with the Communist Party using similar methods to enact genocide, ecocide, and factocide. The government appears ready to do whatever it takes to eliminate any trace of Uyghur and Tibetan culture, heritage, and religious practice—all under the guise of counterterrorism.

In 2016, China enacted a broad-reaching, new counterterrorism law. International human rights groups immediately sounded the alarm about how Chinese officials would use this expansive law to repress religion and civil society, and they were correct. This counterterrorism law is a web of national security directives encompassing military and Communist Party propaganda objectives. All of this is part of a campaign being directed by Chinese Party Secretary and President Xi Jinping to ensure so-called stability.

In practice, China's counterterrorism law prohibits many forms of religious activity that are labeled as terrorism. This is a Communist Party code of sorts that creates the permissions for religicide against Uyghur civilians. China continually presses a false narrative (factocide) that unrest and grievance in both Tibet and East Turkestan (the preferred name for the Xinjiang Uyghur Autonomous Region of China within many Uyghur diaspora communities) are due to outside influences rather than the political and economic grievances of local residents. This allows them to label Muslims and Tibetan Buddhists as domestic terrorists and crackdown on even the mildest expressions of religion identity and culture.

In June 2021, activists in the United Kingdom held a "people's tribunal" to attest to the genocide against Uyghurs in China. Survivors of torture and abuse in Xinjiang courageously told their stories.[162]

One example was Qelbinur Sidik, fifty-one years old. She worked as a Chinese language teacher in the city of Urumqi. In 2017, she was suddenly sent to a detention camp simply because she was a Uyghur. She recounted beatings and serial rape at the hands of her Chinese government captors.[163]

Gulbahar Jelilova, a fifty-seven-year-old Uyghur citizen of Kazakhstan, was arrested by Chinese police in May 2017 as she was traveling to the city of Urumqi, Xinjiang, on routine business for her clothing company. She was shackled in a cell for fifteen months and had to be hospitalized four times after being raped, tortured, and beaten.

Several reports describe how the children of Uyghur detainees are taken en masse to state-run orphanages, where they are subjected to propaganda and indoctrination while desperate parents are coerced in and outside the camps to comply with communist ideology and control.[164]

Survivor testimonies describe powerful and insidious layers of coercion to deny their identity and embrace Chinese communist ideology. Some detainees were forced to take pills every day and receive weekly injections. Zumret Dawut had no idea what was in these medications but says she has not menstruated since her detention.

The injections were once a week.... I got them several times during my two-month stay. When I asked them what it was, they said that it was a vaccine against infectious diseases. After you got it, you'd feel totally empty—not even the thoughts of my children would come to mind. You'd feel very light and relaxed, as if you didn't have a worry in the world. I feel like I got addicted to them—to the point where even now I'll long for one when I feel really stressed.[165]

Anar Sabit, originally from Kuytun, emigrated to Canada in 2014. When she returned to China after her father's death, she was detained for twenty months and sent to a reeducation camp. Her account is adapted from an article by Raffi Khatchadourian in *The New Yorker*, titled "Surviving the Crackdown in Xinjiang."

Sabit's interrogation lasted several hours, as officers recycled the same questions that she had been asked at the airport. While she spoke, she could hear smacks and electric shocks from the Uyghur man's cell across the hall. With his screams filling the room, she found it hard to focus. The lead interrogator turned to his partner. "Tell them to cut it out," he said. "It's affecting our work." The torture quieted, but only for a time.

China's religicide against its minorities echoes the religicidal cases of the Yazidis and the Rohingya. The state is systematically killing, traumatizing, imprisoning, and persecuting hundreds of thousands of families who follow religious teachings and practices contrary to the state ideology. In each case, we can see genocide, ecocide, and factocide in action.

GENOCIDE

In 2020, the US State Department declared that the arbitrary detention and mistreatment of the Uyghurs in Xinjiang constituted genocide. Shortly thereafter, Canadian and Dutch parliaments concurred. According to international lawyers and human rights experts, the Chinese government has breached every article of the UN Genocide Convention. But the Chinese Communist Party continues to deny committing any atrocities despite the growing body of evidence.

The Chinese authorities are not killing Uyghurs en masse. Rather, they serially imprison and punish them for their beliefs and religious practice. To date, over one million Uyghurs have been forced to live in so-called vocational and educational training centers. These are a network of brutal internment camps and prisons surrounded by barbed wire, watchtowers, and armed guards. According to China, these are entirely justified under their anti-terrorism law.

China continues to deny and defend its coercive methods, pointing to the success of the detention centers in reprogramming "terrorists." Some centers have shut down because the Uyghur inhabitants have "graduated." But satellite images and expert interviews reveal that China has built a new eighty-five-acre detention center in Dabancheng for future prisoners.

China is determined to eliminate the Uyghurs's traditions and faith because the Communist Party believes its political ideology should supersede all religious beliefs. Such traditions are considered backward and contrary to the aims of President Xi Jinping.

Uyghurs descend from Turk and Uyghur nomads who originated from the mountains and grasslands of modern-day Mongolia. These nomads were tough horse riders, many of whom settled in northwest China. Most live in Central Asia, where they have a documented Indigenous history going back as far as the eighth century. Their culture draws from diverse groups of that area, as well as those who passed through on the ancient Silk Road. This history of this distinct Muslim Turkic ethnic group has been marked by a series of ineffectual separatist struggles against the Chinese empire from 1759 to 1949.[166]

Today, more than eleven million Uyghurs comprise roughly half the population of Xinjiang in western China. They long for some level of sovereignty and autonomy—the dignity of living their lives and practicing their religion freely.

In the 1980s, Uyghur protests broke out against religious and ethnic discrimination by Han Chinese officials. By the 1990s, the Uyghur resistance movement had become more separatist and violent, culminating in the Ghulja riots and Urumqi bus bombings that killed Han Chinese civilians in 1997.[167] These attacks were the only documented occasions when Uyghur separatists and extremists indiscriminately attacked civilians—a rare but overt act of terrorism. While there were some notable terrorist events in the late 1990s, the threat of Uyghur separatism has long been overestimated by the Chinese Communist Party.[168] Any act of separatism gave China the excuse to crack down on Uyghurs with draconian measures in the name of national security. Absent an official definition of extremism, Chinese officials can condemn any "distorted religious teachings" as the "ideological basis" of terrorism.

GEORGETTE F. BENNETT AND JERRY WHITE

After the 9/11 attacks against the United States, the "war on terror" took off worldwide. China quickly expanded its own network of detention camps, accusing Muslims of terrorism in Xinjiang and abroad. The CCP has since carried out a concerted effort to brand its concern about Uyghur calls for independence as a "terrorist threat" linked to Al-Qaeda post-9/11.[169] This effort successfully built on preexisting stereotypes of Uyghurs as criminals and thieves.[170]

Within a matter of months, the Permanent Mission of the People's Republic of China to the UN released a document entitled, "Terrorist Activities Perpetrated by 'Eastern Turkistan' Organizations and Their Links with Osama bin Laden and the Taliban."[171] This document alleged that there were more than forty Uyghur organizations involved in terrorism under the auspices of the Taliban and Osama bin Laden-affiliated "East Turkistan forces."[172] International experts found such accusations unsubstantiated, but China kept up the pretense.[173]

The state of civil liberties for Uyghurs and other Turkic Muslims in Xinjiang has since deteriorated significantly with China using a state law against terrorism to abuse and imprison its citizens.

In late 2016 and early 2017, two developments accelerated the Chinese government's repressive policies: Chen Quanguo became the new Communist Party Secretary for Xinjiang and the region adopted new "Regulations on De-Extremification."[174] According to Amnesty International, Quanguo has overseen "intrusive surveillance, arbitrary detention, political indoctrination and forced cultural assimilation being carried out there on a massive scale."[175] For years, Quanguo and his supporters have continued to use these tools—obtained through misinformation—to detain, harass, and imprison Uyghurs.

As many as 1.8 million Uyghurs have been held in mass detention camps where they are forced to study Mandarin, sing patriotic communist songs, and disavow their culture and alleged "religious extremism."[176] One survivor testifies:

> The only thing we did was sing Communist songs and memorize the government white papers. The teachers there would instruct the inmates to express gratitude to Xi Jinping and the Party several times a day. 'There is no such ethnic group as the Uyghurs,' they'd tell us. 'They're all a part of the Chinese group.' That was the kind of propaganda they taught us in order to make us reject our identity.[177]

There are ongoing reports of psychological and physical abuse, malnutrition, solitary confinement, and torture for those who resist.[178]

Male survivors told the 2021 UK people's tribunal about rooms inside the detention camps filled with torture equipment such as steel chairs with electric prods. Some testified that prison guards had inserted electric wires into their penises. Others said they were made to stand in underground water rooms in cold water up to their necks. Many survivors, both men and women, said their fingernails were routinely yanked.

The Chinese Communist Party aims to eradicate any Uyghur practice of Islam in the country. This religicide includes official anti-halal campaigns that include making Muslims eat pork to "safeguard ethnic unity" of all Chinese people.[179] Chinese officials have developed the insidious "Pairing Up and Becoming Family" campaign that places Han Chinese monitors inside Uyghur homes.

Violence against women represents an essential component of modern religicide, achieving the goals of ethnic cleansing through the "genocide-in-slow-motion" of reduced birth rates, forced conversions, and intergenerational trauma. As with Rohingya and Yazidi women, rape of Uyghur women has been used as a weapon of war.

Another horrifying practice, which arguably amounts to state-sponsored rape, is forced marriages between Uyghur women and Han Chinese men.[180] Uyghur women are coerced into denouncing their faith, thereby rendered unable to pass on their heritage to offspring.

Along with coerced marriage is the Chinese government's forced reproductive control of Uyghurs. The one-child policy didn't apply to minorities in China. Twenty-six provinces allowed ethnic minorities to have an additional child, but the Uyghurs were not among them. In a systematic attempt to suppress their births, the government has employed forced sterilizations, birth control implants, and other forms of sexual and reproductive violence and control.[181] Recent data suggest that birthrates for minority areas in China fell by more than 50 percent between 2018 and 2019. According to Adrian Zenz, one of the leading researchers on this topic, more recent data remain unavailable because the counties in Xinjiang with the highest rates of forced contraception have stopped sharing data.

In his June 2021 column, "One Woman's Journey Through Chinese Atrocities," Nicholas Kristof expanded on this theme. He related the story of a gynecologist sent to a concentration camp for two years and to prison for six years. Her crime? Removing intrauterine devices (IUDs) from two women for medical reasons. Kristof asserted that 80 percent of the IUD insertions in China are in Xinjiang, which houses only 2 percent of the population. His source goes on to tell him of a relative responsible for family planning work in a Uyghur village. On her watch, a woman became pregnant without permission. That woman's husband was sent to prison for eleven years and the family planning worker was sent to a concentration camp for two years.

ECOCIDE

The Australian Strategic Policy Institute (ASPI) estimates that 65 percent of the mosques—sixteen thousand sites—in Xinjiang, China have been destroyed or damaged. Much of the land on which they sat now remains vacant.[182] The ASPI estimates that 30 percent of Islamic sacred sites (such as cemeteries) have been destroyed and a further 28 percent have been damaged. The *New York Times* reported in 2020 that the Chinese government has enacted destructive policies by arguing that culturally significant sites and buildings are "un-Chinese."[183] This level of religicide takes time and intention. By leveling their sacred sites, China is aiming to erase the Uyghurs's religious customs and practices.

Abduhebir Rejep, a Uyghur survivor who fled to Turkey in 2016, describes the collective trauma he witnessed in his homeland, watching serial attacks on his faith and places of worship:

> Life for a Muslim in East Turkistan [Uyghur Eastern China] is really hard. Now, the Chinese are carrying out a genocide because of the East Turkistanis being Turks and Muslims. Praying is forbidden. Fasting is prohibited. Ablution

also. Women are forbidden to wear the *hijab*.
There used to be 15 mosques in Hotan City, but
now there's only one left. The others were all
destroyed.[184]

In addition to bulldozing places of worship and devotion,
China's ecocide is destroying Uyghur water and food sources. One
of the great historic, ecological, and cultural contributions of the
Uyghur people is the *karez* irrigation system, an Indigenous method
of irrigation that has been practiced throughout the Middle East
and Central and South Asia for more than three thousand years.[185]
The *karez* design advances sustainable water usage by preventing
water table depletion and excess evaporation, modulating salinity
for downstream agriculture, and providing easy drainage to prevent flooding.

The *karez* irrigation network in Western China and Central
Asia reflects a broad ecological ethic that is rooted in a unique
cultural heritage that combines Sunni Islam with traditional
beliefs influenced by Shamanism and Buddhism, among others.[186]
There are myriad examples pointing to the significance of water
and nature in Uyghur culture, including folk songs praising the
Tarim River as a lover.

Karezes are a wonder of ancient civilization and a heritage
worth preserving. But since the 1950s, Chinese government officials have systematically sabotaged the *karez* irrigation system that
connects Uyghur communities. This includes the dismantling of
the *waqf* system of endowments in Islamic law, many of which
were used to provide and maintain sources of clean water for local
Uyghur communities.[187]

The destruction of these ingenious irrigation systems has eradicated centuries of Indigenous knowledge. Destructive Chinese

government policies in this region have made Xinjiang one of the most polluted provinces in China. There is a higher incidence of respiratory diseases, cardiovascular illness, and tumors among the local Uyghur population than elsewhere in China. Dangerously high levels of carbon dioxide, nitrogen dioxide, and sulfur dioxide are the direct result of China's support of coal-burning plants in Xinjiang. These plants provide China with 40.6 percent of its coal supplies, fueling the economic growth of China's regional economic priority, the Belt and Road Initiative (BRI).[188]

Another result is an increase in kidney stones due to excess fluorine contamination of groundwater and water scarcity in major cities, such as Urumqi. The subsequent decline in biodiversity has made traditional Uyghur livelihoods unsustainable, like licorice and carrot harvesting for rabbits.[189]

Nuclear testing sites in Xinjiang and Tibet are another form of ecocide that endanger the health and habitat of China's minority populations in their ancestral land. According to Dr. Enver Tohti, a cancer surgeon who worked in Xinjiang during the late 1990s, nuclear tests conducted in Lop Nor, a dried up salt lake, have led to high rates of cancer and disease among Uyghur patients.

Ecocide in China purposefully destroys the places where Uyghurs can live and practice their religion freely. None of this is accidental. For those who remain in their communities, Chinese security officials punish any display of Uyghur culture and Islamic devotion. For example, in 2014, police searched the homes of Uyghurs during Ramadan to look for "conservative" books or clothing. They detained individuals simply for wearing veils or growing long beards and would not allow Uyghur students or civil servants to fast or pray.[190]

Kayrat Samarkand, a Muslim man, attests that he was held in a reeducation camp in November 2017 for three months. During this time, he alleges he was forced to watch and recite communist propaganda that promulgated falsehoods about his people.[191]

FACTOCIDE

The Chinese government outright denies that the Uyghurs are an Indigenous community in Central Asia with a unique heritage and millennia-long presence. China denies any Uyghur cultural achievements, including the *karez* water system. Many Chinese language websites and academic journals refer to the *karez* as "one of the three Great Ancient Chinese Works," the other two being the Great Wall and the Grand Canal, despite substantial historical evidence that the *karez* originated in modern-day Iran.[192]

China also denies the existence of concentration camps in Xinjiang. Rather, these are described as successful "re-education centers" that have led detainees to "voluntarily" revoke conservative Islamic clothing (such as wearing the burqa) and to choose a more "secular lifestyle."[193] Yet the barbed-wire prison camps are clearly visible in satellite images. Later iterations of the re-education camps emphasized learning Mandarin as a means of integration and assimilation, even though the Uyghurs' own language, which is similar to Turkish, is important to their cultural identity.[194]

The Chinese government frames all criticism from the United States and Europe as anti-communist propaganda. For example: "Based on the history of Western atrocity propaganda...we are skeptical that the US...has any legitimate moral interest or grounds on which to defend Muslim religious rights in Xinjiang."[195]

In 2020 and 2021, both pro-Uyghur and pro-China narratives have competed for attention on social media sites such as Instagram. Online users have called for a boycott of the Disney movie *Mulan* in response to film credits that thank Communist government agencies in Xinjiang. The public outcry on Twitter and Instagram made headlines in the *New York Times*.[196] This growing social media response gave rise to increasing backlash from pro-China groups such as the Qiao Collective, which recently published a slide deck on Instagram:

> Based on a handful of think tank reports and witness testimonies, Western officials have raised allegations of genocide and slavery in Xinjiang Uyghur Autonomous Region. But is the politicization of Chinese anti-terrorism policies in Xinjiang just another front of the US-led hybrid war on China?[197]

Chinese officials may accuse the United States of propagating a double standard, given America's own ill-fated wars on terror with mass suffering inflicted on Muslim-majority populations in both Afghanistan and Iraq, but these were not genocides or religicides as in the case of China.

Denying any culpability, the Chinese government has disseminated more than three thousand propaganda videos claiming to portray unfiltered glimpses of a "peaceful" life in Xinjiang—echoing "Potemkin villages" and the model concentration camp, Theresienstadt, of an earlier era. They circulated most of their messaging via western social media sites like YouTube and Twitter. Jeff Kao and his coauthors in the *New York Times* and *ProPublica* describe this disinformation as one of China's most elaborate

efforts to influence global opinion. The *Times* investigation identifies striking similarities between the clips, such as identical
introductory phrases and English-language captions that reveal an
organized systematic effort by the Chinese Communist Party to
shift global public opinion on this issue. For example, many videos
began with variations on the phrase, "We are very free," and show
clear similarities in content and phrasing that are unlikely to have
arisen by chance.[198] These efforts explicitly deny the tragic reality
of the Uyghur religicide in the face of contrary international evidence and testimony.

Chinese officials understand how lies and factocide are necessary to advance their religicide with impunity. However, the voices
and testimony of courageous survivors inside and outside China
have become one way the international community can understand the truth of what is happening, even with limited access to
information inside the country.

Remember Zumret Dawut, the Uyghur woman detained
in 2018 whom we quoted earlier about mysterious injections. In
challenging China's accounts about the Uyghur camps, she said:
"[What] they're saying that they're teaching the people in those
camps Chinese is a complete lie. They say that just to fool the
world."[199] Uyghur survivors are not keeping silent, as their testimonies bear witness to the ongoing religicide and persecution against
their community.

WHAT CAN BE DONE?

China's religicide against the Uyghurs remains one of the most
intractable religion-related conflicts of our time. There is a place
for naming, blaming, and shaming tactics against the People's

Republic of China for its crimes against the Uyghur people. But confrontational approaches have rarely generated significant or lasting behavior change in such a powerful, proud, and centrally controlled state.

Given the scale, severity, and complexity of China's human rights violations against its religious minorities, ending the Uyghur religicide requires more than a simple plan of action by any one state or civil society group. Ending religicide requires a multi-tiered strategy that reflects the interests and values of all relevant stakeholders—most notably the leadership of China as one of the most powerful and important countries in the world. A strategy for action must be rooted in principles that resonate with key actors ranging from business leaders to Uyghur activists to Chinese officials.

Political

As a member of the United Nations, China has committed itself to certain international legal norms, which it is required to uphold. These are broadly embedded in the UN Charter and the UN Universal Declaration of Human Rights. The People's Republic of China is also a signatory to the 1948 UN Genocide Convention with 151 other countries. The freedom of religion or belief is safeguarded by The International Covenant on Civil and Political Rights, which the People's Republic of China has likewise signed. The Convention of the Rights of the Child was signed and ratified by China, as was the International Covenant on Economic, Social, and Cultural Rights, which addresses the protection of cultural rights that guarantee the freedom to practice one's own culture. All of these are violated in China's religicide against the Uyghurs.

China's permanent position on the UN Security Council allows it to veto any sanctions. Therefore, it is highly unlikely the Security Council will take any action against China. Only another superpower can apply effective political levers against China's violations of UN treaties. In May 2021, the United States, Germany, and Britain clashed with China at the United Nations, rightfully calling out China's treatment of Uyghurs. "We will keep standing up and speaking out until China's government stops its crimes against humanity and the genocide of Uyghurs and other minorities in Xinjiang," said US ambassador to the United Nations, Linda Thomas-Greenfield, at an event attended by fifty countries.[200] More of such diplomacy is needed to increase pressure and public awareness, including the following direct diplomatic requests for the Chinese government:

- Abide by international human rights norms on the right to freedom of association. End interference by officials, Chinese Communist Party representatives, and state security forces in the formation, continuation, and conduct of independent social associations in Uyghur communities.
- Cease alleging, without basis or evidence, that foreign forces are manipulating social groups or activists to get them to express dissenting views or engage in violent or subversive activities.
- Release educators, social activists, and local officials arbitrarily detained for serving their communities.

Parties to the 1951 Refugee Convention and its 1967 Protocols should respect the rights of Uyghur refugees, including the protection from forced repatriation to China and the right to claim asylum. The United States, Canada, the European Union, and other safe third-country states should offer asylum to Uyghurs living abroad who fear persecution by host governments (e.g., Turkey, Central Asian states) or forced repatriation to China. For example, Uyghurs who are longtime residents of Afghanistan fear being deported as part of the Taliban regime's attempt to establish warm relations with China.

International governments should publicly call on China's leaders to reconcile laws and policies restricting the rights to freedom of expression, peaceful assembly, and association with their claims to respect the rule of law. When cooperating with China on law enforcement or counterterrorism efforts, they should publicly condemn the use of false public order, terrorism, or separatism allegations to persecute or otherwise curtail the rights of minorities and nongovernmental groups. One way to do this is to request that Beijing define the specific terrorist groups with which China is not willing to engage, and then make sure the Uyghurs are not on that list.

Diplomats, independent human rights groups, the International Red Cross, humanitarian relief organizations, journalists, and UN special representatives should all press for access to the region.

Economic

The world economy's increasing dependence on China has given that country enough economic and political leverage to avoid the sweeping sanctions and punishments that might otherwise have been levied against a regime perpetrating human rights abuse and crimes against its population.

China's regional power has only increased with its ambitious Belt and Road Initiative (BRI). The BRI is a large-scale, long-term infrastructure project meant to reshape global trade in China's favor, much in the style of the ancient Silk Road. The Chinese government is directly investing in infrastructure projects in countries that have signed onto the BRI, offering generous loans at very low interest rates. Especially important are Muslim partners (for example, Egypt, Turkey, Saudi Arabia, Iran, and Iraq) and Central Asian countries (such as Kazakhstan, Kyrgyzstan, Tajikistan, Turkmenistan, and Uzbekistan). There are more than 130 countries involved in the Belt and Road Initiative. With this much economic gain on the line, it is unlikely that many BRI countries will denounce the Uyghur genocide and risk Chinese reprisal.

That said, China has reduced its investment in BRI projects by more than 50 percent over the past year, and almost every aspect of the BRI has experienced slowdowns.[201] This creates an opening to persuade participating countries to limit their involvement in the BRI contingent on human rights conditions.

Donor nations should offer infrastructure and economic stimulus packages for key Belt and Road Initiative countries to suspend their participation until China ceases its genocide against the Uyghurs. They should impose tariffs on all raw material exports and refined products from the Xinjiang Uyghur Autonomous Region until the Chinese government takes measures to end mass internment of Uyghurs in the Xinjiang region.

The US Agency for International Development (USAID) can take a leading role in increasing foreign direct investment (FDI) to countries in the Belt and Road Initiative to counterbalance the growing Chinese economic and political influence in the region. FDI helps both the United States and the countries receiving the aid. US investment will strengthen the economies of our allies while promoting goodwill between governments and the public. FDI should be dispensed in accordance with human rights behavior, including a willingness to speak out against genocide and refusal to engage with Uyghur forced labor.

Private businesses benefit from the BRI and Uyghur forced labor. As such, they buttress the BRI and Chinese economic power. Human rights diligence, especially regarding China and the persecution of the Uyghurs, should be a precondition for government contracts, export credit licenses, and stock exchange listings. The US State Department should liaise with multinational corporations to enforce such requirements as part of its diplomatic efforts.

Chinese economic influence through the World Bank or the International Monetary Fund (IMF) can be balanced by contributions from other economic powers, such as the United States and the European Union. The World Bank lends money to low- and middle-income countries to aid in development projects such as education or health initiatives. The United States government should invest with the World Bank and the IMF to mitigate China's undue economic influence in BRI countries. Investing in and through these banks increases the likelihood of broader international pressure to stop human rights abuse and atrocities against the Uyghurs.

Although many argue that sanctions are an overused and largely ineffectual blunt instrument, targeted sanctions against Chinese entities can advance the human rights agenda. The United States and European Union have already levied sanctions against specific Chinese officials in Xinjiang. The US government should maintain and expand such targeted sanctions.

This includes the boycott of fashion brands and other businesses that continue to profit from Uyghur forced labor and the active use of social media to interrupt and report disinformation about the Uyghur genocide. According to the Coalition to End Forced Labour in the Uyghur Region, one in five cotton garments in the global apparel market are tainted by forced labor from the Xinjiang region. Brands like Abercrombie & Fitch, Adidas, Gap Inc., Zara, Lululemon, Nike, Nordstrom, Target, and Walmart have all been implicated in the use of forced Uyghur labor and thus far have not taken steps to address human rights abuses in their supply chains.

In December 2021, President Joseph Biden signed into law the Uyghur Forced Labor Prevention Act.[202] This law, which was passed nearly unanimously by the House and Senate, bans projects made with forced labor in China. The burden of proof is on companies to prove that their factories and suppliers do not use slavery or coercion. Because of the critical role that Xinjiang plays in many supply chains, the enforcement of this law could force many companies, and potentially entire industries, to change the way they produce their goods. Other countries could enact similar laws to coalesce against forced labor in Xinjiang.

Cultural

Anti-religion sentiments of the Chinese Communist Party have created an atmosphere that legitimizes religious violence and state crackdowns on traditional faith communities. The future of the Xi Jinping administration is now tied to the preservation of the myth of the one great homogenous, powerful, and prosperous China. As the *Washington Post* reported in 2017, the official party line of local officials to Christian believers is "Jesus Christ won't drag you out of poverty or cure your illnesses, but the Chinese Communist Party will, so take down those pictures of Christ and put up a nice photograph of President Xi Jinping."[203]

Unfortunately, the social stigma against Muslims in China (and elsewhere in Asia, Europe, and the Americas) has led to apathy and inaction by many world leaders and citizens when it comes to speaking out against the suffering of this seemingly obscure Turkic Muslim minority. Powerful elites, including governments and business leaders, evidently prefer to focus on the all-encompassing drive for economic growth in partnership with China, including China's Belt and Road Initiative (BRI).

Social Media

Social media platforms including Facebook, Twitter, and Google, must remove digital disinformation about Xinjiang and the Uyghurs propagated by the Chinese government.

Governments must take action to prevent the targeting of Uyghur activists in diaspora communities, including online and via social media. Immigration officials must consider the targeting of family members still in China and support fast and efficient family reunification processes for Uyghurs and other Muslim minorities targeted by the Communist Party. Other government actions might include the following:

- Recognize violence against women as an essential component of modern religicide. Some have called this a form of "femicide"—dictating control over women's bodies and reproductive rights. It is imperative to address the disparate impacts of violence on Uyghur women and girls through the provision of culturally appropriate native-language psychosocial support and sexual and reproductive health services for Uyghur women.

- Individuals and civil society can help uplift and disseminate the voices of Uyghur-led groups, including the World Uyghur Congress, Uyghur Human Rights Project, and Uyghur American Association, and become cognizant of the importance of preserving language, culture, religious education, and local leadership.

Ending religicide against the Uyghurs in China will require a concerted multilateral effort. The US government is uniquely positioned to harness its influence. By prioritizing an end to the Uyghur genocide, the United States can build a coalition of allies—from the EU to Africa, Asia, and Latin America—and present a package of incentives and disincentives to effect change. With clear talking points, US diplomats at embassies worldwide can protect religious and cultural diversity and promote respect for differences. (But this may require more humility on the part of Americans to admit our own history of slavery and religicide of Indigenous Americans, and the steps we are taking to repair these injustices.) The broader the coalition, the better. China's false claim that this is just anti-China rhetoric coming from a rival power must be discredited.

In 2021, US President Biden made his plans to pursue a foreign policy centered around diplomacy and human rights clear, aiming to reestablish a position of global leadership that he argues was eroded under President Donald Trump's administration. In an early address to diplomats at the State Department, President Biden stated, "We must start with diplomacy rooted in America's most cherished democratic values: defending freedom, championing opportunity, upholding universal rights, respecting the rule of law, and treating every person with dignity."[204]

Repression of religion is hardly a new trend in modern Communist China, but the scale, scope, and specificity of religicidal efforts are alarming and tragically reminiscent of the Cultural Revolution (1966-1976) under then-President Mao Tsetung. A new decade of religicide in China today will lead to the death, displacement, and suffering of millions more.

The effects of religicide are disastrous for victims and perpetrators alike. Ongoing genocide, ecocide, and factocide are unsustainable and harmful to China and its people. Trying to establish a monoculture, whether in agriculture, religion, or politics, is unnatural and ends up harming people and the planet. Diversity and complexity are natural. Permaculture and polyculture are worth protecting and celebrating worldwide. The good news is that, as with climate policy, the People's Republic of China can change course quickly. The country will grow stronger by forging an authentic, new social contract with its diverse minorities, including Indigenous Uyghurs. Politics do not need to eradicate religion and culture. Thankfully, the resilient voices of Uyghur survivors offer a powerful invitation of hope for China to tap into its ancient roots, to emerge as a powerfully generative force for good in the world.

The case for religicide in China is not limited to Uyghurs. Another region in the southwest of greater China have been under threat for decades—the Buddhists in Tibet.

Chapter Seven

TECH-ASSISTED RELIGICIDE: CHINA'S SURVEILLANCE IN TIBET

Chinese government does not let us live as Tibetans....
Whatever we do, our opinions must be what the
government and Party approves.... In fact, to live as
a Tibetan is to take a risk...and some Tibetans get
punished for it.... I can see that Tibetan identity, tra-
ditions which make us proud to be who we are, and
distinguish ourselves from Chinese, is about to disap-
pear from the new generation in Tibet.[205]

—Interview on the Closure of a Rural *Kyidu*.

Tibet, a striking mountainous region that stands between China and its neighbors India, Nepal, and Myanmar, is a strategically valuable 2,500-mile security buffer. It holds valuable minerals and the world's third largest freshwater source. This is why Chinese authorities demand control over it, aiming to suppress any notions of Tibetan claims or aspiration for autonomy and independence.

Plainly stated, the Chinese Communist Party (CCP) is conducting religicide against Tibetan Buddhists. It has been going on for decades. The Communist Party targets the spiritual practice and private lives of Tibetans through a campaign that includes destruction of their cultural heritage, imprisonment, physical and psychological abuse, and high-tech surveillance. Religicide tolerates no dissent, freedom of opinion, or freedom of religion.

For the Chinese Communist Party, patriotism has a very particular meaning: love for the motherland, for Socialism, and for the Communist Party. This does not leave much room for love of God or fealty to any religion.

Tibet was an independent state politically and historically before its invasion by Communist China in 1950. The People's Republic of China (PRC) claims that Tibet has always been part of their country, reaching as far back as the Mongol Yuan dynasty (1271-1368 CE). However, at that time, Tibet was part of the Mongol empire, which was not ruled by the Chinese. During the Qing dynasty (1644-1912), Sino-Tibetan relations were not regulated by formal treaties or agreements. Tibet administered its own affairs, laws, and policies. The 1912 fall of the Qing dynasty resulted in the temporary expulsion of Chinese officials and troops, giving Tibet a forty-year taste of independence. But since 1950, China and Tibet have been in conflict over who controls Tibet.[206]

China's repression of religion in Tibet began with the arrival of Mao Tse-tung's troops. It evolved into a full-out religicide during the Cultural Revolution (1966-1976). The Chinese adopted a brutal policy to destroy the "four olds" of Tibetan society: old ideas, old culture, old customs, and old habits. Among other requirements, nomadic men had to cut their distinctive hair style of bangs and two braids, and women were required to break their tradition of slaughtering animals. Men and women were killed, imprisoned, or displaced for not complying. Their religious practices and rituals were forbidden. Period.

Tibetan Drikung Chetsang Rinpoche recalls in his biography, *From the Heart of Tibet*, how the "Red Guards went into the temple and started ransacking sacred ritual objects and ranting against 'superstition.'"[207] Another Tibetan scholar, who preferred anonymity, recounted his experience in 1968, when he was thirteen. He was required to spy on everyone in his family while they were being "reeducated."

> Every evening we had to go to meetings and read Mao's writings and slogans. We were asked, 'What did your family do today? What did they say?'
>
> They wanted us to spy on our families. I often had to apologize because I hadn't watched all of my family's activities on that day. I told them that I would be careful to do so the next day.[208]

This type of repression has escalated under the rule of President Xi Jinping, which started in 2013. President Xi demands unconditional support for his political ideology to Sinicize 1.4 billion people. That means assimilating one's identity to be loyal to the one Chinese race, *zhonghua minzu*. Quoting Confucius, he vows to "govern with virtue and keep order through punishments."[209] In order to achieve homogenization, Xi is bringing every aspect of life under his state control, including all religions, "to contribute to the realization of the Chinese dream of national rejuvenation."[210] This includes working to "reeducate" roughly six million Buddhists living in Tibet—less than 0.5 percent of China's population.

In China, the official policy of Sinicization of religions was publicly rolled out at the Nineteenth Party Congress in 2017. To accelerate homogenization, Xi Jinping made changes in the party-state system by putting the United Front Work Department (UFWD) in charge of religious policy. The UFWD functions as the propaganda enforcement agency, taking charge of state-level administration, discipline, and punishment.[211]

Unlike the Uyghurs, whom China labels as terrorists to justify its brutality against them, tactics against Tibetans are more about surveillance and control, starting with anyone who practices Buddhism.

Monks and nuns have borne the brunt of the Chinese Communist Party's anti-religion policies. In 2012, the Chinese took control over all monastic management. The CCP described its new policy as "critical for taking the initiative in the struggle against separatism," and to make sure that "monks and nuns do not take part in activities of splitting up the motherland and disturbing social order."[212] Over time, Chinese authorities have imposed heavy surveillance and tight control over nearly all Tibetan monasteries and nunneries. Surveillance of the monastic community is done through a network of human and electronic means.

According to the campaign to save Tibet, CCTV cameras are deployed for surveillance of the monasteries and used by law enforcement agencies to record, control, and suppress any dissent. The cameras are visible and obvious—a constant reminder to monks and nuns that they are being watched.[213]

Current official data are not available publicly, but the state media outlet, *China Daily*, stated in 2015 that more than 6,500 government and party workers are assigned to more than 1,700 monasteries in the Tibet Autonomous Region (TAR).[214] This amounts to nearly three-to-four communist cadres assigned to each monastery. These so-called management committees were installed by the government to establish political stability by ensuring so-called harmonious monasteries. These committees micromanage speech and behaviors of the monastics on a daily basis to ensure full compliance with CCP policies and laws.[215]

In 2012, the Tibet specialist Robert Barnett reported to Radio Free Asia that communist cadres inside monasteries were instructed to "'make friends' with one monk, and keep a file on that monk's thinking."[216] In 2020, Phurbu Sichoe, a party member heading the Toelung Dechen district's United Front Work Department, ordered his underlings to keep a detailed ledger of problems regarding each and every monk, and to rectify them one by one.[217] This has been going on for years.

In 2012, a Chinese tourist to Tibet posted online:

> I visited the Jokhang this morning, just in time
> for the local Shoton festival, and met with some
> extremely devout believers. Inside the square
> there were a lot of weapons: People's Armed
> Police, Special Police, snipers, police, troops
> standing at the ready, it felt like a war was about
> to start. Tour guides say, you can't wear revealing
> clothing, keep your eyes open when you visit, but
> keep your mouth shut! Has life here always been
> like this?![218]

Unfortunately, it has been this way for a while. The Chinese Communist Party prioritizes security and intimidation more than freedom of movement and speech.

By 2018, local reporting suggested there were nineteen thousand CCP organizations assigned to Tibet. Their representatives continually require the monks and nuns to "correct" their thoughts by reciting communist propaganda, like the Uyghurs in their reeducation camps and detention centers. Around this time, Chinese authorities launched new regulations on religious affairs, enforced by the UFWD. These include the four standard policies imposed on monastic communities in rather technocratic yet ominous jargon:

1. Comply with the standard of *political reliability* [emphasis added] and strive to be advanced monks and nuns with a steady and distinctive stance.
2. Obey the *standards on religion* [emphasis added] by creating harmony and strive to be advanced monks and nuns for diligent study and strenuous training.
3. Follow the standards of *moral integrity capable of obedience to the public* [emphasis added] and strive to be advanced monks and nuns for law-abiding and noble morality.
4. Obey the standard that work at the critical times and strive to be advanced monks and nuns for playing active role.[219]

A symposium on "Following the four standards and striving to be advanced monks and nuns" was held in Lhasa, Tibet's capital. The Party Secretary Wu Yingjie, who presided over the meeting, required the monastic community to be grateful to the party for all their so-called benefits and to become loyal followers of the party.[220] He required monks to "firmly establish a correct view of the motherland, nation, history, culture, and religion."[221]

Sadly, this is about control, compliance, and coercion rather than tolerance or religious freedom. The monastic community is prevented from expressing any of their own thoughts. They are required to tow the party line on China's history, culture, and religion. Essentially, Buddhist monks and nuns are required to become party propagandists, not Buddhists.[222] That means acknowledging the primacy of Communist Party leaders over any precept of Buddhism and its religious figures, especially the Dalai Lama.

An anti-Dalai Lama policy has been in place for more than twenty-five years.

That policy demands recognition of a state-approved reincarnation of the Dalai Lama to be built into a new Chinese curriculum that advances "re-education activities" in monasteries.[223] To ensure its control on the naming and approval of reincarnated lamas—most importantly the reincarnation of the current fourteenth Dalai Lama—the CCP has adopted regulations that decree the search for reincarnate lamas should only happen within China's borders and be approved only by the leadership in Beijing. China's aim is to supplant the authority of any legitimate Tibetan religious leaders.[224] Nonetheless, the process set by the Dalai Lama in exile would be followed by Tibetan Buddhists outside of China.

For centuries, reincarnations of the Dalai Lama have been recognized in accordance with traditional Tibetan Buddhist practices.' State regulations now in place will permit the atheistic Chinese government to appoint the next Dalai Lama. In 2019, Tibetan monastics and religious leaders in the diaspora resolved that the "authority of decision concerning...the next reincarnation of the XIV Dalai Lama...solely rests with His Holiness the XIV Dalai Lama himself. No government or otherwise will have such authority. If the Government of the People's Republic of China for political ends chooses a candidate for the Dalai Lama, the Tibetan people will not recognize and respect that candidate."[225] Given the tools the CCP has at its disposal, it's unlikely that such a proclamation will have much impact inside China, while Tibetan Buddhists outside of China can and will abide by it.

Aside from choosing Tibet's next religious leaders, China is abusing and imprisoning its monks and nuns. One Tibetan nun recalled her torture in an interview:

> An especially painful torture consisted of wiring one finger on each of my hands, while I was seated on a chair, and connecting them to an electric installation. As the handle on the installation was turned a full circle, I felt every single part of my body being seized by a powerful electric current. The intensity of the shock would fling me across the room, invariably rendering me unconscious. The interrogators would, however, try to revive me by slapping me and throwing water on me. Often the wires would snap, and then they had to reconnect them. People subjected to this method of torture most often had to be taken directly to the hospital.[226]

This nun is not alone. Many of the worst survivor accounts of abuse and torture, including sexual violation, have emerged from Gutsa, the colloquial name for the notorious Lhasa Public Security Bureau detention center. This secret complex serves as Tibet's frontline center for interrogation. Former prisoners recount beatings by authorities trying to elicit confessions of guilt and pressuring them to name others who deviate from the strictures under which Tibetans live.

Chinese authorities take care to cover up disappearances, detentions, tortures, and killings. Restrictions on Tibetans who are released after serving terms in prison have intensified. It is forbidden for them to speak to their families or friends about what they endured in detention. As such, it may be impossible to provide a comprehensive account of the number of Tibetans detained and their experience at Gutsa.

Satellite images of Lhasa show prison facilities like Gutsa growing in size to accommodate the increase in prisoners. And as Tibet becomes increasingly militarized, its capital Lhasa is being transformed by large infrastructure projects and a network of roads wide enough to serve as runways for planes. [227]

To that end, Chinese technology companies are marketing their high tech, artificial intelligence (AI), and big data capabilities in the name of counterterrorism, public order, and stability. According to a report by *Nikkei Asia*, five tech giants of China—Alibaba, Baidu, Tencent Holdings, iFlytek, and SenseTime—have all established a corporate presence or partnership in Tibet. (It is important to also note that Tencent serves as the parent company to many companies familiar to the Western world, such as WeChat and Epic Games, developer of many popular video games.)

The Communist Party's objective is to leverage big data capabilities to monitor and control China's population, particularly its minorities. In the absence of laws that limit the collection of data for public security, such tools enhance the Ministry of Public Security's ability to cross-reference criminal, social, and medical records with any other data considered relevant to apprehend violators. Improvements in big data analytics directly support the strict monitoring and control of individuals for even minute or imagined signs of disloyalty and transgression.

Surveillance, imprisonment, torture, and control of physical activities are severe enough, but China's war on the inner world of the Tibetan monastic community may be even harder—and more successful. Traditionally, Buddhist monks learn in a spiritual environment of trust, with the close bonds between teacher and student sealed by vows. Intrusive surveillance and intelligence gathering inserts suspicion and compromises the close relational basis of Buddhist spiritual development and meditative progress. In this way, the Chinese government has managed to corrupt the very spiritual nature of Tibetan Buddhism by introducing spies, daily punishment, and imprisonment.

China also prevents Tibetan children from attending monastic schools, blocking the transmission of Buddhist knowledge and language between generations of teachers and students—a hallmark of intergenerational religicide.

Along with the UFWD, the Public Security Bureau (PSB) surveils and controls monks and nuns day-to-day. By permanently placing police inside monasteries, the PSB maintains proactive surveillance of monasteries against any act deemed to transgress vague laws on stability—a practice that began after the Tibet uprising in 2008. Virtually all Tibetan rights activism is considered "separatism" by Chinese authorities and can result in individuals, or their families being blacklisted or imprisoned.[228] Internet surveillance of monks' social media activities has deeply affected the monastic community on the forefront of resistance against the Communist Party's atrocities in Tibet. WeChat was initially popular as the dominant social media app in Tibet, but monks later faced arrest for messages deemed illegal—such as sharing images of the Dalai Lama or simply talking about the Tibetan language.

Gendun Sherab, a fifty-year-old monk, was expelled from a monastery and arrested just for posting online a simple letter from the Dalai Lama that recognized a reincarnate teacher of Sera

Jey Monastery, who lives outside Tibet. Gendun later died in 2020, after he was blacklisted and denied medical treatment.[229]

Monks have been arrested simply for posting photos and articles on WeChat that are deemed illegal.[230] Sonam Palden, for example, a young monk at Kirti monastery, was arrested in 2019 just for posting on the pitiful state of Tibetan language instruction.[231] Rinchen Tsultrim, another twenty-something monk at Nangshig monastery, was arrested the same year and detained incommunicado for more than twelve months for posting on WeChat.[232] WeChat surveillance is not limited to Tibet, but also extends to Tibetan diaspora communities, like those in India, which often rely on WeChat to stay in touch with family and friends.

Given the level of surveillance, monastics live with the never-ending anxiety that anything they do might be considered illegal by local authorities. China's laws can be so vague that it becomes virtually impossible to know when something as generic as "picking quarrels and provoking trouble" might be prosecuted.[233] Tibetans can be reported and found guilty for expressing any dissent from the communist party line. It isn't just monastic houses that are subject to intense surveillance. Chinese Communist Party cadres are stationed in virtually every village in Tibet, extending the oppressive surveillance state to each household. The language you speak at home, how often you pray, and which countries or foreigners you contact are tracked by the government. Cameras with AI-powered facial recognition are nearly ubiquitous.

In 2012, China established a grid of new offices in Tibetan towns to provide tighter security on each residential block. Within a year, there was a comprehensive network set up for local reporting known as the "Advanced Double Linked Household" system. Such government micromanagement and hyper-surveillance happens daily at the household level, along with increased restrictions on any community activities and social meetings not approved by the state. China believes this surveillance grid has been so successful in Tibet that it is deploying similar surveillance tactics in Xinjiang to monitor and control Uyghur families. This is a massive intrusion of personal space. Just imagine if your family and friends were not only monitored by cameras but forced to report daily on your every move and spoken word.

At this stage, the Chinese Communist Party will target any person or group with a voice that differs from state ideology. Today, there are more than twenty types of crime violations that Chinese police can enforce randomly. For example, Tibetans frequently call on lamas and other traditional community leaders to arbitrate disputes over grazing rights and other conflicts, which could lead to bloodshed if left unresolved. Under China's police strictures, any form of family or religious intervention to meddle in local conflicts is deemed illegal.

All activities supporting Tibetan language and environmental rights can be deemed illegal, even if they do not involve protest.

Informal welfare associations known as *kyidu*, which are a traditional feature of Tibetan communities, are deemed illegal, because they are perceived as inimical to the Communist Party.

Chinese law makes it a criminal offense for officials to encroach on minority nationalities' customs or habits (Article 251). Yet no cases have been brought in which a Chinese official in a Tibetan area has been accused of—or punished for—harassing Buddhists. This is despite obvious systemic, ongoing, and widespread persecution.

As for accountability or transparency, China does not allow any outside individuals or organizations to visit its prisons or detention camps on a regular basis. And it refuses to issue statistics on the number and names of prisoners. For years, there has been no way to know how many Tibetans have been charged with crimes for nonviolent political activity. The system has become an impenetrable black box. Even close family members are denied access to basic information about their relatives' welfare or whether family members serving long prison terms are still alive.

The Chinese government maintains that it holds no political prisoners. That's because political offenses are not identified as such in Chinese law. Instead, nonviolent political activity inconsistent with official ideology can be labeled simply as "endangering state security" and "disturbing the public order."[234] In essence, the Chinese government can put anyone in prison at any time and provide little-to-no further information.

China's initial campaign of cracking down on Tibetan social groups was only expected to last three years to allow President Xi Jinping to consolidate the Chinese Communist Party ruling foundation at a community grassroots level. Clearly, that has not been the case. Any hint of political, cultural, legal, or spiritual opposition is suppressed, particularly the practices and rituals by which most Tibetans live.

China's pursuit of long-term stability is framed in neutral-sounding, often misleading terms: "stability maintenance" and "social management." But stability maintenance (known as *weiwen*) has become a security juggernaut made up of policing, internet censorship, blacklisting, informants, surveillance, and big data to "eliminate unseen threats." It includes the collection of blood sample genetics, mandatory photo IDs, facial recognition, and omnipresent cameras. Social management, as a carrot-and-stick policy, seeks to prevent social unrest by empowering the government to suppress all dissent.[235] When all these methods are aimed at Tibetan Buddhists, they advance China's religicidal agenda.

Speaking from Dharamshala in 2009, on the fiftieth anniversary of the failed Tibetan uprising against Chinese rule, the Dalai Lama said, "Today, the religion, culture, language and identity, which successive generations of Tibetans have considered more precious than their lives, are nearing extinction."[236]

GENOCIDE

According to Tibetans, during the Cultural Revolution, China destroyed all but eight of Tibet's 6,259 monasteries and nunneries and intentionally burnt sacred Buddhist texts to obliterate Tibetan culture. This devastating loss of heritage amounts to what Tibetans call "cultural genocide."[237] As with religicide, this term has not yet been recognized as a legal category. But it should be because cultural persecution is already considered a war crime.

In 1960, the International Commission of Jurists (ICJ), based in Geneva, called China's military occupation genocidal. The commission ruled that, prior to the invasion, Tibet had possessed all the attributes of statehood as defined under international law. In 1965, China created a Tibet Autonomous Region (TAR) that included only half the territory of pre-invasion Tibet. The rest of Tibet was basically annexed, incorporated into four southwestern Chinese provinces.

In response to the systematic and targeted nature of the violence and physical destruction in the 1950s, the ICJ published two reports with evidence of genocide in Tibet. This 1960 report found that "acts of genocide had been committed in Tibet in an attempt to destroy the Tibetans as a religious group."[238]

The Tibetan government-in-exile has reported that more than 1.2 million Tibetans died between 1950 and 1979, with causes of death ranging from outright execution to imprisonment, torture, starvation, fighting, and suicide.[239]

In addition to these attempts to kill off a religious minority, there is mounting evidence of ecological disaster in Tibet.

ECOCIDE

The impact of climate change in Tibet is harsh. As the world focuses on climate action at United Nations' COP21 meetings, Tibet should be central to any progress made. The Tibetan plateau needs protecting, not just for Tibetans, but for the environmental health and sustainability of the entire world. As stewards of their own land, Tibetans' expertise should be part of tackling climate change.[240]

—The Dalai Lama

The environmental damage is ongoing. Surrounded by mountains 4,500 meters above sea level, the Tibetan Plateau is known as the earth's "third pole" because of its importance as the largest repository of fresh water outside the North and South Poles. As a landscape of glaciers, lakes, and waterfalls, the plateau is a storehouse of freshwater and a source for the earth's eight largest river systems, which are critical to the world's ten most densely populated nations and neighbors.

But Tibet is warming nearly three times as fast as the rest of the earth. Glaciers are melting and permafrost is disappearing. Instead of protecting this fragile high-altitude ecosystem and addressing the challenges, China's policies are reshaping the Tibetan landscape. Dams are built by state-owned Chinese consortia to control the flow of the major rivers running off the plateau. What some call the greatest water grab in history has gone virtually unnoticed.

China's plans for massive water diversion from Tibet to parched lands in northern China requires an influx of Chinese engineers digging through mountains, building concrete walls across mountain rivers, and flooding the wetlands critical to the plateau's fragile ecosystem. The government's construction of hydropower stations in Tibet will have a lasting negative impact on the environment while displacing thousands of Tibetans.

China's damming and diversion projects in Tibet have intensified downstream concern, generating the potential to spur regional instability and conflict. Dams are being built on high gradients at the meeting point of three of the youngest and most unstable mountain ranges in the world without any assessment of environmental impact. Gouging millions of cubic meters of rock and earth to build dams, roads, and tunnels and storing millions of cubic meters of water threatens to affect the very stability of the earth's crust. This is a global concern, not just national or regional. But the Communist Party government sees water as a strategic asset to be exploited. Because it originates in Tibet, Beijing's policies remain exempt from debate.

In Eastern Tibet, a few compliant environmental groups are allowed to function, but in the western half of the Tibetan Plateau, all initiatives to protect the environment are restricted. China wants no criticism as it seizes more land for government-backed construction and development projects in Tibet. Large-scale mining in copper, chromium, gold, silver, and lithium signals China's desire to integrate remote regions of Tibet into its industrial economy. China and the TAR police force do not allow any kind of protest or resistance and will arrest anyone who interferes with government operations. Tibetans who raise concerns about the environmental impact of toxic waste, deforestation, water pollution, and erosion risk imprisonment or worse.

The Chinese government keeps driving out nomadic pastoralists from the vast Tibetan grasslands, a cruel campaign that threatens to eviscerate the Indigenous way of life on this harsh landscape of the high mountain plateau. This erodes the herd mobility essential to the health of range lands, despite the international scientific consensus that Indigenous stewardship and herd mobility are crucial.

Chinese leadership seeks endorsement from international organizations and governments for the creation of new "national parks" on the Tibetan plateau. The motion provides a pretext for the forced removal of nomads from their ancestral pastures— grasslands they have protected for centuries.

FACTOCIDE

China frames its communication in terms of environmental protection, although the opposite is the case. CCP authorities try to convey the impression that their policies in Tibet are aimed at conservation and dialogue. The state media use opaque terminology to convince governments globally that China's land use policies are aimed at climate change adaption and mitigation. Dam building, for example, is described as "water conservation construction"—a case for factocide, as this is clearly not what they're doing.

China employs digital propaganda in the service of religicide. Factocide permeates China with slanted accounts of how the 1959 invasion of Tibet was a "liberation" and Chinese rule is beneficial to Tibet.

After protests in Lhasa just prior to the 2008 Beijing Olympics, China turned a disinformation effort on radio into a more widespread and intense internet and smartphone censorship battle. In 2009, the University of Toronto's Citizen Lab released *Tracking GhostNet*, a report that revealed the shocking extent of China's cyber-espionage and its infiltration of the Free Tibet movement. The document revealed that 1,295 hosts in 103 countries were affected by Chinese malware spread through email attachments. Tibetan activists pivoted from sending attachments to using more secure services, such as Google Drive and Dropbox, to share their files. China was quick to step up its surveillance game. Soon thereafter, organizations started to receive Google Drive attachments from malicious servers with links that led to malware. This malware kept any dissent, or truth, from being communicated to fellow citizens or the world.

Beyond media tech manipulation, Beijing uses intimidation to spread digital disinformation about Tibetan Buddhists, as well as Uyghur Muslims. In 2018, more than forty journalists were jailed for attempting to report on Beijing's persecution of religious minorities across China.[241]

Chinese state media have spent billions of dollars to expand its strategic communications abroad, broadcasting to foreign audiences and producing content that is sold to media outlets in other countries. "Between September and November 2018, China's official Xinhua News Agency signed news exchange agreements with wire services in Australia, Belarus, Laos, India, and Bangladesh," according to a 2019 Freedom House report.[242]

In some cases, China controls the media platforms used in other countries to broadcast news. In Africa, the Chinese television distribution firm, StarTimes, has helped broadcasters in countries such as Kenya, Nigeria, Uganda, and Zambia transition from analog to digital television. The Chinese company then decides which stations its viewers can watch in those countries. Freedom House reported that, although StarTimes is privately held, it receives subsidies from the Chinese government.[243]

China's rationale for increasing media intrusion, restrictions, and surveillance of Tibetan Buddhists is to stop Tibetan support for their beloved exiled leader, His Holiness the Dalai Lama. Tibet's spiritual leader has resided in Dharamshala, India since 1960. There, in exile, he established the independent Tibetan government known as the Central Tibetan Administration.

The Communist Party line is that the Dalai Lama and his allies internationally are organizing and encouraging a violent separatist movement in Tibet. A 2014 Chinese report points a finger at "the Dalai clique"—China's term for the Dalai Lama and his supporters in exile, for the "psychological peculiarity" of Tibetans that makes them reluctant to adopt modern culture. China impugns the influence of religious figures for the "low educational level, densely religious mentality, [and] little sense of the law" among ordinary Tibetans.[244] A common prejudice by many Han Chinese people characterizes Tibetans as "primitive" people who worship a "feudal slave owner" known as the Dalai Lama.

But the Dalai Lama's nonviolent teachings are about peace, compassion, nonjudgment, and equanimity. Chinese government characterizations of the winner of the 1989 Nobel Peace Prize are ludicrous, inaccurate, and propagate false information—factocide—against Tibetan Buddhists.

Over seventy years of rule, the Communist Party has not been able to win over the loyalty and support of Tibetan Buddhists. Decades of violent oppression have prevented the CCP from establishing legitimacy for its rule over Tibet. China may indeed double down on its genocide, factocide, and ecocide, but Tibetans will likely sustain their resistance, as they have done over centuries. Religicide survivors can be dangerous because their faith remains a powerful source of resilience that enables them to survive.

WHAT CAN BE DONE?

Despite periodic condemnation and sanctions from governments and international organizations, China appears fully committed to advancing full-out religicide against Tibetan Buddhists and Uyghur Muslims. Allowing religicide to continue its spread across China will lead to the death, displacement, and suffering of millions of Tibetans and Uyghurs, as well as smaller religious minorities that lack political power, economic clout, or focused media attention from their diasporas and civil society activists.

Many of the recommendations in our call to action for Uyghurs apply to Tibetan Buddhists as well. We will not repeat them here. But there are additional steps that can be taken to induce China to reflect on its unique place in history by celebrating the dignity of difference, including freedom of opinion and religion for all its citizens and Indigenous cultures.

Political

- One of the root causes of the conflict over Tibet is the absence of a political solution. All governments should publicly and privately encourage China to resolve the issue through direct negotiations with the Dalai Lama.

- The US government should make it consistently clear to China's leadership that compliance with human rights obligations and protection of religious minorities are fundamental priorities for diplomatic relations and economic cooperation.

- The United Nations and member states should request increased access to Tibetan areas for diplomats, foreign journalists, and independent observers; increase multilateral pressure for China to abide by international human rights norms on the right to freedom of association; and end interference by officials, Chinese Communist Party representatives, and state security forces in the formation, continuation, and conduct of independent social associations in Tibetan communities.

- The United Nations and its members should enhance international cooperation on counterterrorism with China by agreeing to clearer definitions of extremism and terrorism; engage in constructive dialogue with China regarding UN efforts to develop a plan of action on countering violent extremism; include the imperative to address the root causes of extremism; clarify legal requirements and policies for countries that are fighting terrorism; address China's vaguely phrased provisions in its counterterrorism law (comprised of more than ninety-five articles in ten chapters) that lead to unnecessary restrictions on freedom of expression, peaceful assembly, and religion in Tibet; urge China to make a clear distinction between acts of dissent and religious observance and acts of terrorism; and reconsider the many counterproductive policies that stoke grievances in Tibet.

- China's leadership should decrease the level of militarization and the deployment of security troops in Tibet and East Turkestan and stress the importance of the rule of law and human rights in all counterterrorism efforts. Counterterrorism should not be used as a pretext to oppress religious and ethnic groups, including Tibetans and Uyghurs.

- EU and its member states should confront Beijing's diplomatic efforts to use the Belt and Road Initiative to divide and conquer in bilateral negotiations with Central and Eastern Europe and coordinate EU diplomacy to present a more united front to engage with China.

- All countries should respect the non-refoulement principle to ensure that individuals wrongly accused of terrorism are not forcibly returned to China. For example, Nepal should not return Tibetans to the PRC against their will.

Economic

- Multinational business coalitions should advocate for corporate responsibility and principles of ethical behavior for companies operating in Tibet. China is luring investments from foreign companies such as the British InterContinental Hotels Group, which opened its first hotel in Lhasa in 2014. It is one of several brands, including St Regis and the Four Points by Sheraton. The InterContinental advertises easy access to Lhasa's most treasured Buddhist landmarks, such as the Potala Palace and the Jokhang Temple, the most sacred and important temple in Tibet. The InterContinental was promoted in a video for tourism in Tibet during a tourism and cultural expo in Lhasa that featured a large imitation Potala Palace in the foyer, with Tibetan dancers performing.[245] As Chinese authorities require global investors to pick an approved local partner, foreign investors need to beware of the strong associations with the Communist Party and state to make sure these partnerships do not aid and abet any religicidal practices.

- Governments and socially responsible business coalitions should pressure companies with offices in Lhasa to stop providing surveillance equipment and services that are reasonably expected to infringe on the rights of Tibetans. Hikvision, a China-controlled entity, is the leading provider of surveillance cameras, specialized software for image processing, and other tech tools used to monitor the whole of Tibet.[246] The *New York Times* reported that Hikvision had begun to phase out its "minority recognition function" in 2018.[247] Still, China has found other surveillance firms to help write, use, and identify ethnic surveillance tracking.[248] The Chinese surveillance company Dahua has signed a deal with Amazon, picking up where Hikvision left off.[249]

- The US government should consider imposing sanctions under the Global Magnitsky Act on Chinese Communist Party leaders found responsible for ordering troops to open fire on unarmed Buddhist dissidents. Additionally, the US should work with a bipartisan coalition of leaders on Capitol Hill to deploy targeted economic sanctions against specific Chinese officials and entities in Tibet, including those who have participated in torture, as documented by the UN Committee Against Torture.[250]

Social

- Tencent, a Chinese tech giant, is known for controlling messaging platforms at home and abroad. WeChat, owned by Tencent, reaches up to two hundred million people outside China. Tencent carefully monitors and censors online posts through their app. All the while, China vehemently maintains that religious freedom and the rights of the monks and nuns are protected under its policies and laws.

- Governments must take action to prevent the targeting of Tibetan activists in diaspora communities, including online and via social media. Immigration officials must also consider the targeting of family members still in China and support fast and efficient family reunification processes for Tibetans targeted by the CCP.

- Individuals and civil society should uplift and disseminate the voices of Tibetan-led groups, including such groups as the International Campaign for Tibet, International Federation for Human Rights, Tibet Justice Center (formerly International Committee of Lawyers for Tibet), Bay Area Friends of Tibet, US Tibet Committee, Canada Tibet Committee, US Tibetan Society for School and Culture, the Tibet Fund, Amnesty International USA campaign department, Tibetan Nuns Project, and Students for a Free Tibet.[251]

- Governments and advocates for human rights and freedom should consider how best to incentivize China to release educators, social activists, journalists, civil society leaders, and local officials arbitrarily detained for peacefully exercising their freedom of expression or lawfully practicing their professions. Journalists are fast exiting their profession because of the restrictions and economic difficulties.

- Social media giants should call for an end to Chinese internet censorship, avoid the dissemination of information with terrorist and extremism content, lobby telecommunications operators to implement information content monitoring systems, and when disinformation is discovered, halt its dissemination immediately.

Cultural

- Diplomats should align foreign policies with respect for human rights and the responsibility to protect—not punish—difference of belief or religion.

- University researchers should engage evidence-based nonprofits such as CureViolence to consider ways to depoliticize violence reduction efforts in China, including a data-driven public health approach that is increasingly adopted in the West, and consider new strategies to shift the narrative to make cultural and religious diversity an economic asset in China—something to celebrate rather than punish. Religion and minorities should not be a taboo subject for academic study and citizen inquiry in China.

- Diplomats, reporters, and pundits should avoid validating Chinese doublespeak by refusing to use positive and bland terms for ecocide or genocide. Social media platforms including Facebook, Twitter, and Google must remove digital disinformation and propaganda about Tibetan Buddhists and the Dalai Lama.
- Religious and interfaith groups should step up cultural exchanges and relationship-building dialogues between followers of Tibetan Buddhism and Chinese Buddhism in China.
- Hundreds of thousands of students from the PRC are studying at US colleges and universities. These universities should design cultural awareness programs about Tibetan Buddhism and offer them as educational supplements to Chinese students.
- The United Nations and diplomats worldwide should increase transparency and accountability when it comes to diagnosing extremism. US Secretary of State Antony Blinken has said, "While there is no single cause, we do see common denominators—common factors that breed or help accelerate violent extremism, including feelings of alienation and exclusion, exposure to vile and rampant propaganda, a lack of critical thinking skills, and experiences with state-sanctioned violence and heavy-handed tactics by security services, and systematic denial of opportunity."[252]

Ending religicide against both Tibetans and Uyghurs in China will require a more concentrated and concerted effort by governments, multilateral organizations, business leaders, media, and civil society, including the voice of the victims of religicide speaking their truth.

As it stands, official Chinese efforts to forge assimilation and integration, including Tibetan cooperation on infrastructure projects, are starting to backfire. China's religicide against Buddhists in Tibet is forging an even stronger sense of Tibetan identity and solidarity, with many saying they are increasingly grateful they are *not* Chinese. As Zeid Ra'ad Al Hussein said in 2016, when he served as UN High Commissioner for Human Rights, "Crushing human freedoms will not protect us from terrorism. It creates dangerous divisions and grievances that will lead to more violence."[253]

Former UN special rapporteur for freedom of religion or belief, Heiner Bielefeldt, notes, "Freedom of religion or belief does not protect religious traditions per se, but instead facilitates the free search and development of faith-related identities in the broadest sense of the word."[254] This means that Tibetan Buddhism can only flourish if its traditions, language, canons, and rules are learned, transmitted, and developed freely, without intervention from the Chinese Communist Party and state, including excessive surveillance.

Chapter Eight

RELIGION AND STATE KILLING RELIGION: MYANMAR AGAINST THE ROHINGYA

> *When Myanmar inflicts enormous suffering on the Rohingya—burns them in their homes, cuts the throats of their children, rapes and terrorizes, sends 700,000 people fleeing to Bangladesh in only three weeks—and the government pays no penalty for this—what are we saying to the perpetrators? Or to the victims? And to other potential perpetrators across the globe?... How much crueler can humanity be, and how much chaos and pain are we fomenting?*[255]

—**Zeid Ra'ad Al Hussein**, UN High Commissioner for Human Rights

On August 25, 2017, the Tatmadaw, Myanmar's military, conducted coordinated clearance operations against the Rohingya. The Rohingya are a Muslim minority who historically have lived in northern Rakhine State in western Myanmar, formerly known as Burma. These attacks and those that followed over the following weeks led to the deaths of thousands of Rohingya and the mass exodus of more than 750,000 Rohingya into neighboring Bangladesh. One refugee living in Bangladesh recalls:

> When our village was burned, we move to another village, and they [the Myanmar military] come to burn that village, and we move another village, and when they come to burn that village we move, and that's how we come here at last.... They use the helicopter to burn the villages. Three helicopters, one red color and another two, military color [khaki].... There were some pregnant, eight months pregnancy, unable to move and they were attacked by the military, and there were some little children, and they threw them on the fire.[256]

The religicide inflicted against the Rohingya in Myanmar is a decades-long, coordinated, intentional displacement and eradication of an Indigenous ethno-religious Islamic group.

The historical origins of the Rohingya crisis date back to the 1400s when Muslim settlers arrived in the independent state of Arakan on the coast of the Bay of Bengal. In 1784, Arakan was conquered by the former Burmese Empire, and in 1824, the territory was seized by the British and incorporated into the colonial territories of British India.[257]

In 1942, Japan invaded Burma (now Myanmar), leading to the expulsion of the British and a subsequent Japanese military occupation from 1945 to 1948.[258] By the time Burma gained its independence in 1948, the succession of British and Japanese military conquests had forced multiple generations of Muslims living in the Arakan state (both the descendants of the fifteenth century

Muslim traders and recent migrants) to flee to surrounding areas, including the Cox's Bazar district in Chittagong, Bangladesh.[259]

The term "Rohingya" may have emerged in the late 1950s among Muslim intellectuals living in northern Arakan who began to identify publicly as Rohingya, intending to distinguish themselves from the majoritarian Buddhist Rakhine ethnic group.[260] However, the etymology of this word can be traced to the late eighteenth century. In a 1799 study on the languages spoken in the former Burmese Empire, Scottish scientist Francis Buchanan described the language "spoken by the Mohammedans, who have long settled in Arakan, and who call themselves Rooinga, or natives of Arakan."[261] Pointing to this narrative, Rohingya scholars and activists estimate that more than 10 percent of Arakans were Muslim in 1823.[262]

The ancestors of the Rohingya have been inhabitants of the Arakan kingdom, the modern-day Rakhine State, for more than one thousand years and have developed a distinctive language, culture, and social organization with the adoption of Islamic culture at large.[263] Despite their mixed-Indigenous ancestry, they self-identify as Rohingya with a distinct linguistic culture, Muslim religious practice, and political reality.

Disregarding this history, the Myanmar government has systematically refused to use the term "Rohingya" or to recognize the Rohingya people as among the 135 official ethnic groups in Myanmar. Instead, they describe them as Bengali, a moniker which erases the history of Muslim communities in Myanmar prior to British rule.[264] In 1982, Myanmar passed a citizenship law that excludes the Rohingya, and since the military came to power in 1962, there have been frequent attacks against Rohingya villages, such as "Operation Clean and Beautiful Nation," which destroyed entire villages in Rakhine and resulted in the forced displacement of two hundred thousand Rohingya.[265] In August 2017, a new wave of violence carried out by the army sparked the largest displacement to date, which led an estimated three quarters of all Rohingya in Rakhine State to flee to Cox's Bazar in Bangladesh yet again, resulting in the current humanitarian crisis.

Rohingya Muslims are being systematically removed and murdered by the Myanmar government. We call this religicide.

GENOCIDE

Perpetrators lie in various ways
While the world still debates on genocide.
You can see the fire but not how we are burnt,
You can read of killings but not how throats were cut.
They grabbed our land and build units and prisons
And there they detain and torture us.
They took our properties and bought weapons
And they murder and kill us.[266]

—**Rahamat**, Rohingya poet,
born in Rakhine State

The Myanmar government and military junta are conducting a genocide against the Rohingya. They are systematically eliminating them using virtually every weapon in their arsenal. One of the most effective is the denial of citizenship status.

The Myanmar government has used citizenship laws to disenfranchise and deny the very existence of the Rohingya, even though previous laws had recognized Rohingya as Indigenous, providing multiple pathways to citizenship. In 1948, the Rohingya were recognized as Indigenous and had the same rights as other citizens of Myanmar.[267] But laws enacted in the post-1962 era altered citizenship and stripped the Rohingya of the rights they had previously held.

After the 1962 coup, laws were driven by religious discrimination. In 1978, a citizenship verification process, Nagamin, was imposed concurrently with a counter insurgency operation, Ye The Ha. Ye The Ha targeted the Rohingya by attacking food, funds, recruits, and information.[268]

The 1982 Citizenship Law, which is still in effect, recognizes three tiers of citizenship: taingyintha, associate, and naturalized citizen, with taingyintha being the highest level of citizenship. Eligibility is determined by a list of 135 "Indigenous" ethnicities that was developed in the 1990s, based on the presence of ethnic groups prior to British colonialism of Burma. The question of Rohingya citizenship was removed because the history of Arakan and the presence of Rohingya as taingyintha did not align with the historical narrative of Burma as an exclusively Buddhist state that Ne Win and the other military authorities promoted.[269]

Despite the Rohingya's claims to a long history in Rakhine State, they have been intentionally left off the list of ethnicities included in taingyintha. In 1989, all residents of Myanmar were required to receive new identification cards. The Rohingya never received them.[270] In 1995, the Rohingya were issued temporary identification cards. These were invalidated in 2015, stripping the Rohingya of their voting rights. To obtain national identification cards, Rohingya are forced to identify themselves as foreigners. Arbitrarily applied laws and citizenship impediments became the norm for the Rohingya under military rule. Even when the military stepped away temporarily from total political control as

Myanmar began a move toward quasi-civilian government, the Rohingya were already the world's largest stateless group.[271]

Another weapon used against Rohingya has been dehumanizing rhetoric. Starting in 2011, there was a significant increase in anti-Rohingya sentiment and speech, including racist slurs that characterized Rohingya as subhuman in the media and Buddhist religious circles.[272]

From 2012 to 2016, there were increasing restrictions on the movement, education, and domestic lives of Rohingya. Police checkpoints halted interactions between Buddhist and Muslim communities, increasing communal tensions, and creating the conditions for future violence against the Rohingya.[273]

The ethnic cleansing and removal of Rohingya to internally displaced persons (IDP) camps have created an untenable situation and crisis. Concentration camps may be a more apt description of the IDP camps where Rohingya have been held since 2012. Within these camps and in many villages, Rohingya have been subjected to systematic discrimination, persecution, and violence. Checkpoints outside of villages prevent the movement of Rohingya.[274] As a result, they face economic stagnation and lack access to even the most basic medical care. The latter is an invisible form of violence as Rohingya die in their homes or camps, unable to get to vital public services.

In October 2016, the Arakan Rohingya Salvation Army (ARSA), a Rohingya militant group, attacked security outposts. In response, the Myanmar military conducted "area clearance operations" that lasted for five months.[275] These actions included curfews, extortion, looting of property, and increased security presence. Violence was committed with impunity.[276] The military systematically killed thousands of Rohingya, burned houses and entire villages, raped women and girls, planted landmines, and targeted children.

Forced By Many
(Based on an account from a rape survivor in Long Don)

First, the soldiers asked for money and gold. I gave
everything I owned, including my earrings. And they
raped me one after another. He who was last, used a
knife instead his shaft.[277]

Long before 2017, there was evidence of killings, rape, arbitrary detentions, land confiscations, forced labor, denial of citizenship, and discrimination, including blocking access to health care, education, employment, movement restrictions, and a state-sanctioned campaign of religious hatred.[278] The Myanmar government and military have enacted laws, policies, and strategies of genocidal persecution over the course of thirty years in coordination with Buddhist nationalists against the Rohingya. The intense vilification of the Rohingya as outsiders, illegal Bengalis, and terrorists enabled this genocide.

Torture
(A survivor of torture from Maungdaw custody)

I was stripped, hands were tied, hung up
  "Say as I say" the officer threatened.
    Each hair of my beard was plucked and my phal-
lus, set fire.

"I'm a terrorist," they wanted me to confess. A confession of their version,
A truth for their ears, a depiction that pleases
their eyes.[279]

The "clearance operations" against the Rohingya began in Rakhine state on August 25, 2017. Early that morning, ARSA launched coordinated attacks on a small number of security and military outposts.[280] The military Tatmadaw responded immediately with violent and disproportionate attacks on hundreds of villages that targeted the entire Rohingya population. The ethnic Rakhine participated in the violence alongside Tatmadaw, often killing their neighbors.

One victim was Mayyu Ali, whose poetry appears throughout this chapter. Ali was born in 1991 in western Rakhine State. His birth certificate was confiscated during a paramilitary operation called "the Nasaka" against the Rohingya. As he grew up, he was denied every human right. In 2010, he tried to be a schoolteacher but was rejected because of his ethnicity. He was forced to drop out of Sittwe University in 2012. In 2017, when his village was burned down, Ali fled to Bangladesh with his parents. They live in the Cox's Bazar refugee camp.

Contrary to the Myanmar government's official narrative—that they were responding to an unexpected assault—the military had been planning attacks against the Rohingya for months and actively recruited non-Rohingya civilians to join their ranks.[281] Officials in refugee camps have estimated 9,208 Rohingya killed, 1,358 presumed dead, 2,157 in detention, and 1,834 victims of rape.[282] These figures are almost certainly an undercount.

The military Tatmadaw continued their attacks on the Rohingya, forcing them to flee across the border to Bangladesh.

Due to the treacherous journey and the lack of supplies, many more people died en route. Within a few weeks, these attacks displaced 750,000 Rohingya. Now, more than one million Rohingya are living in refugee camps in Bangladesh where they face worsening conditions.

The Myanmar government has maintained the narrative that the attacks on the Rohingya were never coordinated. However, interviews with defectors refute this claim. Army Private Myo Win Tun reported that in August 2017 he had acted on orders to "shoot all you see and hear." This led to Private Myo's participation in a massacre of thirty Rohingya who were subsequently buried in a mass grave. In another township, Private Zaw Naing Tun received his orders: "Kill all you see, whether children or adults."[283] The attacks against Rohingya villages followed a uniform pattern of civilian mass murder according to pre-planned, military-led clearance operations.

They also used sexual assault and gender-based violence as a tactic of war. The military systematically selected reproductive-age women and girls for rape, attacks, mutilation, and branding.[284]

Teachers, elders, and religious leaders were singled out for murder, leaving very few community leaders alive to speak out against these atrocities.[285] The religicide in Myanmar was brutal in its detailed planned violence designed to destroy Rohingya people and erase their history, culture, and memory.

ECOCIDE

As Muslims, mosques are a central part of Rohingya village life. Since the campaign of violence's beginning against the Rohingya, the Myanmar government used the destruction of religious sites and places of worship as a tool for driving the Rohingya from Myanmar.

The destruction of Rohingya land and sacred sites began in 2012 with the destruction of community mosques burned in villages across Myanmar.[286] The Jama Mosque—a powerful symbol of the long-term presence of Muslims—was ransacked by the Myanmar government.[287] It is now guarded by government forces, and no Rohingya can enter. The destruction of important cultural and heritage sites enables the rewriting of history while erasing evidence so that the perpetrators of religicide can claim the land and property as their own. The military has burned and bulldozed mosques and villages to allow the government and Buddhist nationalists to settle on land previously inhabited by the Rohingya.

A second wave of destruction began in 2017, when the violence against the Rohingya started to escalate. In September 2017, the Myanmar government placed landmines along the Myanmar border with Bangladesh to target Rohingya fleeing persecution.[288] By that December, 354 villages were partially or completely destroyed and burned down within Rakhine State.[289]

The US Department of State documented that more than thirty-eight thousand buildings in Rohingya villages were destroyed by fire between August and October 2017.[290] Then in December 2017 and January 2018, the looted and destroyed homes were bulldozed by the Myanmar government.[291] In describing the clearance operations, survivor Yae Twin Kyun states: "When the military came, they started shooting at people who got very scared and started running. I saw the military shoot many people and kill two young boys.... There used to be 900 houses in our village, now only 80 are left. There is no one left to even bury the bodies."[292]

The scorched-earth policy and the appropriation of Rohingya property and the military's land grab were meant to destroy evidence of genocide.

The government aimed to eliminate the possibility of the Rohingya ever returning to their previous homes in Rakhine State. In 2018, the military began construction on new villages to replace those previously inhabited by Rohingya. Many Rohingya men were subjected to forced labor by their persecutors to reconstruct their former villages.[293] Much of this new construction in Rakhine State was for the Border Guard Police (BGP) bases and their so-called security cities.

An Amnesty International report on the government's attempt to rebuild Rakhine State revealed: "By early March 2018, there were scores of new structures visible in [Hla Poe Kaung]. As with the security bases in Myo Thu Gyi and Inn Din, the transit center is built directly on land that was previously occupied by a Rohingya village." This is a stark violation of the Myanmar government's repatriation arrangement with Bangladesh from November 2017 that promised to "encourage those who had left Myanmar to return...to their own households and original places of residence or to a safe and secure place nearest to it of their choice."[294]

The Myanmar government has continued to destroy and redevelop Rohingya villages. On May 16, 2020, a fire in Let Kar, a village in Mrauk-U, damaged around two hundred buildings.[295] The Myanmar government wishes to have Mrauk-U designated a world heritage site by UNESCO. It is suspected that this fire was a tool used to clear Rohingya villages from the area. The cause of the fire is still unknown, but eyewitnesses attest that Tatmadaw troops were seen "entering the village around the time the fires began."[296]

The military claimed that the Arakan Army had set twenty homes on fire, leaving the fire's origins uncertain and disputed.[297]

FACTOCIDE

False narratives and hate speech targeting the Rohingya fueled the religicide. Starting in 2011, there was a significant increase in anti-Rohingya propaganda, including racial slurs that cast the dark-skinned Rohingya as subhuman.[298] After the ethnic violence in 2012, existing divisions sharpened, which increased the propensity for violence.

There has been widespread resistance in Myanmar to consider the Rohingya as Indigenous or native born.[299] Colonial-era migration fueled the idea that Muslim migrants from modern-day Bangladesh came to Burma and gained an economic advantage over the Buddhist population. This feeds into the nationalist Buddhist narrative that Rohingya people had adopted their name only to gain political rights in the 1950s. This perception continues to stoke ethnic and religious tensions, justifying human rights abuses against the Rohingya.

Over the past few decades, the Myanmar government and Buddhist nationalists have pushed a message of the "Muslim threat" posed by the Rohingya.[300] The dehumanizing language of "illegal Bengali immigrants," who threaten the stability of the country, has led to ongoing suspicion and violence against the Rohingya.

MaBaTha is a prominent Buddhist nationalist organization that has played a large role in spreading anti-Muslim hate speech.[301] Their anti-Rohingya propaganda against Rohingya is spread through schools, books, magazines, and social media.[302] MaBaTha has gained popular support due to their "charitable" activities.

Other Buddhist nationalist groups have joined forces to shape national legislation, including the Race and Religion Laws.[303] This set of laws codifies prejudices against Muslims and relies on the use of veiled language such as "strengthen[ing] Buddhism" to rationalize hateful rhetoric and discrimination against Muslims.

Social media giants such as Facebook have played a significant role in spreading hate speech against the Rohingya. As Myanmar opened to the outside world during the democratic transition in 2011, personal phones and Facebook were quickly adopted by the masses. Facebook is the primary social medium in Myanmar and plays a huge role in public, civil, and private life.[304] Facebook has been used consistently by Buddhist nationalists to spread anti-Rohingya messages and stoke communal tensions. During the religicide against the Rohingya, Facebook failed to interrupt the proliferation of online hate speech and incitement to violence.[305]

Military personnel used Facebook as a tool for ethnic cleansing. An estimated seven hundred military operatives used accounts to spread anti-Rohingya propaganda, while masquerading as entertainment and businesses.[306] They were used to conduct a systematic covert online campaign to spread anti-Rohingya propaganda.[307] In 2017, Facebook posts inflamed community vulnerability and fears by targeting Muslims and Buddhists with messages about imminent attacks. State-run media supported the Facebook posts with headlines such as "Let Us Eradicate Extremist Terrorists, Destructive Elements Together!" The Tatmadaw used social media to make sure it would have at least the tacit support for Rohingya clearance operations from the majority Buddhist citizens of Myanmar.

WHAT CAN BE DONE?

The Rohingya now suffer from at least three concurrent crises: first, the human rights crisis, including murder, rape, torture, and displacement; second, a development crisis stemming from chronic poverty in Rakhine State and the undermining of economic development caused by the protracted conflict; and third, the security and land ownership crisis, creating segregation and exclusion of Muslim communities in Myanmar.

In the short term, at least, governments must press to end the violence and ensure the human rights of the Rohingya are protected. This includes a need to quell the chaos in refugee camps and in Myanmar. In the medium term, there needs to be a transparent and impartial investigation of the violence, as well as protection and return of stolen land and assets to the Rohingya. This means the facilitation of repatriation for the majority of Rohingya who want to return safely to Myanmar. In the long term, the underlying grievances of all parties must be addressed to prevent cyclical violence in the future.

Political

International organizations, governments, and corporations can play a more positive and proactive role in the justice for the Rohingya. Actions by the United Nations, the International Criminal Court, and the International Court of Justice can all use their power to advocate for the Rohingya and investigate Myanmar. Facebook can play a role in helping to protect the human rights of the Rohingya by diligently monitoring and removing hate speech and online propaganda.

Rohingya representatives have initiated a lawsuit against Facebook for over $150 billion under a class action complaint that the company's online platform helped perpetuate genocide in Myanmar. The allegations lodged in both the United States and United Kingdom courts claim that "Facebook's [now under the name of Meta] algorithms amplified hate speech against the Rohingya people; it failed to invest in local moderators and fact-checkers; it failed to take down specific posts inciting violence against Rohingya people; and it did not shut down specific accounts or delete groups and pages that were encouraging ethnic violence."[308] Despite Facebook's internal investigations highlighting the company's culpability for inciting violence against the Rohingya, at the time of this writing there has been no compensation or reparations offered to the survivors.

Within Myanmar, the centrality of ethnicity to public life must be mitigated to ensure that all people in Myanmar have access to citizenship and basic human rights. The creation of an inclusive national identity can be achieved through citizenship reforms and civilian control of the Tatmadaw. Accordingly, citizenship needs to be separated from ethnicity, as recommended by the Advisory Commission on Rakhine State, chaired by Kofi Annan, in 2017.[309]

Challenges remain to enacting any reforms. On February 1, 2021, unrest struck Myanmar when the Tatmadaw seized power in a coup. Civilian peaceful protests and demonstrations have asked for parliamentary action to oppose the ruthless military coup. However, the crisis has escalated with the military's brutal response to diffuse all pro-democracy movements. Previous democratic civilian leader Aung San Suu Kyi has been ousted and was placed under house arrest by the Tatmadaw following the 2021 November elections and subsequent military coup.

Army Chief General Min Aung Hlaing, currently in power, has overseen years of repression and violence against the Rohingya. The military leaders who have been responsible for religicide have expanded their abuse to all citizens of Myanmar who oppose military rule. Since the coup, the Tatmadaw has killed approximately 1,300 people, arrested more than 10,000, and left an estimated three million in need of humanitarian assistance.[310] To make matters worse, the military continues to target health workers and block external aid resources, heightening the conflict. Insurgency groups are growing to counter the military via training in the jungle using firearms and hand grenades.[311] Ongoing civil war looms.

One flicker of hope is the emergent coalition building among the Rohingya with other minorities in Myanmar and youth activists across the country. Increasingly, activists and citizens are becoming aware of how the military manipulated the view of the Rohingya to justify their gross human rights abuses. One aspect of any new government must be the guarantee of basic rights and protections for all minorities and civilian groups, large and small, so the repatriation of Rohingya can occur safely.

Economic

Rakhine State is a crucial access point to the Indian Ocean, which allows imports to bypass the Strait of Malacca. The Chinese Belt and Road Initiative has recognized its significance and is planning developments via the China-Myanmar economic corridor with the Kyaukphyu Special Economic Zone (SEZ) and a deep-sea port. The BRI's construction of the Southeast Asia oil and gas pipeline runs over 750 kilometers from Maday Island port directly into China, bypassing the Malacca Strait. This will have significant negative social and environmental impacts. It appears that Myanmar is trending to become more and more a Chinese client state, dependent on China for its exports.

In this contentious regional environment, an economic incentive plan to start renewable energy in Rakhine State could be beneficial to Myanmar while helping to employ Rohingyas. The country needs incentives to break free of China's grip and build relationships with other foreign investors. Such actions will build state sovereignty and economic diversification while hopefully combating the impending negative effects of the climate crisis.

The dangling of incentives might compel the Myanmar government to be more open to foreign investment and to become more accountable for the human rights abuses of the Rohingya in Rakhine State. Foreign investment in renewable energy can also provide jobs for Rohingyas, which can be furthered by skill development and an expansion of international actors willing to press for human rights and sustainable development.

Social

Socially, there needs to be reintegration of Muslim and Buddhist communities. This includes new joint activities in the marketplace, employment, and entertainment, including shared soccer games, new business ventures, and more creative partnerships to celebrate diverse culture and the arts.

Part of changing the narrative means a greater role for women. Oxfam International reports that "Rohingya women are leading efforts to support their rights and well-being, along with those of their families and communities. Such roles are also contributing to small but important shifts in gendered norms in the camps, ultimately indicating their transformative possibilities." Increasing the role of women and religious leaders in peacebuilding efforts will help generate lasting social transformation that enables the mutual flourishing of the Rohingya and all citizens of Rakhine State. "However, the active roles women are playing in their communities are not being properly recognized and supported by the range of stakeholders involved in delivering humanitarian assistance and developing political solutions to the crisis. This must change."[312]

Cultural

Mrauk-U is an archaeologically important town in Myanmar's northern Rakhine State, as it is the center of both historic Buddhist and Muslim heritage. It was jointly built by Rakhine Buddhist and Muslims in the fifteenth century. As such, it may have the potential to serve as a shared space to foster interethnic and interreligious reconciliation based on shared historic roots and national identity. Former UN Secretary-General Kofi Annan called it "the greatest physical manifestation of Rakhine's rich history and culture."[313]

The history of Mrauk-U spans from the 1430s to the 1780s, when Muslims and Buddhists served side by side in the royal court and government bureaucracy. Mrauk-U offers a unifying motivation with potential to combat the factocide, including the false narrative that the Rohingya are illegal Bengali immigrants rather than Myanmar citizens with equal rights.

The Mrauk-U interfaith initiative is mobilizing religious minority leaders, interfaith groups, Rohingya bloggers, and the Arakan Rohingya National Organization (ARNO) based in the United Kingdom. Nurul Islam and Razia Sultana are two of the leaders of ARNO skillfully advocating for the rights of the Rohingya community. ARNO also includes Mohib Ullah, the leader of Arakan Rohingya Society for Peace and Human Rights, and Hkalam Samson, a Kachin Baptist and the Kachin Baptist Convention president. Ullah represents the Rohingya minority, while Samson represents and advocates for the rights of marginalized Christian minorities in Myanmar. Connecting minority groups who are advocating for their individual and collective rights will unite a growing coalition to challenge the oppressive military regime.

The Yogyakarta Statement on Shared Values and Commitments represents a summit of over thirty Buddhist and Muslim religious leaders, which promotes nonviolence, religious freedom, and intolerance of hate speech. Their plan of action has the potential to effectively target, dissipate, and prevent religicide in Myanmar, and it reflects the ways in which Muslims and Buddhists can work together to address the religicide against the Rohingya.

Finally, a network of underground bloggers has published eyewitness accounts and video evidence that corroborates systemic discrimination, state-sanctioned violence, and mass murder of the Rohingya at the hands of the Tatmadaw. This network serves as a check on censorship by the Myanmar government and provides evidence via international journalists for the pending ICC case on the Myanmar military.

Chapter Nine

RELIGICIDE AND
INDIGENOUS AMERICANS

Our people have been colonized by foreign govern-
ments. We speak and practice vestiges of our own lan-
guage, culture, and spiritualism; but, the non-Indian
language, religions, mode of living, cultural values,
concepts of individualism, greed, private property, and
the nuclear family system have been forced upon our
societies through governmental and church programs
and policies of extermination, termination, assimila-
tion, acculturation, and enculturation. [314]

—Testimony of **Jewell Praying Wolf**
James, descendant of Chief Seal'th

Hallmarks of religicide can be seen in America's white settler colonialism since the fifteenth century. Along with slavery, this remains one of the founding traumas of US history. Hundreds of Indigenous communities and nations lived and thrived in North America before European explorers set out to conquer them. Over time, the "new" Americans systematically destroyed sacred heritage, stole land, and forced Indigenous Americans and their children to convert to Christianity. In many cases, they had to abandon their traditional way of life or die.

This was not solely an American phenomenon. The conquistadors colonized South America and Mexico, decimating the native Inca, Aztec, and Maya populations. These colonizers preceded the arrival of the British to North America's shores by more than a century. The Aboriginals, thought to be among the oldest people on earth, were initially supplanted by British convicts who were exiled to the Australian penal colony starting in 1788. New Zealand was first colonized by the Dutch in the seventeenth century. Later, the British claimed New Zealand as part of the British Empire. The native Maori were given the same rights as British subjects, making their story somewhat different from that of other Indigenous people. But with that exception, we see the same history repeated among native Alaskans, native Hawaiians, and native Canadians. For the purposes of this book, we will focus on the example of Native Americans[315] in the United States.

By the end of the nineteenth century, the Native American population had shrunk from several million to less than 250,000.[316] Can this devastating decimation of Indigenous peoples be classified as religicide? To qualify, wouldn't their spirituality and traditions have to be the main reason Natives were targeted?

The answers are complicated. In short: yes and no.

It is important to remember that Native Americans do not share one single religion. Each Indigenous tribe has its own distinct belief system, history, economy, language, customs, and community structure. Rather than characterizing their way of life as religious, most share a belief that all creation is interconnected through symbiotic relationships among nature, humans, animals, and the supernatural.[317] But was it the otherness that caused a series of policies by the US government to more or less eradicate Native populations in the 1800s? Or was it generic settler colonialism—oppressing, killing, and taking land from Natives for economic gain and cultural domination?

Let's investigate.

The Native history in North America is complex, littered with misguided good intentions, cruelty, violence, and greed. Indigenous Americans have struggled to survive conflict, displacement, forced conversions, and broken treaties.

In many ways the presidency of Ulysses S. Grant (1869-1877) was an inflection point for the fate of the Native tribes of North America. President Grant appeared sympathetic to the Natives and claimed to know them thoroughly. Earlier in his US Army career, he had lived among West Coast Indians while stationed in Washington Territory. In a note to his wife, he observes that the Natives are "the most harmless people you ever saw. It is really my [opinion] that the whole race would be harmless and peaceable if they were not put upon by the whites."[318] This stands in stark contrast to the feelings of Grant's trusted general Philip Sheridan, who infamously remarked, "The only good Indians I know are dead."[319] These contrasting perceptions of Native Americans reverberated through Grant's years in office and the ensuing decades.

President Grant was allegedly committed to justice for Native Americans. In his first inaugural address, he announced his intention to create an incremental path toward citizenship for them. He was convinced that peace with the Natives could be achieved if they would renounce their nomadic lifestyle, settle in vast protected reservations, and become "civilized" through Christianization. This policy was encapsulated in the words "removal" and "civilizing." At the same time, Grant decried the abuse to which the

American Indians had been subjected by white settlers, profiteers, and the US military. Is Grant's desire to Christianize Native Americans evidence of religicide? Arguments abound.

Grant's supposed respect for the Natives was reportedly manifest in his friendship with General Ely Parker. Parker, a full-blooded Seneca chief, was Grant's adjutant and secretary during the Civil War. It was Parker who drafted the final surrender documents signed by Robert E. Lee at Appomattox. When Grant became president, he appointed Parker to become the US commissioner of Indian affairs, making him the first Native American and non-white person to hold a high-level government post. In the end, Grant's attempts to obtain justice for American Indians were defeated by a tidal wave of the westward settler movement, expansion of railroads, corruption, and the pursuit of gold in the Black Hills of South Dakota. Pursuit of land and gold seem the hallmarks of colonization, but perhaps fall short of religicide.

For years, American Indian policy was divided between two agencies: The Department of the Interior was responsible for negotiating with tribes, distributing funds and supplies, and carrying out the work of "civilizing" the American Indians. The War Department was tasked with enforcing the treaties and waging the Indian Wars. With the move to the War Department, oversight of American Indian Affairs was left to generals such as Phil Sheriden.[320] The debate over civilian versus military control of America's Native tribes played out from the 1850s to the 1870s with disastrous results.[321]

While there were members of Congress who had no objection to an out-and-out genocide against the American Indians, the various commissions that were set up and the reports they submitted revealed many politicians with a conscience. President

Grant himself was determined to deal with the tribes more humanely. However, he never questioned his overall approach to the "Indian problem"—removal and civilizing. Ron Chernow, a Grant biographer, observes, "Grant saw absorption and assimilation as a benign, peaceful process, not one robbing Indians of their rightful culture."[322]

President Grant put forth an Indian Peace Policy in which he replaced, with Quakers, the corrupt traders who had been licensed by the Indian Bureau to provision the Natives. Grant believed he could count on Quakers to set an example of honesty and peace. He deemed this initial effort so successful that he expanded it. He mandated that each reservation would be administered by a single religious denomination—Protestant, Episcopalian, Methodist, Baptist, Mennonite, etc.—giving them a monopoly over "civilizing" (read: proselytizing) its inhabitants. Allocations were supposed to be made based on the number of missionaries already at work in the reservations. Using that criterion, Catholics should have been assigned thirty-eight reservations to administer; they were accorded only eight. They got even by forming their own Bureau of Catholic Indian Missions.[323]

Bear in mind that the official objective was to Christianize Indigenous communities. (Administration by American Jews was not even considered until Grant's liaison to the Jewish community protested the exclusion of his people. Apparently, Grant happily assigned the "Israelite" Dr. Herman Bendell as superintendent of American Indian Affairs in the Arizona territory.)[324] Pressure for Native Americans to convert to the imposing power's dominant religion would be a hallmark of religicide.

In 1874, a rumor of much gold being found in the Black Hills of South Dakota spread. General Sheridan sent the Seventh

Cavalry, led by General George Armstrong Custer, to check it out. Grant, fearing an onslaught of gold miners, ordered them to stay away but knew the army would be unable (or unwilling) to hold them off. In 1875, Grant met with Sioux leaders at the White House to convince them to move further south and sell the Black Hills to the government. The president pledged to protect Sioux rights under the treaty of 1868, but his real goal was to secure title to the Black Hills to open them up to settlement and development of mineral wealth.[325] By November 1875, the military no longer enforced Grant's earlier order and the floodgates opened to miners. Sioux were ordered to abandon their land within two months. Of course, they could not comply with that tight deadline, and the Seventh Cavalry, including Colonel George A. Custer, was sent to oust the Sioux. Confronted by a huge tribal force, the Seventh Cavalry was routed, and Custer was found naked and dead on June 25, 1876, at the hands of Lakota and Cheyenne warriors in Montana Territory at the Battle of the Little Bighorn.[326] Historian Ron Chernow writes, "The national response was a ferocious outcry for Indian blood, bordering on the genocidal." [327]

But again, we ask if this thirst for blood was predicated on Native beliefs—or was it simply a clash of cultures and a fight for control of land? We believe that had the American Indians been Christians, the slaughter and stealing of land and resources would not have taken place on the scale it did. Because the justifications of these attacks were rarely, if ever, given as based on beliefs, we cannot say definitively that this Indigenous population was subject to religicide. What we can say is that the collective trauma experienced by Indigenous Americans has continued over centuries, nearly eradicating their beliefs from US culture.

In 1889, when North and South Dakota became states, nine million acres of the Great Sioux Reservation were sold, leaving six smaller fragmented reservations: Cheyenne River, Standing Rock, Rosebud, Crow Creek, Lower Brule, and Pine Ridge. On December 29, 1890, the US Cavalry killed 146 Sioux at Wounded Knee on the Pine Ridge Reservation.[328] This proved to be the last major confrontation in America's war against the Plains Indians. Most of the Sioux killed at Wounded Knee were buried in a mass grave.

The more recent experience in 2016 of protesters at the Standing Rock Reservation may offer a window into Indigenous history on American soil. During a blizzard in North Dakota, thousands of Native Americans and their allies from across the country came to protest the Dakota Access Pipeline. Running this pipeline under Lake Oahe would jeopardize the primary water source for members of the Standing Rock Sioux Reservation. Multiple graves, prayer sites, and sacred heritage were destroyed by the bulldozing and development around Lake Oahe.[329] Lee Plenty Wolf, an Ogala Lakota elder from the Pine Ridge Reservation, explains, "We've lost a lot of land to history. We have to stand up for our rights. Usually, I get up and I look to the east to pray. You know, even if it's a small prayer. But [on the third morning I was here], I glanced at the east, and I looked to the north, and the first vision that came to me was Wounded Knee, the first massacre. You know? I got a little emotional. That's when I decided I couldn't leave."[330]

Let's apply our factors of religicide to the Indigenous history of the United States, and let the reader decide where it falls on our scale of eradicating a population because of their beliefs.

GENOCIDE

"Where today are the Pequot?
Where are the Narragansett, the Mohican, the Pokanoket,
and many other once powerful tribes of our people?
They have vanished before the variance and the
oppression of the White Man,
as snow before the summer sun."[331]

—Tecumseh

Millions of Native Americans died from violence, forced assimilation, enslavement, displacement, and starvation. Entire cultures were destroyed, and those Natives who have survived continue to face an uphill battle to heal, reclaim their rights, and rebuild their traditional way of life in the modern era.[332]

Indigenous rights scholar and author Roxanne Dunbar-Oritz sums up the intention of settler colonialism in her award-winning book, *An Indigenous Peoples' History of the United States*:

> Settler colonization is inherently genocidal in terms of the genocide convention. In the case of the British North American colonies and the United States, not only extermination and removal were practiced but also the disappearing of the prior existence of Indigenous peoples—and this continues to be perpetrated in local histories....Documented policies of genocide on the part of US administrations can be identified in at least four distinct periods: the Jacksonian era of forced removal; the California gold rush in

Northern California; the post-Civil War era of the so-called Indian wars in the Great Plains; and the 1950s termination period.[333]

It is true that settler colonialism systemically reinforced violence against Indigenous Americans. Forms and tactics of colonialism evolved over time and came to include residential schools, allotment politics, and legal institutionalized discrimination. Over time, these degrading policies and practices have contributed to higher levels of poverty, sickness, marginalization, and suicide among Native Americans.

Indigenous Americans' social health and group continuity require more than the mere survival of individuals. They require local and ecological knowledge systems, practice of spiritual rituals, oral tradition—including traditional languages, music, and art—as well as governance and legal systems. Without these, the result is a slow and steady social death—an inability to maintain group identity and community resilience to survive.[334]

Some settlers who considered themselves "friends of the Indian" admitted that the most humane way to achieve their aims would be to "kill the Indian but save the man."[335] This meant eradicating traditional Indigenous culture and peoples by supposedly civilizing, colonizing, re-educating, and Christianizing them. Some of these Christian reformers spoke of a "final solution" well before the Nazis used this ominous phrase.[336]

The role of the Catholic Church in perpetrating religicidal acts is often whitewashed. In California, for example, the church aimed to convert all Indigenous Americans. Between 1769 and 1784, Father Junipero Serra headed missions in northern California to establish nine communities where Natives lived under the supervision of priests. They were expected to assimilate by becoming

Catholic and adopting European-style agriculture. To this day, American students are taught to view Father Serra as California's benevolent founding father and savior of the Natives.[337]

The California Natives were among tens of thousands of Native Americans absorbed into Catholic missions. Under the guise of charity lay brutality, forced labor in mission farming projects, and separation from family. Natives were rarely allowed to leave the missions.

In Canada, as late as the 1970s, more than 150,000 children were forced to attend state-funded Christian boarding schools to assimilate them to Canadian society. These schools were run as cheaply as possible, fostering dangerous conditions with children subjected to forced labor.[338] Many children died of disease, and many were never returned to their families. Three quarters of the schools were run by Roman Catholic missionaries bent on Christianizing and baptizing the "uncivilized" kids forced to reside in their schools. Institutionalized discrimination against Indigenous Americans was not confined to colonial times, as these state-funded residential schools stayed open until the 1980s.[339]

ECOCIDE

My people live in and use every inch of that land. We have lived here for so long that everything has a name: every stream, every hill, almost every rock.[340]

—**Matthew Coon Come**, Grand Chief, Crees of Northern Quebec

Indigenous culture—its traditions and spiritual practice—is normally inextricably linked to reverence for nature and all living beings.[341] During the 1840s, American immigrants on the Oregon Trail wreaked ecological havoc on Lakota country by driving away buffalo, importing disease, and polluting the land.

One well known example of ecocide was the mass murder of bison. Before the 1700s, millions of American bison roamed the Great Plains. These huge shaggy beasts were originally hunted by Indigenous Americans, who sought to waste nothing. Natives traditionally killed only as much as they could eat or carry with them. Every part of a bison was used, including hides for warmth and homes, bones for tools, and meat for food. As Natives endeavored to kill only as many bison as they needed in a particular season, there were always plenty of these animals.

White settlers had a different approach. They killed bison en masse for their hides, which fetched a lot of money. In the winter of 1872, more than 1.5 million hides were shipped from the Great Plains back east, leaving rotting bodies, including wasted meat and bones. This wasn't just entrepreneurship; it was US policy. A directive from President Grant declared that killing bison was a solution to the "Indian Problem."[342] This was direct evidence that the US government aimed to subjugate (at best) or eliminate (at worst) the livelihood of Native Americans. This scorched-earth strategy starved Sioux tribes into submission. The army was directed to destroy the economic base of the Plains Nations—the bison—to create economic dependency and starve the Natives. But bison weren't just a food source, they also had deep spiritual meaning. Historian Roxanne Dunbar-Oritz relays the poignant Indigenous lament from Old Lady Horse of the Kiowa Tribe:

Everything the Kiowas had came from the buffalo.... Most of all, the buffalo was part of the
Kiowa religion. A white buffalo calf must be sacrificed in the Sun Dance. The priests used parts
of the buffalo to make their prayers when they
healed people or when they sang to the powers
above. So, when the white men wanted to build
railroads, or when they wanted to farm or raise
cattle, the buffalo still protected the Kiowas.
They tore up the railroad tracks and the gardens.
They chased the cattle off the ranges. The buffalo loved their people as much as the Kiowas
loved them.[343]

These animals were crucial to Native beliefs and practices. By
1880, the bison had almost disappeared—a form of animal ecocide
that harmed Indigenous communities, their spirituality, and the
environment. Killing the bison was part of the murder of traditional communities on the Great Plains. Animal rights aside, the
pattern of ecocide was clear from the earliest interaction with
European colonizers. Indigenous Americans witnessed their natural ecosystems and land stolen and degraded over time.

The federal creation of national parks—two of them created by President Grant—was lauded by most Americans as
a wilderness conservation effort. It was, in fact, accomplished
through land taken by fiat (stolen), triggering the displacement
of entire Indigenous communities. Most Americans agree the
Grand Canyon is a national treasure. But it was taken from the
Havasupai people who were forcibly displaced. In the same fashion, the picturesque Apostle Islands National Lakeshore was also
stolen without compensation from the homelands of the Ojibwe.

The creation of Olympic National Park prevented Quinault tribal members from exercising their treaty rights. And the Everglades National Park was created on Seminole land on which the tribe depended for food.[344] The list goes on.

The rapid growth of the United States industrial economy in the nineteenth century involved an ongoing confiscation of Native American land. With the growth of free-enterprise capitalism, rapid technological change and the exploitation of natural resources damaged the environment, which in turn harmed Indigenous livelihood and spirituality aligned with nature.[345]

The continual usurping and destruction of Native land are well documented. Whether it constitutes religicide depends on where one stands. To those who lost the land, it is clearly theft meant to eradicate a people. To those taking the land, it is preservation of natural beauty and economic expansion. Whether the intention was religicide or not, the result is the same—land and resources were stolen, exploited, and ruined, and a Native population was left fragmented and adrift.

There are too many examples of environmental injustice to recount here, but a few egregious cases will have to suffice. Without any Indigenous community consultation or warning, the US government turned the Inuit homeland on the northwest coast of Alaska into a nuclear dumpsite. This experiment, designed to test the toxicity of radiation in an arctic environment, led to high PCB levels, thinning herds, and the poisoning and depletion of Inuit food sources. Point Hope, the closest settlement to the nuclear waste site, is one of the oldest continuously occupied town sites in North America. The high cancer rates among Native people of Alaska are more likely due to radioactive pollution than to the "high-risk" lifestyle of the Inuits, as the Alaska Department of Health and Social Services would have us believe.[346]

Nearly thirty million tons of radioactive uranium ore was extracted from the Lakota's sacred site of Paha Sapa—an ongoing threat to the health and well-being of the Navajo Nation.[347] The development of the world's largest hydro-electric project has restructured the ecosystem of the Cree's James Bay area of Northern Quebec. Crees, the only permanent inhabitants of the locality, have hunted, fished, and gathered in Northern Quebec for tens of thousands of years. Now the area's fish are contaminated with high mercury levels. Animal migration patterns have rerouted and the ancient burial sites of ancestral Crees are literally under water.[348]

In the Klamath River basin, there is no longer enough water to sustain the farmers, Native Americans, or wildlife. For generations, Native Americans lived in this region until the Klamath Project was started in 1906 and completely changed the natural ecosystem. The Klamath Tribes have fought for the ability to fish and hunt on their ancestral land, but contamination by farmers in the area has endangered culturally important fish such as the C'waam and Koptu fish. In 2021, extreme drought caused canals and wells to run dry, which has harmed the farmers, tribes, plants, and animals that depend on the basin. Part of restoring this ecosystem, and many others, is returning the land to the tribes, who believe a return to their Indigenous farming and herding practices will help regenerate the soil.[349]

Native Americans were not the perpetrators of these environmental atrocities. They did not instigate disputes over the fishing rights in the Pacific Northwest and the Great Lakes. Nor did they cause the pervasive pollution on the Akwesasne Mohawk

Reservation. Systematic commodification of natural resources and industrial growth have produced long-term ecological destruction on Native lands and contributed to climate change.[350] Native Americans, like many Indigenous peoples who live in poverty worldwide, have contributed the least to the global climate crisis but now suffer some of its worst impacts.[351] For example, the climate crisis has brought the Navajo Nation in Arizona, New Mexico, and Utah prolonged drought since the 1990s. With ongoing soil degradation, traditional crops and medicinal plants have also started to die off for the Cherokee Nation in present-day Oklahoma. Native Americans' hopes to reclaim land, health, water, food, livelihood, and traditional culture remain under threat from ecocide and worsening climate trends. An Indigenous member of the Point Hope settlement, living near US nuclear waste in northwest Alaska, puts it plainly: "When the land dies, our people do, too."[352]

FACTOCIDE

Violence against Indigenous Americans has been obfuscated and perpetrated by the misleading use of quasi-positive language, such as "expansion," "development" (read: Manifest Destiny and industrial growth), "civilizing," and "re-education." This is not unlike euphemisms used by China in the case of the Uyghurs and Tibetans. Such euphemisms cover racialization of Indigenous groups and justify settler colonialism, including tearing Native children from their parents to attend forced residential boarding schools.[353]

Too often the story of Indigenous Americans has been presented in history books and our general cultural narrative as a quaint village of Natives who shared Thanksgiving with white people and got angry when they wouldn't leave. Indigenous peoples lived and thrived for millennia before they were colonized and displaced to reservations.

The narrative origin story of the United States is that the country was born in rebellion against oppression and empirical despots. The narrative is one of overcoming, being morally just, striving for progress, and a manifest destiny. The revised story belatedly included the role and contributions of women, African Americans, and immigrants. But this narrative of plucky immigrants and equality under the law can obscure the history of colonization.

On November 29, 1864, the Third Colorado Cavalry killed several hundred Cheyenne and Arapaho people. Years before this massacre, the local paper had called for the "extermination against the red devils" to stoke hatred against Native Americans.[354] Until June of 2020, the man who led this attack had a statue outside of the Colorado State Capitol Building, and he continues to have a town named in his honor.[355]

In 1891, General William Tecumseh Sherman wrote, "Our only safety depends upon the total extermination of the Indians. Having wronged them for centuries we had better, in order to protect our civilization, follow it up by one more wrong and wipe these untamed and untamable creatures from the face of the earth." [356] Interviewed shortly before the massacre at Wounded Knee, Sherman showed no regrets for his religicidal intent, insisting that "Injins must either work or starve. They never have worked; they won't work now, and they will never work."[357] Such disinformation—claiming that Native Americans did not use the land that was taken from them—is a blatant fallacy used to justify conquest and the colonial redistribution of land.

Factocide and other hallmarks of religicide are evident in the US government's historic treatment of its Indigenous peoples. It is fair to say that the Native population could be violent too. Intertribal warfare was brutal. And they were certainly not passive in their retaliation against the colonial settlers and the government. The Powhatan killed nearly 350 members of the Jamestown Colony—one of many attacks on settler colonies in the 1600s and 1700s. In the 1800s, the battles shifted West. Treatment of captives included burning, genital mutilation, pulling of fingernails, flaying, and beating. Ignorant of Indigenous culture, most settlers were terrified of the Natives they viewed as savages. There was never a government-wide or systematic policy to accommodate or understand the Native populations—only that they must be dealt with accordingly.

Military historian John Grenier connects the history of the first white settlement in North America with today and the future:

> US people are taught that their military culture does not approve of or encourage targeting and killing civilians and know little or nothing about the nearly three centuries of warfare—before and after the founding of the US—that reduced the Indigenous peoples of the continent to a few reservations by burning their towns and fields and killing civilians, driving the refugees out—step by step—across the continent.[358]

For centuries, systemic violence in America has been a chronic tragedy desecrating Indigenous peoples and their way of life.

Native American historian and scientist, Robin Wall Kimmerer, sums it up in her best-selling book, *Braiding Sweetgrass: Indigenous Wisdom, Scientific Knowledge and the Teachings of Plants*:

> Children, language, lands: almost everything was stripped away, stolen when you weren't looking, because you were trying to stay alive. In the face of such loss, one thing our people could not surrender was the meaning of land. In the settler mind, land was property, real estate, capital, or natural resources. But to our people, it was everything: identity, the connection to our ancestors, the home of our nonhuman kinfolk, our pharmacy, our library, the source of all that sustained us. Our lands were where our responsibility to the world was enacted, sacred ground. It belonged to itself; it was a gift, not a commodity, so it could never be bought or sold.[359]

WHAT CAN BE DONE?

How might the United States come to terms with its arguably religicidal treatment of Indigenous people? This is not easy for any country, whether it's Germany, China, Myanmar, Iraq, or Turkey. While living persons are not responsible for what their ancestors did, we are responsible for the society we live in now.

Political

- United Nations and relevant national governmental ministries should investigate the status of treaties and agreements between Indigenous nations, the original colonial powers, and the national governments that now claim authority over Indigenous nations. The UN study on treaties, completed in 1999, is a useful tool for Indigenous peoples in the United States in their continuing struggle for land restoration and sovereignty.

- US government agencies should honor the international treaties that aim to protect the human rights of Indigenous peoples, which the United States has failed to endorse or sign. The United States voted against the UN Declaration on the Rights of Indigenous Peoples in 2007, but then agreed in 2010 to use the declaration as moral guidance. That moral guidance needs to be reflected in national legislation that protects those who identify as Native American or Alaskan Native.

- The Organization of American States (OAS), a regional organization of all thirty-five independent states of the Americas, has adopted the American Declaration on the Rights of Indigenous Peoples. The American declaration offers specific protections for the Indigenous peoples in North America, Central America, South America, and the Caribbean, while affirming their rights to self-determination, education, health, self-government, culture, and land. The declaration specifically states that Indigenous peoples have the right not to be subjected to any form of genocide and have the right to the protection of a healthy environment.[360]

- The United States government should ratify (and urge more countries to follow suit) the International Labor Organization (ILO) Convention 169—an international legal instrument that specifically addresses the rights of Indigenous peoples.[361] The ILO is the only tripartite UN agency that works with governments, employers, and worker representatives to set labor standards and promote decent work for all people.[362] ILO Convention 169 is also known as the Indigenous and Tribal Peoples Convention, 1989, and has been ratified by only twenty-four countries.[363] It is the only international treaty open for ratification that deals exclusively with the rights of Indigenous peoples.[364] It holds governments accountable for recognizing the rights of Indigenous peoples and their rights to self-determination within a nation-state.[365]

- US agencies should increase funding for federal, state, and local policy initiatives led by Native Americans to address food insecurity. Indigenous knowledge is particularly effective in coping with climate change and food security.[366] Examples of these contributions include Incan traditions of crop diversification and Sahel use of water harvesting. Such programming can be led by Indigenous people and scaled to address these issues nationally.

Economic

- The United States should support efforts that respect indigenous values and embedded practices around reciprocal, instead of extractive, relationships. Indigenous leader Winona LaDuke declares that "the only compensation for land is land."[367] In her call to action, LaDuke acknowledges a tendency of the American government to make amends through transactional payments, but what is of value to Indigenous people is the actual land, not the compensation for stolen land.

- US agencies should offer Indigenous people permanent unencumbered access to their homeland by returning most of the eighty-five million acres of national parks to a consortium of federally recognized tribes.[368] This consortium would govern the parks for Native people and all Americans. (There is precedent for this type of Indigenous land transfer in Australia and New Zealand.) Returning the national parks would be a meaningful form of restitution and would benefit the land due to Indigenous stewardship practices.

- American business and government should redesign technologies, incentivize markets, and align values to shift away from continued colonization and environmental degradation as part of vital regenerative response to the climate crisis. Colonization today continues through logging, mining, drilling, and other detrimental and exploitative processes that are conducted under the guise of economic development. Such activities undermine the prosperity and health of both Indigenous people and non-Indigenous people.[369]

- Investors and state officials should engage Indigenous people in an urgent energy system redesign—an overdue process that will require radical inclusion and equity. There is an opportunity to do more than replace the energy system by actively engaging Indigenous people in this process. One example is the closure of the Navajo Generating Station in 2019 and the shift toward solar energy as is shown in the film *Current Revolution: Nation in*

Transition. At the very least, this transition can help bring prosperity, employment opportunities, and renewable energy to fragmented Native American reservations.

- The energy industry is deeply connected to inequality, and emerging clean energy markets can be designed to become generators of economic security. This shift can be accomplished by creating sustainable employment opportunities for generations to come—aligning industry with cultural and Indigenous values that respect the planet and its people.

- US farmers and nonprofit organizations should advocate to reform local food production with training to shift away from monoculture to regenerative farming and permaculture. Recultivate Indigenous foods for trade such as the Native Foodways Program run by the Cultural Conservancy at their bases in Heron Shadow and the Indian Valley Organic Farm and Garden.[370] This program includes distribution of Native foods, medicines, and organic produce through partnerships with Native communities and local farms. The land base houses a seed library where culturally important plants and crops are stored to maintain traditions, and the space serves as an excellent location for public events to connect community members.

- Scale up similar programs across the country. Treaty concessions, forced under conditions of epidemics and starvation, eviscerated Native American territory.[371] For Indigenous people, food sovereignty is political, cultural, nutritional, and "cosmological."[372]

Cultural and Social

- US historians and teachers should work with Indigenous educators to amend and rewrite textbooks guilty of factocide to reflect a more balanced history of American settler colonialism and the historic genocide against Native Americans.
- The US Congress and corporations should reroute or ban pipelines and mining that can irreversibly harm the earth and its Indigenous communities. Native spirituality is intimately tied to the environment. Cultural roots, practices, heritage, and forms of expression, such as art and music, are linked to the relationship between Indigenous peoples and their natural environment. Philanthropies and corporations should fund cultural revitalization and collective healing through art and stories of individuals and citizens rooted in ancestral tradition. The aim is to preserve traditional wisdom and spiritual practices that build community and promote a sense of connectedness and belonging.
- Television producers and donors should support diverse Native media programming—including documentaries, podcasts, and public exhibitions—aimed to advance public awareness and community education done in collaboration with Indigenous communities.
- Educational, environmental, and conservation groups should set aside public space for traditional practices that celebrate Native cultures and open space for social solidarity and connection. The Cultural Conservancy offers a Native Arts program designed to revitalize culture

through carving, weaving workshops, regenerative farming, youth internships, and public exhibits.

Indigenous communities can chart a way forward to a post-colonial life that doesn't erase the crimes of the past. It requires respectful reclamation of the language of survivors. As the author of *Braiding Sweetgrass* puts it, "When a language dies, so much more than words are lost. Language is the dwelling place of ideas that do not exist anywhere else. It is a prism through which to see the world."[373]

Words often fail us in the face of the unspeakable crimes committed against humanity, including the atrocities of religicide. But our collective aim must be for reconciliation, truth, and equity for all people, including the Indigenous communities who have been victimized over centuries.

There is a growing body of international law, policies, and practice to build upon. In 2007, the UN Declaration on the Rights of Indigenous Peoples (UNDRIP) was adopted by the UN General Assembly.[374] This declaration outlaws discrimination, promotes the full and active participation of Indigenous peoples in all matters that concern them, and protects their rights to pursue their own distinct economic and social development. The declaration addresses both individual and collective rights, including cultural rights, rights to education, health, employment, and language. Indigenous peoples have the right to enjoy all human rights and fundamental freedoms protected by international human rights law.

There are additional protections granted to Indigenous peoples to shield them from any form of discrimination based on their ancestry. This includes the right to maintain and strengthen their distinct economic, political, social, cultural, and legal institutions.

Article 37 of UNDRIP explicitly mandates the right to recognition and enforcement of treaties and agreements with States.

The declaration invites the direct input of Indigenous peoples in decision-making and meaningful participation in all decisions that will affect their lives. UNDRIP affirms the rights of Indigenous peoples to self-determination and recognizes rights to lands, territories, and resources. When the declaration was adopted, Australia, Canada, New Zealand, and the United States initially voted against it but later reversed their positions and expressed support for UNDRIP.

The World Bank has also established some procedures for protecting the rights of Indigenous peoples.[375] Their manual states the World Bank's policy on the development process in relation to the dignity, human rights, economies, and cultures of Indigenous peoples. This includes identifying impacts on Indigenous peoples and providing free, prior, and informed consultation with affected communities. If there is not broad support for the project among Indigenous peoples, the World Bank does not proceed further with project processing. This process also provides special considerations for lands and natural resources based on close ties between Indigenous peoples and their land.

Within the United Nations, there are bodies that report on the rights and issues affecting Indigenous peoples. The UN special rapporteur on the situation of human rights and fundamental freedoms of Indigenous peoples promotes laws, programs, and agreements between Indigenous peoples and states to implement international standards.[376] The special rapporteur periodically reports on the overall human rights situation of Indigenous people, addresses cases of rights violations, and contributes to studies on the protection of Indigenous peoples' rights. The expert mechanisms on the rights of Indigenous peoples also provides the UN Human Rights Council with thematic advice on the rights of Indigenous peoples.[377] Finally, the UN Permanent Forum on Indigenous Issues is an advisory body to the Economic and Social Council and can submit recommendations to the Council, raising awareness and prioritizing activities related to the advancement of Indigenous peoples.[378]

This is good news. Indigenous rights and reporting are now inextricably linked to our international system of human rights. They signal a way forward in preventing religicide and protecting the freedom of practice by Indigenous minorities.

Chapter Ten

GAPS IN THE PROTECTION OF RELIGION AND BELIEF

There are hundreds of intertwined laws, resolutions, declarations, and mandates designed to protect our right to believe what we want, how we want, where we want, and with whom we want. In addition to human rights laws, several other regimes of international law address aspects of religicide, including international criminal, humanitarian, refugee, and Indigenous peoples laws and treaties. Unfortunately for those experiencing religious persecution, the various laws all have their gaps, troubling histories, and political and internal disputes, which often leave them impotent and ineffective.

We make the case here that anti-religious persecution and violence fall between the cracks of these elaborate laws and procedures. We believe religicide warrants its own category with an innovative and coherent regime designed to protect religious minorities and cultural heritage at risk of extinction.

INTERNATIONAL HUMAN RIGHTS LAW

An extensive, dynamic, and complex human rights law network and ecosystem blankets the world. It's made up of diverse activists, lawyers, subject matter experts, scholars, the UN and other public officials, civil society organizations, philanthropists, businesses, journalists, religious groups, brave citizen activists, and most courageous of all, the survivors of cruelty and abuse themselves, including their families and loved ones. In most cases, the jurisdiction, legal obligations, and authority to protect rights and punish abuse are carefully delineated internationally, regionally, and nationally.

The thirty articles of the 1948 Universal Declaration of Human Rights (UDHR) enumerate the inalienable rights to which all people are entitled—regardless of "race, color, sex, language, religion, political or other opinion, national or social origin, property, birth or other status."[379] Yet, on a daily basis, virtually all these rights itemized in the UDHR are violated by governments and non-state actors perpetrating religicide:

- Everyone has the right to life, liberty, and the security of person.
- No one shall be subjected to torture or to cruel, inhuman, or degrading treatment.
- All are entitled without any discrimination to equal protection of the law.
- No one shall be subjected to arbitrary arrest, detention, or exile.
- No one shall be subjected to arbitrary interference with his privacy, family, home, or correspondence, nor to attacks upon his honor and reputation.
- Everyone has the right to freedom of movement and residence within the borders of each state.
- Everyone has the right to leave any country, including his own, and to return to his country.

- Everyone has the right to freedom of thought, conscience, and religion.
- Everyone has the right to change his religion or belief.
- Everyone has the freedom to manifest his religion or belief in teaching, practice, worship, and observance in public or private.
- Everyone has the right to freedom of peaceful assembly and association.
- Everyone has the right to equal access to public service in his country.
- Everyone has the right to education that shall promote understanding, tolerance, and friendship among all nations, racial, or religious groups.

This abridged litany of rights concludes by saying no "state, group or person [has] any right to engage in any activity or to perform any act aimed at the destruction of any of [these] rights and freedoms." This book is filled with examples of egregious violations of this declaration, particularly when it comes to religious minorities facing genocide.

In his introduction to the 2015 illustrated edition of the 1948 Universal Declaration of Human Rights, then-UN High Commissioner for Human Rights Prince Zeid Ra'ad Al Hussein, acknowledged:

> Human rights abuses did not end when the Universal Declaration was adopted. But since then, countless people have gained greater freedom. Violations have been prevented; independence and autonomy have been attained. Many people—though not all—have been able to secure

freedom from torture, unjustified imprisonment, summary execution, enforced disappearance, persecution, and unjust discrimination, as well as fair access to education, economic opportunities, and adequate resources and health care. They have obtained justice for wrongs, and national and international protection for their rights, through the strong architecture of the international human rights legal system.[380]

Prince Zeid Ra'ad Al Hussein of Jordan is right to commend the declaration's myriad contributions to humanity. With 530 translations, from Abkhaz to Zulu, the declaration is the most translated document in the world.[381] But it is a declaration, not a convention or treaty. As such, it sets important standards, values, and principles, but they are not legally binding on nation-states. While vital and necessary, they have been and are insufficient to reverse the proliferation of genocide, ecocide, and factocide today.

That's because there are numerous gaps in laws, authorities, and political will to enforce international obligations. This is not a criticism per se. It is a conundrum, particularly at a time when liberal democratic principles are under attack, and authoritarian countries such as China, Russia, and Iran are joining forces in their campaigns to challenge Western liberal concepts such as human rights.

The United Nations built on the Universal Declaration of Human Rights by enacting a series of conventions and covenants, which do have strong mechanisms to enforce the law. Between 1948 and 2006, laudable progress was made. At least nine UN covenants and conventions have addressed specific rights enumerated in the declaration: civil and political rights; economic, social, and cultural rights; protection from torture and other degrading treatments; rights of the child; protection of migrant workers; rights of persons with disabilities; protection of all persons from enforced disappearances; and discrimination against women. All of these have been incorporated into human rights laws.

In the 1960s, the UN General Assembly debated two specific forms of discrimination—race and religion—even though both were already identified or "covered" by the Universal Declaration of Human Rights. The International Convention on Elimination of All Forms of Racial Discrimination was introduced in 1962 and ratified in 1965. Unfortunately, the convention on the Elimination of All Forms of Religious Intolerance faltered and failed to materialize. To this day, it remains the most ambitious UN attempt to make religion a subject of international law.[382] Though negotiated simultaneously alongside the efforts to end racial discrimination, the convention concerning religious intolerance was eventually dropped. At the time, many countries in the global south and west were advocating strongly for an international framework to end anti-religious intolerance and violence. But Communist states preferred criticizing the West for its systemic racism than advancing any religious freedoms back home. The Soviets, in particular, considered race a priority in their appeal to so-called third world countries advancing an anti-colonialist agenda.[383]

The stage for the development of a convention to end religious intolerance had been set in 1960 with the negotiation of the International Covenant on Civil and Political Rights. Article 18 of the covenant is specifically worded to protect freedom of religion and belief worldwide:

1.   Everyone shall have the right to freedom of thought, conscience, and religion. This right shall include freedom

to have or to adopt a religion or belief of his choice, and freedom, either individually or in community with others and in public or private, to manifest his religion or belief in worship, observance, practice, and teaching.

2. No one shall be subject to coercion which would impair his freedom to have or to adopt a religion or belief of his choice.

This language would seem clear and straightforward. Yet religicide violates each of these provisions with impunity. Paragraph three of Article 19 gives states wanting to excuse their discriminatory behavior on other grounds some wiggle room:

3. Freedom to manifest one's religion or beliefs may be subject only to such limitations as are prescribed by law and are necessary to protect public safety, order, health, or morals or the fundamental rights and freedoms of others.

Article 19 of the covenant further enables abusive states to evade accountability by hiding behind their stated needs for "national security" or "reputation."

Even a cursory survey of the applications of international law suggests there is no enforceable international statute that sufficiently protects religious minorities and their sacred heritage from ongoing attack or persecution.

The failed draft convention on religious discrimination went much further than the 1960 International Covenant on Civil and Political Rights. It added, importantly, the freedom to learn about and change religions, enjoying equal legal protection, and freedom from compulsion.[384]

During the 1967 session of the UN General Assembly, there was a debate on whether incitement to hatred should be subject to punishment. The United States objected, but Israel and many European countries supported its inclusion. It was the Jamaican UN Ambassador Egerton Richardson who distilled the core issue:

> The purpose of the convention was to say that religion and belief were matters for the conscience of the individual and that every individual should be free to decide whether he wished to believe or not, to worship or not, and to observe or not to observe any particular religion. In short, it was the purpose of the convention to declare that, in such matters, the State had no authority to interfere with the individual and to urge every State to grant equal freedom to all individuals. It was the individuals who were thus placed on an equal footing, not the religious or beliefs themselves.[385]

The convention left it to governments to take their own measures to prevent and eliminate discrimination.[386] This is one of the ways the United Nations sidestepped requests by several member states to make religious discrimination a crime, punishable by law. It would be a local decision, naively assuming that countries would police themselves.

The Pakistani delegation made the case for a new UN convention against religious discrimination, noting that the founding Charter of the United Nations had already proclaimed the principle of nondiscrimination, but it only "did so in a general way, so that a convention on the subject would in no way be superfluous."[387]

The oft-heard refrain that religious discrimination is "already covered" by other conventions has kept the issue of religious persecution at a general level, without any teeth, national accountability, or resources to enforce or punish ongoing human rights violations related to religion. We reiterate, religion-related hostilities are the fastest growing category of violence in the world today.

Another attempt at protecting religious freedom came from the Vatican in 1963. The papal bill of rights that emerged from Vatican Council II had legitimized the codification of freedom of religion in international human rights law.[388] Citing the Vatican Council, René Cassin, the French jurist who coauthored the Universal Declaration of Human Rights, argued that the United Nations should prioritize a convention on religion. However, negotiations to that end fell apart by 1967.

This was a historic lost opportunity to birth a new and more accountable framework to prevent and reduce religion-related violence worldwide. There are many reasons it was lost. Consider the political tensions of the 1960s, many of them rooted in religion. For starters, freedom of religion was at odds with the ideology of communist countries, so the convention fell victim to Cold War politics. Then the International Court of Justice refused to rule on the legality of apartheid in South Africa, which dampened confidence in the efficacy of international bodies. The aftermath of the Six-Day War further poisoned the chances for progress, with Israel accused of religious fanaticism and the destruction of Islam's sacred sites. The "Troubles" in Northern Ireland cast religion in a bad light, as did rising Hindu-Muslim violence in India and Pakistan. According to scholar Steven L.B. Jensen, in his groundbreaking analysis of *The Making of International Human Rights*, "International relations were at a low after the war in the Middle East, and the Convention on religious intolerance was part of the collateral damage."[389] Had the convention been successful, it would have established international legal standards, international monitoring and reporting, and obligations on states to change and/or adopt laws related to freedom of religion and belief.

A Convention on the Elimination of All Forms of Religious Intolerance would have brought to bear greater legal attention and awareness to inhibit the spread of anti-religious violence. We will never know how many thousands of lives such a convention might have saved.

It was not until 1981 that the UN General Assembly would finally ratify a watered-down resolution on the Declaration on the Elimination of All Forms of Intolerance and of Discrimination Based on Religion or Belief. But, once again, it was enacted as a declaration, not a convention. Like the Universal Declaration on Human Rights, it is important and aspirational, but lacks the force of law.

There are other gaps as well.

International human rights law and the UN statutes are directed at state actors. In the case of the religicides discussed in this book, that would apply to China and Myanmar, but what about non-state actors, like ISIS? There is nothing in the existing statutes that brings them to justice. In such cases, we are completely dependent on states—some of which are failed, some of which are authoritarian, and some of which lack legitimacy.

We have identified factocide as an indelible feature of religicide. Factocide includes hate speech, disinformation, and incitement. Previously, we discussed the link between hate speech, incitement, and violence. Under Article 20 (2) of the International Covenant on Civil and Political Rights, states parties are obligated to prohibit by law "any advocacy of national, racial or religious hatred that constitutes incitement to discrimination, hostility or violence." [390] States are not obligated to criminalize such kinds of expression.

Ironically, when statutes are used to criminalize incitement, they are often used as a bludgeon against secular and civil society human rights activists rather than a means to bring the perpetrators of anti-religious violence to justice.

Hate speech is more difficult to manage and the subject of intense debate in human rights law. Its vague definition makes it hard to prosecute without violating legitimate freedom of expression. As such, the international human rights framework has evolved with competing norms: freedom of expression vs. anti-discrimination and equality. The kind of expression captured in Article 20 of the International Covenant on Civil and Political Rights and Article 4 of the International Convention on the Elimination of All Forms of Racial Discrimination presents challenges to both sets of norms. "Restrictions on the right to freedom of expression must be exceptional, and the State bears the burden of demonstrating the consistency of such restrictions with international law...and States should generally deploy tools at their disposal other than criminalization and prohibition, such as education, counter-speech and the promotion of pluralism, to address all kinds of hate speech." [391]

Respect for freedom of speech and human rights are fundamentally important for world order. Human rights laws set appropriately high standards that tend to evolve and grow progressively after mass violence has wrought catastrophe on millions of innocent people. When it comes to existential threats to survival, citizens and civilians can't afford to hold their breath, waiting for human rights declarations to save them. There is also a duty for governments and the international community to protect civilians, including religious minorities under siege.

However, in criminalizing and prosecuting incitement to violence against religious groups, we run into more gaps in international law and find more roadblocks in bringing the perpetrators to justice.

INTERNATIONAL CRIMINAL LAW

While human rights law specifies the legal duties of states, international criminal law serves to criminalize and punish individual violators of human rights. The International Criminal Court (ICC), as structured by the Rome Statute, is the implementing arm of such criminal prosecutions. The Rome Statute was drafted in July 1998 and went into force in July 2002. These dates are important because, per Article 24, the statute is not retroactive. No person can be held criminally responsible for conduct prior to the entry of the Rome Statute in 2002. That means that previous religicidal attacks against Tibetan Buddhists, for example, would be excluded—even if China were a party to the statute, which it is not.

The Rome Statute went into force with 123 countries. Of these, thirty-three are African states, nineteen are Asia-Pacific states, eighteen are from Eastern Europe, twenty-eight are from Latin American and Caribbean States, and twenty-five are from Western European and other states.[392] Of the cases cited in our book, only Bosnia and Herzegovina and Germany are parties to the Rome Statute. None of the religicidal countries profiled in this book—China, Iraq, Myanmar, Turkey, and the United States—fall under the jurisdiction of the ICC. Indeed, in 1998, the United States was one of only seven countries, along with China, Iraq, Israel, Libya, Qatar, and Yemen, that voted *against* the Rome Statute becoming law. In reviewing ICC cases over the past twenty years, it is disturbingly clear that all of them are of people of color, overwhelmingly from African countries. There are virtually no cases from Asia.[393] The main offenders in Asia—China, Myanmar, and increasingly, India—are not parties to the Rome Statute, and the ICC has no jurisdiction over countries that are not signatories to the agreement.

There are more gaps. For one thing, the International Criminal Court tries persons, not states, organizations, or groups. This makes Article 33 particularly important. Consistent with the Nuremberg Principles, a crime committed pursuant to an order of government or of a superior does not relieve that person of criminal responsibility. But there are two exceptions that directly contradict this tenet: first, if the perpetrator was under legal obligation to obey orders of the government or superior, and second, if the perpetrator did not know the order was unlawful. These exceptions obscure rather than clarify the question of criminal responsibility. What is the definition of a legal obligation? What is the definition of unlawful? Can official government policy be unlawful? The actions of the Nazis were completely legal under German law.

The ICC can try only persons whose crimes were, at the time committed, under the jurisdiction of the court. Those crimes are limited to genocide, crimes against humanity, war crimes, and aggression. In the interest of flexibility for future prosecutions, these crimes were defined broadly. Only clearer actionable definitions would make it possible or easier to prosecute. Today's religicides don't fit neatly into any one of these categories, though they include elements of all of them.

While grievous religious persecution is a crime under the Rome Statute, ICC trials have focused mostly on violence rather than persecution. A stronger focus on grievous religious persecution might not fit easily into the ICC framework, but states can prosecute this crime under their national laws.[394]

But do they? Will they?

Even if grievous religious persecution was fully covered by the four crimes in the ICC's jurisdiction, prosecutions would be hampered by the two required elements of proof: material (actus reus) and mental (mens rea). Material elements include conduct, result, state of affairs, or an omission. In other words, everything other than the perpetrator's state of mind. Article 30 of the Rome Statute requires proof of the intent to commit, and knowledge of, the crimes under the ICC's jurisdiction. So, if future defendants simply assert that they acted in the interest of national unification or security (rather than with the intent to commit a genocide or religicide), then the mental element (read: intention) for their crimes would be absent. Even if China were a future member of the ICC, it most certainly would use this defense. Had Germany's and Turkey's historic crimes of genocide been subject to ICC jurisdiction, they could have asserted self-defense, as they had done publicly to justify their crimes. In this scenario, with the required mental element lacking, the court could not have convicted the perpetrators and officials who stood trial. The requirement of intent, which can be easy to sidestep, leaves a huge gap for egregious crimes that cannot be prosecuted.

But what if the defendants have instigated massacres, rapes, pillaging, and torture—and continue to perpetrate such crimes? Why not prosecute them based on the outcome of their actions instead of their intentions? Shouldn't this material element of documented action be sufficient? No. Article 15 specifies that the UN Security Council must determine whether a state has committed aggression before the International Criminal Court can act. Given that China, Russia, and the United States hold permanent seats on the Security Council, this makes prosecution of them or their allies highly improbable. China and the United States are not signatories, and Russia signed but never ratified its membership. As nonmembers, why should these countries have the power to obstruct or circumvent the ICC, which is supported by most countries?

If there is no determination within six months of notifying the Security Council, the ICC prosecutor may proceed. But the states' investigations get the first shot at bringing an action. While the ICC has the right to override if a state takes no action, it defers to, and is dependent on, the states. It is the states that must make arrests, enforce warrants, provide evidence, collect assets for payments of fines, and incarcerate the convicted criminals. But what if government officials are the perpetrators? They can characterize their policies and actions as necessary or justified for national security reasons—i.e., countering terrorism and promoting stability. Even if abundant evidence reveals the mechanics of a systematic religicide—such as China's surveillance of Muslim Uyghurs and Tibetan Buddhists—would that genuinely advance China's national security interests? How so? Leaving essential policing, prosecutorial, and incarceration functions to the states introduces a dangerously subjective arbitrariness, even though state parties are obliged to cooperate.

If a state refuses to cooperate, what happens then? The ICC may inform the Assembly of States Parties (the court's management oversight and legislative body composed of the states that have ratified or acceded to the Rome Statute) or inform the Security Council. Would the Security Council ever take action given each member's veto power and national interest? Highly unlikely.

And what of reparations for victims? Article 75 allows the ICC to make an order directly against a convicted person, but what if that person has no assets? Who then provides restitution, compensation, and rehabilitation? That's also unclear.

There is a big escape hatch in the Rome Statute. Article 124 allows any member state to declare that it is not subject to the jurisdiction of the court when a crime is alleged to have been committed by its nationals or on its territory. And Article 127 allows a member state to withdraw entirely from the International Criminal Court (as long as they pay any outstanding financial obligations as of the date of its withdrawal).

All these limitations make the ICC an unlikely venue for responding to religicide—especially the anti-religious violence waged by a state against its own population. There are provisions to revise the Rome Statute over time if two-thirds of the members vote to submit an amendment to the UN secretary-general.

For now, the ICC would certainly benefit from more funding. As it stands, the ICC receives its money from assessed contributions by state parties, UN funds, and voluntary contributions. If a state is in arrears, it loses its vote in the Assembly of State Parties. With more funding, the ICC could potentially take on more investigations and cases and become less dependent on the states for enforcement.

There is another aspect of religicide that is better covered but less prioritized by international criminal law: the destruction of cultural heritage. Although Raphael Lemkin lobbied for including the destruction of cultural heritage in the 1948 Genocide Convention, it was omitted from the final version.[395] As the treaty was being finalized, debates emerged over the inclusion of the phrase "cultural genocide." Many state representatives understood cultural genocide to be a distinct problem. Diplomats argued that it was illogical "to include in the same convention both mass murders in gas chambers and the closing of libraries."[396] It wasn't until the 1954 Hague Convention for the Protection of Cultural Property in the Event of Armed Conflict that systematic attempts to erase history and memory were eventually addressed. This convention, overseen by UNESCO, has been described as "the first and the most comprehensive multilateral treaty dedicated exclusively to the protection of cultural heritage in times of peace as well as during an armed conflict."[397]

There is a catch. Cultural property must be registered and marked with a specific emblem for protection. This ignores sacred lands, rivers, and mountains in favor of large cultural landmarks already recognized by UNESCO as a World Heritage Site. But what about smaller sites, cemeteries, and articles of religious custom and practice that may reside inside homes for ritual use? What about scriptures and sacred books? And what if the state charged with protecting cultural artifacts is the very force that wants to loot, burn, or trash them? And how does one protect or prosecute when the culprit is a non-state actor, such as ISIS, trying to wipe out the religion to which those artifacts are connected?

In its preamble, the 1954 Hague Convention was the first multilateral agreement to refer to cultural heritage, not just cultural property.[398] As such, it laid the groundwork for the 2003 UNESCO Declaration Concerning the Intentional Destruction of Cultural Heritage and the 2003 Convention for the Safeguarding of the Intangible Cultural Heritage. The 2003 convention reinforces the importance of cultural heritage as a right, including the protection of oral traditions, performing arts, social practices, rituals, festive events, traditional knowledge, and practices concerning nature and the universe.[399] All signatories are required to make an inventory of the intangible cultural heritage in their territories. The convention is an expression of good will. It provides for technical support and conferences. Yet again, there is no enforcement mechanism.

The International Criminal Tribunal for the former Yugoslavia, whose mandate ran from 1993-2017, brought eleven cases dealing with cultural heritage. Previously, we described the sacking of Bosnia's national library as part of the Serbs' ethnic cleansing campaign. "Attacks on cultural treasures are an attack on collective memory, as if what came before never existed." [400] For acts like these, Slobodan Milosevic, along with others, was charged with three counts of destruction and willful damage of historical monuments and institutions. However, as with the ICC, cultural destruction must be intentional if it is to be considered a crime against humanity. In other words, the perpetrator must know that it is a cultural property. And the destruction must be widespread and not justified by military necessity.[401]

INTERNATIONAL HUMANITARIAN LAW

International humanitarian law is a body of rules enacted to limit the effects of armed conflict and to protect civilians and unarmed groups acting in their humanitarian or civil capacities. Humanitarian laws also call for the protection of medical personnel, hospitals, ambulances, and supplies. Humanitarian law is rooted in the Geneva Conventions of 1949 and the Additional Protocols of 1977. These cover conduct of warfare, including the treatment of the wounded, prisoners of war, and civilians. More specifically, the Geneva Conventions prohibit:

> Violence to life and person, in particular torture, mutilations or cruel treatment; the taking of hostages; deportations; outrages upon personal dignity, in particular humiliating or degrading treatment, or adverse treatment founded on differences of race, colour, nationality, religion, beliefs, sex, birth, or social status.[402]

In theory, these prohibitions should protect victims of religicide, but they haven't, and they don't. These laws apply only during armed conflicts, and they distinguish between conflicts that involve at least two states and those that occur internally within a single state. In the case of internal armed conflict, the rules are more limited. Most religicides don't fall into the category of armed conflicts. It is hardly a level playing field when only one side of the conflict is fully armed.

The conventions protect only those "in the hands of a Party to the conflict or Occupying Power of which they are not nationals."[403] In the case of religicide, victims are generally nationals of the state that is oppressing them. One could make a case that the Geneva Conventions do apply to the Rohingya as an exception, since Myanmar is claiming that Rohingya are not nationals of that country. But that would mean accepting Myanmar's systemic marginalizing of that ethnic group as nonindigenous and not worthy of citizenship. Does the ethnic cleansing of the Rohingya violate the Geneva Convention prohibitions against mass transfers of population?

If your country has not signed onto these conventions, you are not protected. As China is not at war, apparently the same rules do not apply to protecting the Uyghurs. Does the enslavement of Yazidis by ISIS violate the prohibitions against the taking of hostages? No, because Iraq is technically not in a state of armed conflict. All religious minorities facing religicide are from, or live in, countries that are bound by the UN Geneva Conventions. The question arises whether these conventions can be adapted to address ongoing anti-religious persecution, not just limited to persecution during war.

The Additional Protocols cover aspects of humanitarian aid, such as siege and starvation. But in a paper for the *Naval War College Review*, Yoram Dinstein writes:

> In reality...there is no clear-cut right under existing international law to humanitarian assistance in peacetime.... To the extent that the right to humanitarian assistance is vouchsafed by binding norms of international law (customary or conventional), this is so only in certain contexts of armed conflict. During an armed conflict (whether international or internal), the issue of humanitarian assistance arises solely as regards

the indispensable needs of the civilian population.... Clothing, bedding, and means of shelter are of particular relevance to refugees and displaced persons, but all civilians in a devastated area (including those with roofs over their heads) may be in dire need of food, water, and medications.[404]

Dinstein distinguishes between humanitarian *intervention*—which requires approval by the Security Council when there is a threat to peace—and humanitarian *assistance*, which is a moral obligation to provide relief to innocent victims. In all the protocols he cites, assistance is subject to an agreement between the warring parties. "Consent—the expression of sovereignty—is hence a basic principle in the exercise of the right to humanitarian assistance in armed conflicts."[405] Declining consent is easy, so this requirement obviates any legal obligation to provide humanitarian assistance to religious minorities facing an existential threat and in dire need of outside help to survive.

The Security Council is empowered to require unimpeded delivery of aid to civilian populations. This can be done through escalating resolutions that can become binding after all other forms of pressure and encouragement have failed. Such was the case with Bosnia and Herzegovina. After several nonbinding resolutions failed to clear the way for humanitarian assistance, the Security Council established a ban on all military flights in Bosnia and Herzegovina's airspace to clear the way for the delivery of aid.[406]

The Security Council can act based on the binding language in Chapter VII of the UN Charter. But unless peace and security are threatened by a conflict, the principal of nonintervention—including humanitarian intervention—remains sacrosanct. The UN Charter requires that humanitarian aid is distributed through the government of the state in which it is needed. In the case of Syria, among others, that means aid goes only to those areas within the state's control, while others legitimately and urgently in desperate need of aid are left to freeze, starve, and suffer without recourse.

The UN Charter prohibits the unilateral use of force against a state that interferes with humanitarian assistance. Only the Security Council can approve an enforcement action against a recalcitrant state, and that is highly unlikely given the politics of its permanent members.

Significant gaps remain.

INTERNATIONAL REFUGEE LAW

The 1951 Refugee Convention and its 1967 Protocol are the main global legal instruments that explicitly cover the protection of refugees. They define a refugee as a person who is outside his or her country of nationality or habitual residence because of a "well-founded fear of being persecuted for reasons of race, religion, nationality, membership of a particular social group or political opinion...and is unable or, owing to such fear, is unwilling to avail himself of the protection of that country; or who, not having a nationality and being outside the country of his former habitual residence as a result of such events, is unable or, owing to such fear, is unwilling to return to it."[407]

The core principle is known as non-refoulement, which prohibits the return of a refugee to a territory where his or her life or freedom is threatened. The 1951 convention and 1967 Protocol were signed by 149 states. But non-refoulement is considered a rule of customary international law (even though unwritten). As such, it is binding on all states, whether or not they are signatories. A refugee seeking protection must not be prevented from entering a country to seek sanctuary, as this would amount to refoulement.[408]

As mentioned earlier, Article 13 of the Universal Declaration of Human Rights asserts the right of emigration for those denied the free exercise of religion. But refugee law becomes relevant only if a persecuted individual actually manages to escape their country of oppression. The Rohingya have been driven and escaped en masse from Myanmar. But the recognition of a refugee hinges on the word "persecuted." This is where we find further gaps in international law. "Despite its extensive acceptance as an enumerated inhumane act of crimes against humanity under customary international law, the complexity and inconsistency of a substantive understanding of persecution may well be its prime debilitating factor."[409] The crime of religious persecution remains underdeveloped in international criminal law and is therefore left under-prosecuted.

The recognition of persecution as a crime against humanity dates to the Nuremberg Principles. As with other aspects of international criminal law, proving persecution requires evidence of a conscious and deliberate discriminatory intent against a group based on their identity. The Protecting Civilians in Conflict Program, from the Washington-based think tank Stimson Center, finds that the main conflict risk for interreligious violence is the intersectionality with other identity markers.[410] These include cultural persecution, gender, poverty, ethnicity, nationality, political affiliation, and sexual orientation. The intersections among these markers have yet to be tackled by International criminal law.[411]

Because the ICC's rulings are not a binding source of law, there is an opening here to revisit and reconceptualize persecution as a crime. By connecting persecution to intersecting identities, prosecutions may have a greater chance of success.

CHALLENGES

At present, we clearly lack an effective toolkit of laws, practice, and norms to reverse the rising tide of anti-religious violence. A complex web of international legal standards, authorities, and customs have failed to prevent the rise of religicide. This is due in part to legal and definitional vagueness as well as issues of jurisdiction and sovereignty. Governments with an inclination to persecute religious minorities or eradicate religion will not police themselves and are highly unlikely to enforce their legal obligations under international law. Despite seventy-five years of trial and error, the ecosystem needed to prevent religious persecution and to repair the damage done to religious minorities and their sacred sites remains underdeveloped and under-prosecuted. A new category of grievous religious persecution is needed with tighter definitions for anti-religious violence and religicide in order to strengthen the ability to enforce international criminal prosecutions.

That said, many will argue that expanding international law isn't necessarily the answer to filling gaps. One needs to keep assessing whether the gap is a gap in the law or a gap in its enforcement and application. The implementation gap may be definitional and conceptual. What do we really mean by genocide, crimes against humanity, and persecution? Or the gap could be political, given that those in power deliberately choose to overlook or override legal complaints when related to religion and violence. We need to start by strengthening and building upon what already exists. This includes a significant boost in anemic budgets for legal research, training, implementation, and reporting. Advancing the law is normally achieved case by case, in an incremental way. Most of the human rights conventions grew out of declarations. Many of the provisions in the Universal Declaration on Human Rights were later enshrined in binding conventions. So, we could push for additional UN declarations because they are far easier to negotiate and enact than conventions. We will continue to advocate the advancement of a new international convention to protect the rights of all people to enjoy religious freedom and belief.

But time is not on our side.

Years, even decades, may pass while we await more jurisprudence and much-needed resources. Meanwhile, tens of millions of people who affiliate with religion face persecution, torture, imprisonment, and death. The status quo is not working, at least when it comes to religicide.

Perhaps we need not be overly dependent on global human rights bodies for recourse to action. Since most provisions of international law are dependent on states for cooperation and enforcement, perhaps one can work more impactfully with regional human rights organizations—and, of course, with religious institutions, civil society, and community organizations.

A 2020 Stimson Center report puts all this into context. It asserts that religion-related violence is largely underrecognized by the international community—even though there are increases in such violence, especially government violence against ethno-religious minorities. Mass death due to state violence in twenty countries has increased 25 percent since 2007. Property damage inflicted by government has been reported in sixty-nine countries. China, Myanmar, and Turkey were responsible for more than ten thousand incidents of force against religious minorities in 2018 alone. Eritrea, Iran, Iraq, Rwanda, Syria, and Uzbekistan each had between one thousand and ten thousand such incidents. Mobs of non-state actors committed acts of violence against religious minorities in forty-one countries.[412]

Three UN bodies—the Human Rights Council, the General Assembly, and the Security Council—have all tackled anti-religious discrimination and violence with various resolutions and calls to action, all of which are nonbinding and ineffectual. The credibility of the UN Human Rights Council has been damaged by the abysmal human rights record of some of its members, including China, Nepal, Pakistan, India, and Russia—all of whom are serial violators of religious freedom.

The real power player in this triumvirate is the UN Security Council. The UNSC has been slow to make the connection between religion-related violence and international security—and even slower to act on it. As previously discussed, China and Russia make liberal use of their veto power to ensure their own domestic aggressions will not be challenged.

The Stimson Center has proposed several ways to deal with these limitations. One is to create a salaried full-time special rapporteur for religion-based violence to report systematically and objectively to the three UN bodies. Another is for member states to create confidential and accessible mechanisms for civil society to report violations of freedom of religion. A third is to weave religion-based violence into other human rights agendas with which it overlaps, such as gender, peace, and genocide. This would entail using intersectionality to bring more attention to religion-related human rights violations.[413]

We urgently need to devise a fresh approach as most cases of anti-religious violence and persecution are slipping through the cracks of international law. Religious leaders and other non-state actors will have an especially important role to play to prevent anti-religious violence and advance peacebuilding worldwide. The final two chapters will describe how diverse faith groups, public officials, and civil society can join forces to reverse religicide with an integrated top-down, middle-out, and bottom-up approach.

Chapter Eleven

A MULTI-TIERED APPROACH TO PREVENT RELIGICIDE

Left unchecked, the ongoing murder of religious minorities will result in millions of deaths, immense human suffering, and ecological disaster.

Perpetrators of religion-related violence will continue to dehumanize, blame, and victimize their perceived enemies to justify mass murder, scorched earth, and disinformation. Unfortunately, this violence is now abetted by technology, artificial intelligence, and social media. The risks are enormous, and a global response is necessary.

How can governments, businesses, civil society, and individuals join forces to bring some much-needed cooling to this burning problem?

Previous chapters offered historic context for religicide, closing with actionable policy prescriptions—political, economic, cultural, and social. If ignored, religicide against the Uyghurs, Tibetans, Yazidis, and Rohingya (not to mention other emerging cases, such as Christians being persecuted in the Middle East and Muslims in India) will mean that more than twenty million innocent people could be murdered, along with their cultures.

Our proposed short-term fixes—economic sanctions, political pressure, public education, and media reform—are indeed necessary tactics. But protecting people's rights and beliefs will not be easy because we must change the predominant public mindset about religion as the cause of violence. We must recognize how religious and Indigenous wisdom can help us build a more sustainable and equitable future. So, as we seek ways to curb violence in society, we must also seek ways to simultaneously protect religious diversity and biodiversity.

That means coming up with solutions that are more powerful and impactful than another UN treaty or interreligious decree denouncing violence for the umpteenth time. We must go beyond anemic corporate social responsibility pledges that, while important, often lack courage and accountability. We propose instead an integrated multi-prong strategy designed to engage and inspire political, business, and civil society changemakers, including traditional and Indigenous religious groups. Survivors of religicide worldwide hold the power of conscience but need powerful allies at all levels to heal and transform their communities and our broader societies. What binds them to each other is what we call covenantalism.

Community-based religious and Indigenous groups should lead the way. What has worked, what is missing, and what might we try differently to reverse religicide?

There are at least three tiers that can be mobilized: the "top-down" government policymakers and industry; the "middle-out" capacity of civil society and faith-based groups to make change; and the "bottom-up" community grassroots strategies to amplify the voice of Indigenous people and the survivors of religicide.

TOP-DOWN

Rampant human rights abuses are often the prelude to violence. They reflect a breakdown in the rule of law, and if they are allowed to continue unchecked, the result will be weakened confidence in states' commitment to the protection of human rights, democratic governance, and international treaties. [414]

—Carnegie Commission on Preventing Deadly Conflict

Most top-down approaches involving government and corporate elites rely on short-term transactional fixes that do not address the underlying causes of religion-related violence. Invoking international human rights and legal obligations among nation-states does not stop religicide. The status quo is difficult to change, as most multinational corporations prefer noncontroversial incremental change rather than radical transformation.

As far back as the seventeenth century, the Peace of Westphalia, which ended the Thirty-Years' War between the Protestants and Catholics in Europe, established the norms of sovereignty among nations. While those norms ended a religious war, they lacked a broader moral appeal to engage communities and people of faith. The treaties' declaration of "religious tolerance" and the "private right" of citizens within sovereign nations to worship as Catholic, Lutheran, or Calvinist may have been a welcome reform to stem Christian-on-Christian violence. But it also served to privatize religion and establish the supremacy of the state.

Today, freedom of religion is seen as an individual human right—not a shield for collective or communal cultural heritage and practice. As such, it has tended to favor the right of individuals to proselytize their faith more than it has offered real protection for all religious communities and traditions from abuse or persecution. Relegating religion to private life and positioning the nation-state as the supreme unifier of its people produced an unintended consequence. It prioritized protection of sovereign states and governments over and above the people who live under their rule.

Nation-state agreements fail to protect victims of religicide because Article 2 (4) of the UN Charter forbids the threat or use of force against sovereign states. When atrocities, such as religicide, take place within the borders of a single state, international action is prohibited. Only when a conflict spills over into neighboring states is it viewed as a threat to international peace and security, and it becomes subject to intervention. But interstate, cross-border conflict is not the main source of violence in the modern era. It's what happens inside nation-states.

So, let's look at what needs to be done at the UN level to protect victims of religicide and end anti-religious violence. There are two important exceptions to Article 2 (4): individual defense or collective self-defense in response to an armed attack; and uses of force authorized by the Security Council under Chapter VII of the UN Charter. On the face of it, that sounds quite sensible. However, the Security Council is a political body. Its members vote in ways that preserve their alliances, not in ways that preserve human rights. Any one member can veto a resolution. Once a veto is issued, the Security Council cannot act. Such vetoes have a long history of thwarting humanitarian action—as they have in Syria, Rwanda, and many other crisis zones. For instance, China is a permanent member of the Security Council. When it comes to religicide, China is almost certain to veto any UN intervention on behalf of Uyghurs. No political body should control the enforcement of religion-related rights. Therefore, protecting victims of religicide must require an ability to override the Security Council. A 2013 paper prepared for the UK Parliament argues that human security supersedes the national security of the state.[415] To be legitimate, the nation-state has a duty to protect its citizens. In an ideal world, when a state violates the rights of its people, it should lose its shield against intervention by other states. But as things stand, humanitarian intervention that violates the borders of a sovereign state—unless it is an act of self-defense—is illegal under international law. And self-defense is rarely invoked. That must change.

The preamble to the UN Charter affirms "faith in fundamental human rights." But the actual operations of the Security Council conflict with that noble goal. In 2001, the International Commission on Intervention and State Sovereignty (ICISS) issued a report making the case that sovereignty is not a right; it is a responsibility to protect. But the report's attempt to create a right of humanitarian intervention was rejected by the international community because few states are ready to risk any part of their sovereignty. In the absence of such a right, and in the absence of action by the Security Council, the report recommended that the General Assembly should invoke the "Uniting for Peace" Resolution 377(V).

Uniting for Peace was adopted in 1950 as an emergency measure "if the Security Council, because of lack of unanimity among the permanent members, fails to exercise its primary responsibility for the maintenance of international peace and security."[416] In that case, the General Assembly can call an emergency session to consider the matter and make recommendations to the members.

In short, the United Nation's second principal organ, the General Assembly, should be given a more prominent role in the maintenance of international peace and security. The General Assembly is more democratic and representative than the hyper-political fifteen-member Security Council and could play a bigger role in the domain of international peace and human rights. Unfortunately, in recent years, the General Assembly proved completely ineffectual in overriding the vetoes of China and Russia in relation to emergencies such as the war in Syria.

Barring a change in rules to deny the veto right in the Security Council, no proposed resolution, convention, or treaty to curb anti-religious violence and end religicide would succeed in those states. When it comes to proposing any draft UN resolution against religicide, the General Assembly would be the only forum to engage or ultimately approve such an initiative. Otherwise, the resolution would surely be vetoed by the partisan and self-protective Security Council, including the "Permanent Five": China, Russia, Britain, France, and the United States.

We must also consider economic incentives to ensure protection of religion and rights. It turns out mass violence is less likely when there is economic interconnection between a perpetrating state and other states. The less isolated a state, the less likely it is to engage in mass violence.[417] Therefore, top-down pressure can be exerted with economic incentives, sanctions, and conditionality. Among incentives, we have advised that the World Bank and International Monetary Fund invest in countries that distance themselves from religicidal states. To these, we add "most favored nation" status and trade agreements, along with tariff reductions and direct purchases. Boycotts and sanctions can be effective because they signal international disapproval for religicidal acts and punish bad behavior. For example, we have called for boycotts of goods and services performed by forced Uyghur labor in China.

The Islamic State (ISIS) was fueled by oil revenues from the fields it controlled in Syria. With periodic oil gluts, it would have been feasible to boycott oil from ISIS-controlled Syria. Once ISIS was driven from that area, it lost a major source of income and provided leverage to the US, which took control of the oil fields. (Unfortunately, the United States failed to use its leverage to shrink the crisis and protect those who were being assaulted by ISIS.)

Impact investing and sustainable development goals are other tools that enable businesses to rethink their supply chains and move them away from exploited labor. Apple has been called to account for a supply chain that includes seven companies said to use forced Uyghur labor. The revulsion for blood diamonds is another case in point. Finally, conditionality, as explained by the Carnegie Commission, involves "the forging of links between responsible nonviolent behavior and the promise of greater reward through growing integration into the community of market democracies."[418]

Preventive diplomacy can also play a role in engaging religicidal states and non-state actors. While it's tempting for states to suspend diplomatic relations with bad actors, it's important to maintain communications with both the victimizers and the victimized. Diplomats can make the case for how religicidal policies impact their own country's interests. In doing so, they make it clear that there's a much bigger dog in the picture than the one that the offending state is beating. Their ability to forge multilateral alliances greatly strengthens the response to religicide. However, diplomacy fails if diplomats don't fully understand the collective trauma of the large groups with which they're negotiating, as well as the long-lasting economic, cultural, social, and environmental costs of religicide. For most of US history, diplomats have avoided dealing with religion, thinking the separation of church and state in America prevented them from negotiating with religious leaders. Until about 2012, our foreign policy institute conducted rigorous language training for diplomats going overseas but lacked any meaningful education in religious literacy or outreach.

This must change. Diplomats serving in any region must be taught basic religious literacy regarding the traditions and cultures of that region. Beyond these government and business solutions, we must activate the religious communities and faith leaders around the world.

This is the context for the emergence of a Global Covenant. Religious actors can become effective peacebuilders and interrupters of systemic violence. Along with diplomats and civil society networks, they play a key role in the quest to delegitimize religious justifications for mass violence. The backing of religious powerhouses—like those in the "Ring of Faiths" convened by Jordan's King Abdullah II—provides the moral underpinning for a multi-prong strategy to stop religicide: top-down, middle-out, and bottom-up.

Shaykh Abdallah bin Bayyah, the widely respected Mauritanian-born Sunni Muslim scholar, spoke forcefully against violence and in favor of interfaith action: "I am calling upon the religious leaders from all of our various traditions to take resolute steps to remove these elements of incitement, and to distance these inflammatory interpretations from our religious practices.... It is incumbent upon the religious leaders to grasp that an attack on any religion is an attack on all religions. The reconciliation among religions without which...peace cannot be achieved, is not enough unless religious solidarity is realized."[419]

The late Pope John Paul II was another case in point. In 1993, he proclaimed, "When all the options offered by diplomatic negotiations...have been carried out and, despite this, entire populations are on the point of succumbing to the blows of an unjust aggressor, states have no right to indifference any longer. It appears to be their duty to disarm this aggressor."[420] The voice of such a prominent and respected religious leader causes people to listen.

The late pope explained that intervention need not be military. But if so, it must be a defensive operation "aimed at protecting populations and humanitarian aids."[421] And, if military, it must not cause more harm than the war in progress. We need more prominent spiritual leaders to speak up and speak out. Gross violations of human rights provide just cause to use force to reestablish protections. But armed intervention should not itself violate those same rights.

Pope John Paul II's articulation of these criteria is a restatement of the just war doctrine, which traces its roots from ancient Egypt, through Greek and Roman philosophers, to Deuteronomy 20, Saint Augustine, and beyond. The just war tradition is the foundation of international law. It allows for retaking what was wrongly taken and the punishment of evil. Its two components, paraphrased here, consider both ethics and consequences.[422]

> *Jus ad bellum* governs decisions to go to war, based on several criteria: a just cause; a sovereign authority; probability of success; proportionality of good accomplished versus harm done; and war as a last resort.

Jus in bello governs the conduct of war and requires distinguishing between combatants and noncombatants, as well as proportionality within each military operation.[423]

Under just war doctrines, it is unclear whether the United Nations has the sovereign authority to use force, and therein lies that body's ultimate ineffectiveness. Nor, according to some, can a military alliance, like NATO, claim to be the international community. Therefore, it cannot be regarded as the legitimate authority required by just war criteria.[424] This brings us back to the important role of non-state actors, such as religious leaders, civil society, and businesses, working across faith boundaries and borders to end religicide.

MIDDLE-OUT

Whether we like it or not, religion is an essential component of international politics and peace. The misuse of religion can fuel violent conflicts, making them more difficult to resolve. But religions also can advance fruitful peacebuilding, including regenerative approaches to climate activism. This goes beyond simply promoting the seventeen UN Sustainable Development Goals (SDGs), which are important priorities, but don't specifically involve religion.

The time is now to engage more deeply with faith-based organizations, religious institutions, and civil society to save the planet from violence, oppression, and mass destruction. If religion is not welcomed as part of the solution for peace and progress, it will continue to be erroneously perceived by secular leaders in the West as the cause of the problem.

For decades, diverse faith leaders have been uniting to denounce the holy terror of violence and mass atrocities. Nongovernmental organizations such as Religions for Peace, the Elijah Institute, United Religions Initiative, and the Parliament of the World's Religions have issued interreligious statements objecting to anti-religious violence and calling for peace and justice.

The vital role of religious actors lies in providing wisdom and moral guidance, rather than mastering data science and politics. It is critical for faith leaders to take a values-centered stand against all violent atrocities, particularly those done in the name of God. Many faith leaders work tirelessly to clarify the toxic texts, which are endemic to all the great faiths, by emphasizing the overriding call for compassion, mercy, and peace. Religious leaders share a responsibility to be decision-making role models, deep listening, and speaking responsibly to their followers. The words they use matter, and their teachings can have a profound impact on the resort to violence.

Middle-out approaches to violence reduction must do more than just complement top-down governmental negotiations. Religious actors and civil society must push hard for policy change to protect communities at risk for religicide. This means that civil society, religious institutions, and academia need to work together. Too often these middle-out initiatives take place in silos and therefore lack the aggregate power to effect lasting change. But they can have power when coupled with more top-down approaches.

In April 2015, H.M. King Abdullah II convened a top tier "Ring of Faiths" steering group in Amman. The group had the participation of the Vatican, Lambeth Palace, scholars from Cambridge and Oman, His Royal Highness Prince Ghazi bin Muhammad of Jordan, and representatives to the Organization of Islamic Cooperation, along with world leaders such as Pope Francis, the Prince of Wales, and the archbishop of Canterbury. His Majesty King Abdullah of Jordan had invited religious scholars, faith leaders, and diplomats to work together on recommendations for a UN resolution that would identify and make religicide a crime under international law. The charge from these leaders was to lay out an actionable legal framework to reduce interreligious and sectarian violence and create a code of conduct regarding protection of religious belief, practice, and sacred heritage.

This unprecedented initiative to name and denounce religicide was important but never got off the ground. The effort, though noble, was top-down, siloed, elite, and rushed. Significantly more time was needed to build bridges among faith leaders and diplomats, as well as to socialize and discuss the concept of religicide and deliberate on the implications for international security, human rights, and humanitarian law. The UN Security Council, for reasons described earlier, was not the right place to introduce a religicide resolution, because it was likely that the United States, China, and others would block it at the outset. And that's precisely what happened. Jordan's draft resolution, even with the significant support and approval of religious leaders, never saw the light of day.

This taught us that any one sector or group, working in a silo on its own, will not mobilize the power needed to expose and end religicide. At the middle-out level, there are several impressive interfaith organizations who have been working over decades to promote interreligious peacebuilding. Among them are the United Religions Initiative, Religions for Peace, Parliament of the World's Religions, the Elijah Institute, Network of Religious and

Traditional Peacemakers, the Tanenbaum Center for Interreligious Understanding, and the Multifaith Alliance for Syrian Refugees. Each has done remarkable and courageous work fostering interfaith action and solidarity. All these organizations are vital to future transformation. But without deeper simultaneous engagement, coalition building, and policymaking aligned with top-down and grassroots "bottom-up" community-based players, their laudable efforts will remain insufficient to effect lasting transformative change.

Traditionally, most middle-out civil society players have shied away from taking on the issue of religious freedom and other religion-related rights. International advocacy groups, such as Human Rights Watch, Human Rights First, and Amnesty International—along with their traditional funders, such as the Carnegie Corporation, the Ford Foundation, the Rockefeller Foundation, and the Open Society Foundations—have lacked the religious literacy and confidence to engage long term with faith-based actors. Indeed, some eschew funding any programs that contain the word "religion." For the most part, secular institutions, as with governments, display a conventional bias that continues to view religion as the problem rather than an opportunity for strategic peacebuilding.

But what if there were a concerted effort to protect the rights of the religious that could in fact unify all these levels of effort? A Global Covenant of Religions could emerge as something dynamic, authentic, flexible, and alive—something that is relationally and spiritually motivated, as well as something outside the current constraints of nation-state legal frameworks, including the United Nations and other multilateral or regional bodies.

So why would a new Global Covenant, or any nonlegal agreement, potentially lead to more impact? Because it could go beyond the letter of the international law and rely on the power of the spirit and the heart—faith, hospitality, and love of our neighbors—the promises rooted deeply in religious traditions and spiritual beliefs of the vast majority of the world's citizens who believe in something bigger than themselves.

Community-based religious leaders can have a tremendous impact on local conflict. First, they carry a clear message that can resonate with their followers. International multifaith networks of peacemakers offset their isolation, providing these quiet heroes with affirmation and support. For instance, the Tanenbaum Center for Interreligious Understanding can work in parallel with other innovative peacemaking networks such as Search for Common Ground, the United Religions Initiative, Religions for Peace, Peace Direct, Ashoka, Catholic Peacebuilding Network, Kroc Institute for Peace and Justice, the Network of Religious and Traditional Peacemakers, Global Covenant Partners, and the Community of Sant'Egidio, among many others. Working in concert, networks such as these can harness the power of the collective to take a values-driven stand to mediate and disrupt violent conflict.

Many are skeptical that violent religious conflict can be interrupted. Research indicates there are early warning signals of religiously motivated conflict. Summoning the intellectual powers of faculty and student researchers at the University of Virginia (UVA) in Charlottesville, author Jerry White and religious studies professor Peter Ochs launched a three-year research lab to examine religion, politics, and conflict (RPC). The RPC research lab generated significant results through unprecedented transdisciplinary research among scholars from a diverse range of sciences—data science, ethnolinguistics, politics, literature, history, and religious studies.

Working in field settings in South Asia and the United States, the researchers discovered correlations between linguistic signals in the speech and writing of faith leaders and religious stakeholder groups. Put more simply, us-versus-them dehumanizing speech was often a precursor to violence. Monitoring the use of language provided clues to likely types of near-future group behavior. On one hand, black-and-white polarizing speech, with little room for interpretation or nuance, can be an early warning for the emergence of religicidal violence. This is not surprising. On the other hand, it is also important to note any lack of response, or vague speech, that permits any interpretation whatsoever. Linguistic vagueness offers an early warning sign of passivity or indifference in the face of others' violence. We saw this, for example, in President Trump's reaction to the insurrection and violent assault on the US Capitol on January 2020. Even vaguely approving language can be an early linguistic clue, indicating that bystanders and witnesses to conflict would allow mass violence on their watch, putting up no resistance. Violence is not just about the perpetrators but also the context and enabling social conditions that fail to interrupt or counter that violence.

Analysts at the University of Virginia successfully field-tested these linguistic discoveries in regions of tension and social hostilities related to religion. UVA researchers confirmed their findings through computational analyses conducted by university data scientists. Individual faculty members from a broad range of academic disciplines researched prototypical features of religion in conflict, including the post-colonial settings of religious conflict, modern Europe and non-modern religions, foreign affairs and religion, racism and the modern state, modern war and religion, religious discourse and peacekeeping, religious conflict over sacred sites, human rights and modern policing, refugees and immigration, and portable housing for refugees, conflict, trauma, and nursing.

After field-testing our research in many regions of the world, the authors concluded that Western researchers and policymakers have largely failed to design successful responses to religion-related conflicts because, for the most part, they insisted that religious behavior was not a unique category of human activity worthy of inquiry. Instead, they deemed that religion-related conflicts were best studied through the current tools of political and social science. Our research showed that sophisticated analysis of religion-specific behavior would contribute to more successful policy and better outcomes for conflict mediation and peacebuilding in all the situations we studied.

UVA Professor Peter Ochs, the author of *Religion without Violence: The Practice and Philosophy of Scriptural Reasoning*, developed a data-driven early warning tool that would not repeat the typical measures used by defense analysts at the Pentagon or diplomats at the State Department to track hate speech and sentiment analysis.

Even more interesting, our research at the University of Virginia demonstrated how binaries (i.e., good versus evil) are too simplistic and obvious. We discovered new ways to enable peacekeepers and negotiators to anticipate in advance whether a religious group was likely to behave aggressively toward other groups, when they would be open to dialogue, or when they would show signs of fragility and chaos. It is all based on what language these groups are using about themselves and about "the other." Language and linguistics are key to forecasting the onset of violence. They are also critical to predicting the prospects for peaceful engagement and negotiation with adversarial groups in conflict settings.[425]

Scholar Ervin Straub points out that a central feature of mass violence is that it evolves over time. That means there is time to intervene and interrupt religicide. If only we would heed the obvious signs and symptoms of impending violence: uncompromising language, previous intergroup violence and organized killing, systemic human rights abuse, escalating oppression, stockpiling of weapons, and worsening economic conditions. As we've learned from examining cases of religicide, disinformation combined with hate speech and weaponized language are precursors to religion-related violence. Violent language must be monitored closely and challenged promptly with alternative narratives.

Bystanders and witnesses to religicide can play a crucial role in halting the evolution of mass violence. But it takes empathy and courage. Negotiation guru William Ury at Harvard calls this the "third side." There needs to be someone or some group that interrupts the violent cycle of victim and victimizer. There are a range of roles the third side can play, including mediator, witness, or negotiator, among others. The bystander or witness can be a special envoy representing an international response or a respected authority figure—such as the religious peacemakers described above.

A Global Covenant could include training to empower survivors of religicide and a network of faith leaders to become community-based interrupters in their own cycles of violence. Data-driven research led Dr. Gary Slutkin, an epidemiologist, and the founder of Cure Violence Global, observed how city gang violence in Chicago behaved and spread like an HIV/AIDS epidemic Slutkin had tracked in Uganda. He realized violence can be treated like one treats a growing epidemic. Like the spread of a disease, violence can be stopped with early intervention. His data-driven research demonstrated how a public health approach can be designed to interrupt and reduce violence. Cure Violence stops the spread of violence by using methods and strategies associated with disease control and developed over the past twenty years:

- *Detecting and interrupting the spread of conflicts*: Trained violence interrupters and outreach workers prevent shootings by identifying and mediating potentially lethal conflicts in the community and following up to ensure that the conflict does not reignite.[426]
- Identifying and treating the highest risk individuals: Trained, culturally appropriate outreach workers work with the highest risk members to make them less likely to commit violence. They do so by meeting them where they are at, talking to them about the costs of using violence, and helping them to obtain the social services they need— such as job training and drug treatment.427
- Changing social norms: Trained workers engage community leaders and residents, local business owners, faith leaders, service providers, and the high risk, conveying the message that the residents, groups, and the community do not support the use of violence.[428]

Cure Violence is an important example of an effective approach that combines middle-out and bottom-up work to stop retaliatory killings and the spread of community violence. This public health methodology to violence prevention serves to deescalate it and engages a system-wide approach for detecting and preventing it. This is a pragmatic method to protecting human rights and the dignity of all those involved in a violent conflict, ranging from police, schools, and prisons, to courts, social services, and community health.[429]

The efficacy of this approach has been demonstrated through independently funded and conducted multi-year, multi-site, mixed-method scientific evaluations that show 40-70 percent reductions in shootings and killings in the hardest hit communities in the United States. In some cases, killings and shootings drop by 90 percent, and retaliation killings stopped completely.

This health-based approach not only reduces and prevents violence, but it also builds local capacity and promotes social and economic growth. A core part of the approach involves connecting high-risk individuals with resources for job readiness, education, and health services. Such a transformative investment in the public health approach to violence prevention can be applied more broadly—especially when it includes religious leaders to help build community resilience, capacity for early warning, and rapid response to mitigate conflict.

The question is whether such a data-driven public health model could in fact help prevent and stop religicide in Myanmar, Iraq, China, and the United States. We believe it could be appealing to countries that resent the moralism of human rights activists but are comfortable with nonjudgmental, data-driven approaches that can end terrorism and reduce community-based violence.

BOTTOM-UP

Top-down and middle-out efforts are essential but insufficient to end religicide. The bottom-up component may prove the most critical for durable systemic impact, especially when it comes from the faithful who are "on the ground." It is here that one finds authentic leaders who have experienced religicide as well as other individuals and small groups that are determined to make change happen.

This is an approach that had impact on one of the most enduring religion-related conflicts of the past fifty years. When "the Troubles" in Northern Ireland first gained momentum in the 1970s, vigilantes on both the loyalist and Irish Republican Army (IRA) sides patrolled the streets to protect their communities, instilling widespread fear. Reverend Roy Magee, a Protestant Belfast pastor, anticipated that the assembled crowds, armed with sticks, would explode into violence. He convinced his Protestant constituents to go home and assured them that he would personally patrol the streets every night to keep them safe. That was the beginning of twenty-five years of peace activism. "My actions were established when I examined in detail the example of the Lord Jesus Christ as recorded in the Gospels," explained Magee.[430]

Reverend Magee delivered a very clear message to a top fighter in the loyalist paramilitary. Magee warned him that the paramilitaries "were breaking the law of God, as well as the law of man, and that one day they would be held accountable."[431] That message carried some weight, but it wasn't the message alone. It was Magee's long-standing pervasive moral presence on the ground that gave him street credentials. Or, as the Carnegie Commission puts it, the "legitimacy for speaking out on crisis issues."[432]

Magee's counterpart on the Catholic side was Father Alec Reid, known as "the IRA priest." Reid didn't just preach; he got down in the trenches. Reid established his own street cred by repeatedly responding to violence where it was happening and working in the notorious Maze Prison with IRA hunger strikers and their families. Although his ministry was IRA-focused, an iconic photo of him went viral around the world. In that photo, he is kneeling over a fallen British soldier on the street, administering last rites to the enemy. Such compassion illustrates the "traditional orientation to peace and good-will" and ultimate respect for humanity that the Carnegie Commission cites among the assets that religious leaders bring to the table, and that can interrupt narratives of anger, victimhood, and hate.[433]

It was these two clergymen, each named one of the Tanenbaum Center's Peacemakers in Action, who negotiated the IRA and loyalist paramilitary ceasefires that made Northern Ireland's Good Friday Agreement possible. Alex Reid and Roy Magee weren't the ones who received the Nobel Peace Prize, but it was their behind-the-scenes, bottom-up, street-level work that hastened the end of "the Troubles" in Northern Ireland.

Local religious actors remain long after wars have ended or UN peacekeeping forces have left. Such was the case in Bosnia and Herzegovina, where UN peacekeepers were present for three and a half years. Although they were helpful in distributing humanitarian aid, they were unable to intervene in the carnage, but Friar Ivo Markovic did, a Franciscan friar—and so did a Bosnian Croat.

Markovic lived in a Serb (mostly Orthodox Christian) area. In 1992, a Serb paramilitary unit stormed his seminary. Markovic escaped with his life and spent the next months trying to tamp down violence between Croats (mostly Catholics) and

Bosniaks (mostly Muslims). His most daring act is documented by the Tanenbaum Center for Interreligious Understanding, where Markovic became the first member of its Peacemakers in Action Network.

"The Croat and Muslim armies were...facing each other across a field when we decided to walk through their lines and go from a Croat village...to the Muslim one...in order to ask the imam to help us. Soldiers on both sides challenged us. When approaching the Muslim side, dressed in Franciscan habit, I was told to stop or they would shoot. I became angry and ran toward them saying, 'What, shoot? Would you shoot me, you idiot?'"[434]

The soldiers stood down and some followed the Franciscans into the village, which was under attack by Croats. The Bosniaks were preparing to return fire when the Franciscans found the imam and proposed bringing together the Croat and Bosnian commanders to prevent the violence from escalating. One of the Franciscans offered to stay in the village as a "guarantee of good will," but the imam refused to hold hostages. Markovic and his colleagues met with the two commanders in a local café and negotiated an agreement to refrain from fighting. Although the region was later overrun, no fighting took place in this corner where Friar Markovic had created "an oasis of peace."

Markovic fostered honest dialogues about religion and faith as an antidote to religiopolitical ideologies. As of this writing, Markovic heads Sarajevo-based Oci u Oci ("Face to Face") Interreligious Service, which works to foster a pluralistic Bosnia. This work is reinforced by the multiethnic, interreligious Pontanima Choir and Chamber Orchestra, which tours the world with its message of peaceful coexistence.

At their best, faith leaders connect with deep humanity in a way that state and business actors simply will not or cannot. Many of these practitioners operate outside the mainstream of their religious institutions. Alex Reid was told by his Catholic hierarchy that he was on his own. Magee said his church didn't want to dirty its hands by working with murderers. In Bosnia, religion and ethnic identity were so conflated that many statements made by religious leaders inflamed, rather than tamped down, emotions—and ended up legitimizing the violence.[435] Having diverse religious leaders call for peace and calm was an important counterforce.

Survivors can also be leaders in stopping the perpetration of violence. Rehumanizing the dehumanized victims of religicide is a big step in preventing further atrocities. That means hearing the voices of the survivors and calling nations to account. At the grassroots level, it also means eschewing name-blame-shame attacks and instead engaging with the perpetrators—just as Ivo Markovic did in Bosnia and like Alex Reid and Roy Magee did in Northern Ireland. Hating your enemy may feel good or righteous, but it won't solve the problem. Counter-messaging based on sound social psychological principles, some of which are intuited by religious leaders, is an important part of the response to religicide. It means acknowledging our common humanity and overcoming the hate that dehumanizes the other.

Social psychologist Jonathan Haidt, founder of OpenMind, has developed an evidence-based approach to constructive dialogue for finding the humanity in the "other." He distinguishes between automatic thinking and controlled thinking. The first consists of emotions, intuitions, and other unconscious processes that are quick. It is here that our instinctive hatreds and preconceptions reside. Controlled thinking is conscious rational thinking.

As such, it functions more slowly than the automatic mind. It's the reason that it's harder to convince people through arguments and facts than it is to win them over through their emotions and intuitions. Our "naïve realism" presumes that anyone who doesn't see the world as we do is crazy, stupid, or evil. Therefore, Haidt focuses on the moral foundations that we all share: care, fairness, liberty, loyalty, authority, and sanctity. The way we interpret those foundations is influenced by culture, upbringing, and unique life experiences. Understanding those interpretations is the key to truly hearing each other and building on our common humanity.

How we identify ourselves and our groups can also impact conflict. Vamik Volkan, a Turkish Cypriot and emeritus professor of psychiatry at the University of Virginia, has for forty years applied psychoanalysis to conflicts between countries, cultures, and individuals. His political psychology theories—chosen trauma, large group identity, transgenerational transmission of trauma, individual and societal mourning—are crucial to tapping into the motivation for religicide as well as guiding how its victims can recover.

He posits that large group identity is often defined by what its members mourn. ISIS, for example, mourns the loss of the caliphate to a secularized Turkey. Its terrorist activities, in the service of reestablishing the caliphate, are their exercise of what Volkan calls "reactive power." Chosen trauma—that is, those past traumas around which a group coheres—is another marker of large group identity. Volkan cites the Battle of Kosovo in which the Ottomans killed the Serbian Prince Lazar. That battle took place nearly six hundred years ago, but it was a humiliation the Serbs have never forgotten. It remained a powerful rallying cry that Slobodan Milosevic exploited to justify the Serbs' genocide against Bosnian

Muslims. Milosevic equated Bosnian Muslims with fifteenth century Ottoman Muslims and killing them was a way for Serbs to recover what they lost centuries ago. Similarly, Volkan calls out Wounded Knee, described in a previous chapter, as the chosen trauma around which Native American tribes coalesce.

The botched attempt by the Seventh Cavalry to disarm a band of 350 Lakota tribespeople, including women and children, ended in a massacre. In the aftermath, L. Frank Baum, the newspaper editor of the *Aberdeen Saturday Pioneer*, (who was to become the author of *The Wonderful Wizard of Oz*) wrote:

> The Pioneer has before declared that our only safety depends upon the total extermination of the Indians. Having wronged them for centuries, we had better, in order to protect our civilization.[436]

It's not clear whether the massacre was intentional, but Wounded Knee became the symbol of the attempt to wipe out Native Americans, and the site is now a protected National Historic Landmark.

Similarly, Volkan cites Osama bin Laden's consistent references to three historical traumas to justify his terrorism against Americans: US intrusion into holy places in Saudi Arabia, UN sanctions against Iraq, and US support for Israel.[437]

Karen Armstrong, a prolific writer on the history of religion, observes the "feelings" of religious persecution: "Every one of the movements I have studied is rooted in the fear...that modern society is out to destroy not only their faith but also themselves and their entire way of life.... When people fear annihilation, their horizons tend to shrink and they can lash out violently."[438] This observation, along with Volkan's work, implies that one must understand the deep fear that accompanies any extremism. There are truly evil people with whom one cannot work. But Tanenbaum-recognized peacemaker Canon Andrew White believes many violent actors can be reached because they have experienced a profound sense of loss. "When one comes to know one's adversaries, their humanness and likeness to oneself is revealed, thereby opening a door to cooperation and action...directly tied to the teachings of Jesus."[439]

Similarly, Tanenbaum peacemaker Bishop Nkulu Ntanda Ntambo of the Democratic Republic of Congo received a feared and brutal warlord into his home. He was fully aware of, and detested, the suffering the warlord had inflicted on his people. But he believed that God demanded of him this kind of radical hospitality.[440]

The idea of oppressors and the oppressed confronting each other on the level playing field of a truth and reconciliation commission is at the heart of conflict transformation. When oppressors acknowledge the pain they have inflicted, and each side feels somewhat rehumanized, victims of religicide may find a slow healing path to move forward in the direction of reconciliation. This is never an easy path. The healing way forward, we believe, will not come through endless therapy sessions or confessions, but will require deeper collective community-based work and reflecting on our ancestors while thinking through the impact of our daily actions on future generations.

Elders in Aboriginal communities in Canada wisely think ahead in terms of seven generations. The expression has found its way into mainstream usage, in discussions about sustainability, economic development, philanthropy, ecosystem science, and green energy. Mi'kmaw elders in Nova Scotia, including Murdena Marshall and her colleague Cheryl Bartlett, the Canada Research Chair in Integrative Science, consider a single generation as 120 years. So, seven generations mean thinking ahead 840 years.

David Rieff, author of *In Praise of Forgetting*, argues that moving forward must sometimes mean disremembering. Rieff posits that virtually every great crime of the twentieth century has been committed in an atmosphere of fear and with the justification of self-defense.[441] "Few phenomena [are] more uncontrollable socially and, hence, more dangerous politically than a people or a social group that believes itself to be a victim."[442] This was amply demonstrated in chapters 1 through 3, with the examples of the Armenian genocide and the Holocaust, among others. In the Bosnian case, Milosevic whipped up violence by invoking the Serbian collective memory of having been brutalized by the Croats during World War II. Rieff argues that such memories legitimize "a particular worldview and political and social agenda." Consistent with Volkan's theories, he goes so far as to say that group identity is a function of what and how the past is remembered.[443]

This would seem to imply that victims of religicide should forget their trauma. But to forget, they must heal. To heal, they must be given tools for mourning their trauma. Volkan talks about the importance of monuments and objects as avatars of the losses being mourned. But they can also evoke feelings of victimization and revenge. By keeping the mourning process alive, "They can continue to stoke tensions or help bring the mourning process to an end, as is the case with the Vietnam Veterans Memorial."[444]

The perpetrators are generally acting like the aggressors because of their own collective memories. Groups like ISIS are ultimately the product of colonization and its humiliations. China clings to a memory of one violent episode coming out of Uyghur protests. The Burmese Buddhists have a memory of Muslim support of the Ottoman Empire and their attempt to create an independent state as well as the defeat of Burma by the British in 1824. Per Volkan, memories like these are hardwired into the social DNA and transmitted across generations. Eventually, they can be evoked to justify the eradication of a religion.

Omar Shaukat interviewed ISIS fighters to understand what drives them. He found that they are motivated by revolutionary fervor rather than texts. Indeed, he observed that they aren't particularly literate when it comes to Islam. Therefore, his solution is to offer them a "nonviolent or non-hateful way to being radical" and more effective strategies for changing the world than those offered by ISIS.[445] This is consistent with Eric Hoffer's theory, described previously, in which he posits the interchangeability of causes for the true believer. "Mass movements draw their adherents from the same type of humanity and appeal to the same types of mind...one mass movement readily transforms itself into another."[446]

Shaukat points out that indoctrination often preceded, rather than followed, Qur'an reading. He takes this as evidence that ISIS adherents would be amenable to alternative, nonviolent interpretations of their holy book.[447] Here is yet another role for religious leaders.

To stop religicide in our day we will need to strengthen these top-down, middle-out, and bottom-up approaches. Truth be told, all are needed. But incremental improvements will not suffice. We need to consider a root-based approach to cocreate a visionary Global Covenant to halt religicide, honor creation, and celebrate difference. The covenant requires the Indigenous leadership of those most impacted by religicide. It must be operationalized through civil society in partnership with interreligious institutions and support from moral leaders.

Since the Enlightenment, all things Indigenous (religious, tribal, subjective) have had a tendency to be viewed as somehow primitive, simple, irrelevant, and outdated. Rituals and beliefs are sometimes considered quaint or superstitious, but never really on par with modern science. Thanks to Darwinism, including social Darwinism, there has long been a sense that the less complex evolves into the more complex. Evolution is understood as one thing morphing into something else, rather than something that carries everything within its DNA even as it changes and transforms.

The more we understand the nature of DNA, the physical environment, the realities of evolution, and the limits of the planet, the more we realize that this attitude is based on incomplete assumptions about how the natural world functions. Since Charles Darwin, we have learned a lot more about how everything in the universe is interconnected and interdependent. This is something that most Indigenous cultures have always believed and respected.

False information and propaganda underpinned the US religicide against Indigenous Americans. Understanding local culture with at least some basic religious and cultural literacy really does matter. For example, the United States needs to better understand the Taliban in Afghanistan, including its current form of dealmaking—from buying off farmers with opium taxes to bribing Afghan military commanders and officials. US diplomats need to understand the role of religion in tribal dynamics by listening more deeply to local voices on the ground.

Chapter Twelve

A GLOBAL COVENANT:
THE MISSING PIECE

In 1984, Father Thomas Keating, the late Christian mystic and interfaith pioneer, invited a diverse group of spiritual leaders—Buddhist, Hindu, Jewish, Islamic, Native American, Russian Orthodox, Protestant, and Roman Catholic—to gather at St. Benedict's Monastery, on the side of a mountain in Snowmass, Colorado. The invitation was explicit. Participants would meditate together in silence and share their spiritual journeys, especially those elements in their respective traditions that have proved most helpful. Its agenda? Simply to explore their similarities and talk honestly about their differences. Originally, they kept no record and published no papers. They met for a week or so each year for twenty years. Eventually, they released some of their reflections in a small book, *The Common Heart*, summarizing the shared wisdom of their beliefs, including several significant points of interreligious agreement:

> World religions bear witness to the experience of
> an "Ultimate Reality" to which they give various
> names (though this Ultimate Reality cannot be
> limited by any name or concept).

Faith is opening, accepting, and responding to Ultimate Reality.

The potential for human wholeness—or in other frames of reference, enlightenment, salvation, transcendence, transformation, blessedness—is present in every human being.

Ultimate Reality can be experienced through religious practice and through nature, art, human relationships, and service to others.

Disciplined practice is essential to the spiritual life; yet spiritual attainment is not the result of one's own efforts, but the result of an experience of oneness with Ultimate Reality.[448]

These broad agreeable concepts recognize that the silos of our different religious beliefs do not hinder our experience of Ultimate Reality, and that oneness with that reality and each other is possible no matter our labels. One of the participants in these Snowmass gatherings explained how different faiths do not have to share exact beliefs or agree on interpretations of scriptures to be in deep friendship or conversation.

People often think that to do interreligious dialogue you have to come to some bland, low-level common denominator and never disagree. However, we know one another well enough to really disagree, fundamentally, and not be affected negatively in our relationship. I never had to water down my feelings or my tradition.[449]

Instead of a need for agreement or control, it is a healthy respect for difference that strengthens our shared humanity. As we pursue our respective efforts at religious and spiritual expression, it helps to recognize the differences in approach as well as our interdependence. Peace is predicated on balance and diversity (polyculture) not on conformity to one power or control (monoculture). If we are to solve, or at least calm religion-related violence around the globe, we need to acknowledge the right of all religions to exist. And that means reaching out and connecting because of our beliefs, not despite them. Meaningful outreach among diverse faith groups is critical to building bridges for peace and justice as we disrupt our baser temptations to violence and revenge.

Solving a complex problem requires teamwork. Diplomats, lawyers, and international agencies are critical to advance a coherent set of legal obligations and policies to protect people and the planet. Civil society networks are critical to help build community resilience and capacities for early warning and response to conflict. Survivors of religious persecution are critical to speak truth to power, decrying and documenting the horrors they have witnessed and experienced firsthand. Indigenous communities who have been assaulted by religious persecution over decades and centuries are critical as sources of wisdom to guide our collective healing. All these elements are needed; none is sufficient alone.

Steven Charleston, a voice of justice for Indigenous peoples and a member of the Choctaw Nation, shares his wisdom in *Ladder to the Light: An Indigenous Elder's Meditations on Hope and Courage*. He describes how his ancestors survived for millennia by following a spiritual path that was respectful of the earth and all humanity; noting that his tradition has survived as one of the oldest continuous spiritual paths on earth.

My ancestors' faith continues to this day despite
every hardship and persecution it has been forced
to endure.... In historic memory, we have seen our
reality come crashing down as invaders destroyed
our homeland. We have lived through genocide,
concentration camps, religious persecution, and
every human rights abuse imaginable. Yet we are
still here. No darkness—not even the end of the
world as we knew it—had the power to overcome
us. So, our message is powerful not because it is
only for us, but because it speaks to and for every
human heart that longs for light over darkness.[450]

We believe these ingredients—Indigenous, spiritual, traditional, and religious—can and must work together.

How can we pull these diverse actors, faiths, and traditions
together to work in concert to enable sustainable peace? We propose a covenant to stand against anti-religious violence, bring an
end to religicide, and point the way to human flourishing.

Where to begin? How about starting with the truth?

Very often it's difficult to admit the facts in front of us: systemic violence is happening on a daily basis. Factocide about
"those people" and lies about harm being inflicted have created
cultural beliefs that must be dismantled by uncovering the truth.
We must name the crime, face the facts, and take action guided by
conscience. A growing number of survivors and their allies have
demonstrated great courage in raising their voices and telling the
truth about the horrors they have witnessed. We need to listen
attentively, hear them, and commit ourselves to act. Ending religicide and reversing its devastating consequences begins with telling
the truth.

Next, we must rebuild community among former neighbors who have been taught to mistrust and even hate each other. Again, a member of the Indigenous Choctaw Nation describes the messy challenge of community building:

> Spiritual community is sometimes portrayed as a sing-along around a campfire. It seems sweet and sentimental, but nothing could be farther from the truth. A spiritual community is more like a labor union. It is a community of workers, drawn together by the pressure exerted on them by the darkness, who are determined to protect the weak and uphold justice. The community is tough and accustomed to struggle. It is designed to face the powers of injustice and privilege—and doing that is no sing-along.[451]

Unfortunately, Indigenous victims of religicide, on their own, do not possess the power to stop these atrocities against them. They have learned to mistrust and fear those who have persecuted them. They are understandably frustrated by the world's seeming indifference to their suffering. They have watched the serial failure of government and business leaders to stand in solidarity to protect them. So, where are our persistent calls to the United Nations and public officials to do more to stop documented mass violence? Where are the efforts to heal and repair the consequences of religicide? To help build more equitable and peaceful communities?

One Indigenous group working to rebuild truth and community are the Yazidis in Iraq. We chronicled their struggles in an earlier chapter. The Yazidis who fled genocide and sought asylum in Germany desperately reached out to a Catholic abbey and got some help from an organization whose purpose is to work in covenant with any and all religions to rebuild faith communities and regenerate damaged its land. So, why aren't there more groups doing this? Because everyone thinks "the system" or governments will help. It's not working.

Twentieth century interstate diplomatic tools are failing to stop intrastate atrocities in the twenty-first century. The current international system is centered on protecting nation-state sovereignty at the expense of human rights. Humanitarian and human rights laws favor the protection of individual rights over collective or group rights. These don't adequately address collective rights or environmental justice and ecological rights. We need a renewed focus on our shared human responsibilities to protect all people, regardless of their beliefs. Who better to bear this responsibility than people of faith? People who share the universal values of compassion, equity, and dignity can unite in a common powerful voice calling for an end to religicide. Their ties to each other are less a treaty and more of a covenant.

Instead of relying on governments to police their own human rights record and systemic violence (unlikely), we need to expand the role of religious actors and people of conscience worldwide.

That is why we are proposing the creation of a Global Covenant of Religions. This would serve as an interreligious peace promise signed and agreed to by people of faith calling on their coreligionists, governments, policymakers, and industries to work together to end religicide and address the roots of anti-religious violence.

We believe this will save millions of lives and protect shared cultural and ecological heritage worldwide. Such a covenant, led by survivors of religicide and rooted in Indigenous wisdom and practice, calls on world leaders and nation-states to repair and heal the injustice of religious persecution.

We believe a covenantal framework has the potential to bind diverse communities together—top-down, middle-out, but primarily bottom-up—in relationship to a set of shared values and commitments that demonstrate a deep reverence for life and biodiversity. Such an approach would engage people, spirit, and land simultaneously. It would generate new ways of protecting and caring for our neighbors.

Tribalism and religion are not receding in the modern era. They are growing. By now, we understand how they can combust into religion-related conflict in the face of existential threats. But they also can serve as powerful survival mechanisms built into our social DNA, our very evolution. We survive and flourish in groups. But these groups too often compete for dominance rather than community. How do we remain true to our social nature of wanting to be part of a group, but still want the best for other groups? And can we do that while aligning ourselves with living systems and our natural habitats, thereby reversing ecocide?

A covenantal approach, tapping the strengths of religion, Indigenous spirituality, wisdom, and ecology, is showing us the way forward.

Governments aren't sufficient. They come with inherent self-interest and a need for power, control, and competition. If we are to end genocide, ecocide, and factocide, a different approach is needed.

We believe a Global Covenant is the missing piece. We would ask its adherents to fulfill the following promises, while simultaneously pressing governments and international organizations to do the same:

- Protect members of religious groups who do not threaten violence against other groups or individuals, including the right to study and practice their religious beliefs.

- Protect against religious groups who threaten others with violence because they do not share the beliefs of such groups, or because they are unwilling to cede property, religious sites, or other items or allegiances demanded by aggressors.

- Protect sacred sites identified by an international commission of religious history, in concert with UNESCO efforts, to protect world heritage.

- Uphold the right to religious education. Protect members of religious groups who are persecuted solely for seeking to become educated in their religious traditions or to be educated through sources that differ from those favored by dominant groups.

- Mobilize international resources to report, monitor, and evaluate the approaches, practices, and tools that have been most effective in promoting interfaith harmony and reducing violence.

- Train international organizations and monitors to detect and take early action against emergent signals of noncompromising communication and media disinformation, elements that often predict onset of violence.

- Educate diplomats and secular civil society leaders on the constructive role religion can play to mediate and mitigate conflict. Religion can offer deep resources for resilience, stability, and strategic peacebuilding.

Each of these improvements are important incremental steps that align with the preexisting commitments governments have already made as member states of the United Nations.

WHY A COVENANT, NOT A TREATY?

We envision an interreligious Global Covenant to go beyond any secular interstate agreement. Such a covenant would be cocreated first and foremost by religious actors and Indigenous peoples worldwide to inspire new creative mechanisms to advance peace and flourishing beyond what the United Nations and governments are able to accomplish through their seventeen UN Sustainable Development Goals.

We cannot be too prescriptive here. A covenant must emerge organically as a growing network of relationships, something that is intentionally flexible, dynamic, and alive. And individuals across different faiths can project and dream what they ideally wish it will become.

The concept of covenantal promises is already familiar to more than four billion people who are members of the Abrahamic monotheistic traditions of Judaism, Christianity, and Islam, at the very least. It evokes for the descendants of Abraham some form of divine promise and participation. In the Hebrew Bible, for example, covenant refers to several promises God made to the Jewish people. They remain an aspirational work in progress, often expressed as a collective effort to "repair the world"—*tikkun olam*. God also made covenantal promises with non-Jewish people, including the descendants of Ishmael, gentiles, and creation itself.

Covenant is a way to generate partnership without power and competition. This holistic approach, which we call covenantalism, respects the dignity of everyone to believe what they want, with whom they want, and how they want. Covenantalism enables its partners to accomplish together what they can't achieve on their own. This is not unlike a marital promise with its mutual long-term commitment to work through difficulties and remain in relationship for better or worse. Covenantal relationships require reciprocal generosity and teamwork, with no one person or religious group dominating the conversation. Some Indigenous groups assert there isn't even a word for "domination" to be found in their native languages.

Covenants are inherently pluralistic, welcoming, and hospitable to difference. Covenantalism requires an affirmative values-infused vision to inspire even adversarial groups to coalesce and commit to action in service to a higher good, not just their self-interest or power. Covenantalism builds on the universal calling to "love thy neighbor." This concept is central to important international interfaith efforts, including A Common Word Between Us and You, The Amman Message, and World Interfaith Harmony Week—all initiated by descendants of the Prophet Muhammad living in the Hashemite Kingdom of Jordan.

The creation of a Global Covenant arises from three main points of understanding:

- Religious covenants represent ties that bind communities together in an enduring relationship by what they call "Ultimate Reality," "God," "Goodness," the "Sacred," or some combination of shared transcendent values.
- Secular state institutions are transactional or political by nature, and are not designed to address the underlying roots of anti-religious conflict. (Yet they remain essential

when it comes to protecting their citizens, including religious minorities under threat.)

- A Global Covenant would go beyond nation-state institutions as an enduring source of connection and communication across religions working toward peace, justice, and environmental regeneration.

A Global Covenant will seed a cross-faith movement of grassroots religious actors to redouble their efforts to promote interfaith cooperation and harmony, and to renounce violence committed in the name of God or group ideology. Major faith leaders must consistently appeal to their followers, including religiously motivated youth, with an affirmative call to action that offers a compelling invitation to community service as an alternative to extremist calls for violence.

Over the past few decades, there have been attempts by remarkable individuals and organizations to coalesce interreligious leadership around various declarations to stop violence and even sign onto a compassion charter. But this work has not yet scaled to match or keep up with the accelerated spread of anti-religious violence. And most top-down elite initiatives from faith leaders as revered as His Holiness Pope Francis, His Holiness the Dalai Lama, or the late Desmond Tutu, do not address the root causes of anti-religious violence nor take hold on the ground where violence takes place. Violence, like politics, is local. Therefore, a Global Covenant must prioritize local interfaith organizing bottom-up, starting with survivors of anti-religious violence and their allies working at the community level.

A new covenant would present a higher calling than mere tolerance or some sort of nonaggression pacts between and among religious groups. It means committing to the protection of difference, the freedom of believing what one believes, and the insistence on nonviolence locally, nationally, regionally, and globally. It aligns powerfully with nature, creation, social evolution, and principles of survivorship: the ability to live positively and dynamically even in the face of disease, disability, disaster, and death.

It is critical that cross-faith relationships are developed deeply and locally, not just through international workshops but neighbor to neighbor. No one technique is sufficient to make this happen. What is needed is to support and practice a blend of intercommunal dialogue, mutual study of scriptural wisdom, basic religious literacy and education, and joint community service designed to benefit the larger community, not just one sect or faction. Engaging in a common task for the common good strengthens communities, while breaking down stereotypes and misinformation.

Millions of people of faith belonging to religious communities worldwide have been experiencing a relentless onslaught of disinformation over the past two decades. This incites systemic violence that reveals gaps in current international laws, political frameworks, and global responses. A new covenantal approach would help fill those gaps with more constructive ways to counter ongoing slander and ignorance, such as:

- *Study*: Research the underlying causes and drivers of violence and test tools that can detect and mitigate the risk of religion-related conflict.
- *Dialogue*: Participate in local volunteer interfaith circles to study across traditions and convert learning into action.

- *Media*: Amplify inspired storytelling by survivors, their allies, and subject experts with particular attention to youth engagement and truth-telling.
- *Action*: Mobilize networks of partners and interfaith allies to take concrete steps to prevent religicide and reduce other religion-related violence.

These practical activities will help debunk misinformation and disinformation. In this way, a Global Covenant has the potential to generate new educational, media, scriptural, and jurisprudential resources to guide participants in their respective obligations to protect and care for their neighbors, even those who are differently faithed. The aim is to proliferate interfaith interaction, relationships, and collaboration at all levels (top-down, middle-out, and bottom-up). But we believe that without a strong commitment to survivor-led grassroots interfaith organizing (bottom-up), there won't be sufficient authenticity and credibility for religious elites to find the courage to confront the roots of anti-religious violence and to challenge their governments to change their discriminatory laws, budgets, and behavior.

Where does one start?

A Global Covenant needs to prioritize halting the most egregious cases of religicide happening today, including those we have highlighted in previous chapters. Entire communities, their heritage, and way of life are tragically being destroyed before our eyes. We know that no one religion, organization, or government can succeed in this work alone. It will require values-driven concerted action among all participating religious, educational, political, and civil society groups.

Will diverse religious groups and tribes really learn to get along and work together for a common cause? We believe they will. Indigenous practices over centuries—including Native Americans, Yazidis, Tibetans, Uyghurs, Rohingya—offer lessons on how to reach consensus in decision-making. Revisiting Native governance practices may help us understand respectful ways to promote peace and restorative justice going forward.

For example, present-day Indigenous psychotherapy and restorative justice circles endeavor to heal trauma simultaneously on the individual, communal, ancestral, and spiritual levels. According to shamanic healer and mediator, Dr. Myron Eshowsky, healing is not so much the treatment of disease and disability as it is a holistic educational process of discovery that generates reconnection to community. A covenantal approach would reaffirm the Indigenous therapeutic belief that we belong to a wider community, and to heal we must act collectively as an antidote to the chronic and rising rates of depression, suicide, and addiction that we observe in communities facing religicide.

Judy Atkinson, a researcher of Aboriginal descent who studies Indigenous healing practices, describes this community approach simply, but powerfully:

> I will listen to you, share with you, as you listen to
> [me], share with me. Our shared experiences are
> different, but in the inner deep listening to, and
> quiet, still awareness of each other, we learn to
> grow together. In this we create community, and
> our shared knowledge and wisdom are expanded
> from our communication with each other.[452]

This notion of community building, of enemies eventually breaking bread together and learning to bless each other's differences, is simple but powerful. It's simply asking all members of the faith community to come together and learn about each other with respect for difference.

What might it look like for a few Chinese Han and Chinese Uyghurs to speak together, listen, and share more deeply about what is happening with each other? Yes, this requires courage to speak openly about the diversity of China, the wisdom of Confucianism, as well as Islam's contributions to culture and civilization.

What might happen if Myanmar military and Rohingya met each other and connected in empathy?

Could Sunni and Shia Muslims in Iraq learn from another monotheistic tradition called Yazidism, let alone the remnant of Christians who remain in the country?

Yes, adversaries—victims and perpetrators alike—must eventually sit down together and listen. We are already in relationship to one another, inextricably linked whether we like it or not.

There are tried and true practices of governance and dialogue that we need to resurrect in our modern era. When forming a circle, for example, there is normally a ritualized opening and closing that affirms everyone's interconnectedness. The practice of deep listening engages all our senses. Each person has an opportunity to share without disruption, criticism, or judgment, often holding a stick, feather, or stone, when it is time to talk. The potential for what we call covenantalism among Indigenous elders and diverse community leaders responds holistically to heal collective trauma such as religicide.

It is time for more listening and hearing in the present while learning from the past.

Healing religious divides and protecting religious freedom are also good for business and economics. Brian Grim, founder of the Religious Freedom & Business Foundation (RFBF), is one of the world's leading experts on the relationship between religious freedom and the economy. RFBF is dedicated to educating the global business community, policymakers, nongovernment organizations, and consumers about the positive power that faith and religious freedom for all (including those with no religious faith) has on business and the economy.

In the United States alone, Brian Grim estimates that religion provides more than $1 trillion in value to the economy and society each year. These contributions include billions spent on charitable projects, educational institutions, and health care. Over 150 million Americans (nearly half the US population) make up the membership of over 344,000 congregations.[453] Congregations and faith-based institutions enhance the economy of every town and city throughout the country. Each year, 7.5 million volunteers are coordinated by congregations to support or manage 1.5 million social projects across the country. Despite a decline in religious affiliation among Americans, religious groups have increased their spending 300 percent on social initiatives over the previous fifteen years, reaching $9 billion.[454] Measured in terms of GDP, religion in the United States would rank as the world's fifteenth largest national economy.

Even in China, the active engagement of religious minorities in society typically fosters economic innovation.[455] China today has the world's second-largest religious population after India.[456] It seems unwise and unrealistic to try to eradicate religion in such a large and diverse country. Research by Qunyong Wang and Xinyu Lin published in the *China Economic Review* examined the impact of religious beliefs on economic growth in China using province data from 2001 to 2011. Of all the religions studied, Christianity contributed most to China's economic growth.[457] Government-recognized Christian congregations and institutions, accounting for roughly 16 percent of all religious institutions, enjoy economic advantage over the tens of millions of Christians who are not recognized by the Communist Party.[458]

Ultimately, religion is here to stay. This should be cause for celebration and appreciation for cultural diversity and creativity worldwide. Tapping religion as a source for peace and community building seems a far better approach than letting it fuel violence, division, and harm. People survive, adapt, and evolve in social groups, not in isolation. Consider religion's staying power: Judaism has survived for nearly 6,000 years, Christianity more than 2,000, and Islam more than 1,500. Today, there are estimated to be more than four hundred million Indigenous peoples worldwide, from America to Africa to Australia, living in more than ninety countries. These are individuals who practice diverse spiritual traditions and speak more than four thousand languages.[459] Indigenous people such as Aboriginals, who have been present in Australia for an estimated fifty thousand years, make them one of the world's oldest civilizations. By comparison, economic and political empires may have a good run for only a century or two, as with France in the eighteenth century, Britain in the nineteenth century, and the United States in the twentieth century. Nation-states lose power much more quickly than religious groups.

Religions are a fundamental source of resilience. Research conducted at Yale University by Dr. Dennis Charney and Dr. Stephen

Southwick reveals the top ten hallmarks of resilience: optimism, altruism, having a moral compass, faith and spirituality, humor, having a role model, social support, facing fear, having a mission, and training.[460] Aside from optimism perhaps, these hallmarks are all things we can do and cultivate, mostly in groups, socially. After all, we build resilience *together*. But where? At a rock concert? A political rally? On Zoom? No, historically and traditionally, these ingredients for resilience are found in the religious or spiritual community.

Religion, rather than being something that teaches exclusivity, can help teach the importance of diversity and creation. Hinduism, for example, is internally diverse, containing within it an expansive range of beliefs and practices. Gandhi presciently said that India's ability "to reach unity in diversity will be the beauty and the test of our civilization."[461] India is now being tested in the twenty-first century with a surge in religion-related violence targeting Christian and Muslim minorities. Far more robust interfaith efforts, state by state, will be needed to interrupt the disturbing trend of religious beliefs being politicized and used to justify violence across India.

In January 2021, the *New York Times* and *Foreign Policy* magazine suggested that ongoing persecution of Christians in India could emerge as the next case of genocide if we don't heed the early warnings and take action. Violence against Christians seems part of a broader shift in India in which minorities face increasing threats of persecution as Hindu nationalists pursue the Hindutva ideology of turning India into a "pure" Hindu nation.[462] What might this mean for more than thirty million Christians and two hundred million Muslims living in India?

Attacks on Christians and Muslims have increased significantly since Narendra Modi became prime minister in 2014.[463] Father Anand, an Indian priest in Uttar Pradesh, reports that "every Sunday is a day of terror and trauma for Christians."[464]

This growing crisis must be interrupted. Though the violence appears interreligious, we must reiterate that the root causes of anti-religious violence are mainly political and economic, *not* religious. It is inappropriate to label terrorists and extremists with generic characterizations as "Hindu" or "Christian" or "Muslim." Those who commit violence in the name of God are in fact a miniscule fraction of any religious group. We must continue to call out these religious hotspots—reminding all actors that the great preponderance of scripture calls for meeting the "other" with love, compassion, and hospitality, not violence.

Religious scholars often point out that one of the most powerful scriptural affirmations of diversity and pluralism is found in Islam: "O Mankind, We have created you from a male and a female, and made you into races and tribes so that you may know each other." (Qur'an 49:13)[465] We welcome such encouragement in these polarizing times to get to know each other, becoming more compassionate and more covenantal. Religious traditions, in various ways, are all called to celebrate difference, even when this feels counterintuitive. Only together, connecting with our neighbors inside and outside our tribal faith, do we increase our prospects for human flourishing.

It doesn't matter whether you call yourself religious, spiritual, or neither. The challenge is to discover the distinct value and dignity of all human beings, including those who don't look, act, think, and pray like we do. Monoculture, whether expressed through religious fundamentalism or single-party communism, violates the natural order. Insisting on one crop to plant or one interpretation of scripture is damaging to our planet. The stifling danger of religicide is wanting everyone to be the same.

Ultimately, we believe covenantalism offers an effective antidote to religicide. As our final argument, we'll contrast covenant with religicide. Which would you choose?

Covenant opens possibility to foster curiosity and respect difference. Religicide propagates sameness and certainty.

Covenant frames a hopeful pluralistic vision for our shared future of humanity and all living systems. Religicide wants to revise history on its own terms.

Covenant respects dissent and learning from differences. Religicide punishes disagreement, diversity, and dissent.

Covenant seeks the freedom to harmonize and share humanity. Religicide seeks power and control over others.

Covenant welcomes polyculture and permaculture as natural and essential to the health and well-being of people and the planet. Religicide strives for monoculture, which is proven to harm people and the planet.

Covenant encourages people to fulfill their diverse potential and voice. Religicide forces citizens to surrender and obey with no distinct voice.

Covenant aligns with nature, evolving complexity, and diversity. Religicide exerts destructive power over nature, extracting and paving over change.

This covenantal approach contrasts completely with a religicidal march to eradicate difference en route to mass death and destruction of religion and people.

A Global Covenant will emerge in the coming years first and foremost as an invitation rather than some top-down legal directive or prescriptive blueprint.

We invite all religious communities to mobilize their deepest wisdom and resources to inhibit violence and to become part of an international movement that connects them to humanity—to diverse civil society partners and government actors.

We invite religicide survivors, particularly women and youth, to lead the design and implementation of initiatives to prevent and alleviate victimization and suffering.

We invite scholars across different traditions to advance quantitative and qualitative analysis to diagnose the underlying social, economic, political, and theological factors that may contribute to religicide.

We invite diplomats and government actors to address the gaps in laws and policies and provide protections and partnerships with religious communities and civil society organizations.

We invite civil society and local service providers to share their experience and successful methods of practice for building more stable resilient communities with all the previously mentioned actors.

Above all, we invite actors from all of these different groups to engage with, learn from, and be inspired by one another in service to humanity and our stressed planet.

It can be done. Healing, reintegration, living side by side with those who persecuted you is not some high-minded fantasy. We'll end with the example of Yazidis, who we met earlier—the victims of ISIS that were murdered, raped, persecuted, and driven from their homeland. They have returned to their ancestral land. They are rebuilding. They choose daily to heal and recover from religicide, step-by-step, brick by brick, plant by plant.

In the middle of the pandemic, thousands of Yazidis, living as internally displaced people in camps, decided to pack up what little they had and return to their sacred homeland in Shingal. They preferred to die at home than in a God-forsaken, infected camp. It is breathtaking to see what Yazidi families have accomplished with so few resources, thanks to their deep faith and Indigenous knowledge of the land. One family began by restoring the only two ransacked rooms available to them, expanding them to accommodate thirteen family members.

Their priority was to find water—to restore the community well in Jidale. ISIS had done everything they could to destroy this vital source of life. After pulling out as much rubbish as ISIS could throw into one well, the Yazidi families dug down to the original depth. Disappointingly, only a few drops of water trickled out. They soon understood what they needed to do: *Dig deeper!* Dig deeper than ISIS. When they went down another fifty feet, the water started to flow. They are now able to irrigate eight hundred olive trees and ultimately provide water security in the town as needed.

The Yazidi returnees then dug a second well. This time in the nearby village of Wardia to rehabilitate and develop a smaller property to farm there. Whereas the terrain in Jidale is hilly and well-suited for trees and sheep, they knew they could more easily plant vegetables in Wardia. This was a priority for their food security as well as an opportunity to share this blessing with their impoverished neighbors. In March 2021, they planted five hundred fruit trees, a promise for the future. Then, after laying down a drip irrigation system in both Jidale and Wardia, they set up a protective fence and planted three acres of vegetables, also building a small pond in the middle of the orchard. In September 2021, they were finally able to connect to the central electrical grid.

Recovering from religicide, obviously and evidentially, takes daily hard work, and there is still a long way to go. It hardly rained at all in the past year. The climate crisis is a real challenge. The trees in Jidale sprouted healthy leaves, but after seven years without much water, they did not bear fruit. Not yet. There is still so much to restore and replant: housing, barns, sheep, bees, more trees, and more vegetables—and cultural heritage and memory, mass graves and shrines, and schools. This is not traditional development work. It is the powerful work of regeneration—transforming soil and society by tapping into the roots of Yazidism: sharing an ecology of blessing and hospitality in the Middle East. They're now asking for advice on efficient practices like drip irrigation and the advantages of micro-climates such as the one in their orchard. These Yazidis have become covenantal partners sharing the fruits of their knowledge, hospitality, and labor, including watermelons, vegetables, and honey. Their religious tradition compels them to experience blessing once again, including being blessed by interfaith allies who are in relationship with them in a mini-global covenant of sorts.

As one Yazidi puts it modestly, "We haven't done very much yet. We just dug a well and planted a few trees."[466] But he understands how a little can become a lot. Over the course of one year, they have dug deep, and have planted hope. It is starting to bear fruit.

Since our Yazidi friends have returned to Shingal, they were able to clean out and reopen a guesthouse in Tal Azeer. This is now a space where people gather for tea, water, or something to eat. More than that, it's a safe place where they can find community and solidarity—a sense of belonging. On August 14, 2021, the anniversary of a lethal car bomb attack that took place in 2007, they were able to host the local community in this space for the first time since ISIS attacked. People came from all around to mourn together and to honor the dead but also to be together after seven years of displacement. On September 26, 2021, the community was able to host the Yazidi spiritual leader, Baba Sheikh, in this sacred regenerative space.

There is much more to say about the tenacious resilience of Yazidi religicide survivors and how they are rebuilding their community in Nineveh Province in Iraq. But our point here is simply to show there are ways to heal and recover with support from allies. More importantly, there are ways to prevent religicide and anti-religious violence. Whether one is a religious leader, scholar, diplomat, or activist, we all have a role to play to disrupt violence and advocate against monoculture.

Interfaith collaboration expressed through covenantalism will remind us to bless and honor our differences and biodiversity.

Indigenous Americans remind us, for example, that they have no linguistic concept for a weed—that everything has a purpose, a place.

With this hopeful vision of unity in diversity and a willingness to cocreate and learn together, we can reverse the wretched consequences of greed, exploitation, colonialism, slavery, and religicide. We stand in solidarity alongside the survivors of religicide, grateful for their tenacity and resilience, pointing the way forward.

Our survival as a planet and a people depends on it.

BIBLIOGRAPHY

Abu Bakr Naji. *The Management of Savagery: The Most Critical Stage Through Which the Umma Will Pass*. Translated by William McCants. John M. Olin Institute for Strategic Studies at Harvard University, May 2006.

Abudu, Shalamu, et al. "A Karez System's Dilemma." *Socio-Environmental Dynamics along the Historical Silk Road*. Springer, 2019.

Adorno, Theodor W. *The Authoritarian Personality*. Norton, 1950.

Advisory Commission on Rakhine State. "Towards a Peaceful, Fair and Prosperous Future for the People of Rakhine." August 2017.

Aivazian, Haroutune. "Testimonies: Haroutune Aivazian." United States Holocaust Museum.

Albert, Eleanor, and Lindsay Maizland. "Religion in China." The Council on Foreign Relations, September 2020.

Alvarez, Alex. *Native America and the Question of Genocide*. Rowman & Littlefield Publishers, 2014.

Arendt, Hannah. *The Origins of Totalitarianism*. Meridian Books, 1958.

Amnesty International. "Iraq: Dead Land: Islamic State's Deliberate Destruction of Iraq's Farmland." Amnesty International, December 2018.

Amnesty International. "Myanmar: New Landmine Blasts Point to Deliberate Targeting of the Rohingya." Amnesty International, September 2017.

Amnesty International. "Remaking Rakhine State." Amnesty International, March 2018.

Anti-Defamation League. "The ADL Global 100: An Index of Antisemitism." 2021.

Andreopoulos, George J. "Ethnic cleansing." *Encyclopædia Britannica*, December 28, 2018.

Arab News. "Amal Clooney brings to justice Daesh woman who oversaw rape, enslavement of Yazidis." Saudi Research & Publishing Company, June 2021.

Armstrong, Karen. *Fields of Blood: Religion and the History of Violence*. Alfred A. Knopf Inc., 2014.

Arnold, Dan and Alicia Turner. "Why Are We Surprised When Buddhists Are Violent?" *The New York Times*, March 2018.

Arya, T.G. "China was only a part of the Mongol Yuan Dynasty, it was neither the authority nor the inheritor of the dynasty." Central Tibetan Administration, November 2019.

Asher-Schapiro, Avi. "China found using surveillance firms to help write ethnic-tracking specs." *Reuters*, March 2021.

Bader, Jeffrey A. "China's Role in East Asia: Now and the Future." The Brookings Institution, September 2005.

Barnett, Victoria. "A Prelude to the Nazi Genocide of the Jews: The Rise of Religious Ethno-nationalism in Interwar Europe." United States Holocaust Memorial Museum, conference presentation at "Preventing Polarization, Building Bridges and Fostering Inclusivity: The Role of Religious Actors." United Nations Office on Genocide Prevention and the Responsibility to Protect, New York, March 4–5, 2019.

Baumeister, Roy F., Brad J. Bushman and W. Keith Campbell. "Self-Esteem, Narcissism, and Aggression: Does Violence Result from Low Self-Esteem or From Threatened Egotism?" Sage Publications, Inc., February 2000.

Beech, Hannah, Saw Nang and Marlise Simons. "'Kill All you See': In a First, Myanmar Soldiers Tell of Rohingya Slaughter." *The New York Times*, September 2020.

Bennett, Georgette F. *Thou Shalt Not Stand Idly By: How One Woman Confronted the Greatest Humanitarian Crisis of Our Time.* Wicked Son/Post Hill Press, 2021.

Biden, Joe. "Remarks by President Biden on America's Place in the World." U.S. State Department, February 2021.

Blakemore, Erin. "Who are the Rohingya people?" *National Geographic*, February 8, 2019.

Bohman, Sarah. "Laying Down One's Swords – Judaism's Just War." University of St. Thomas Journal of Law and Public Policy, Volume 3, Issue 1, January 2009.

Borak, Masha. "Chinese surveillance giant expanding in the US attracts scrutiny over possible targeting of Uygurs." *South China Morning Post*, November 2020.

Bovingdon, Gardner. *The Uyghurs: Strangers in Their Own Land.* Columbia University Press, 2010.

Broecker, Christen (ed.). *Manual on Human Rights and the Prevention of Genocide.* Jacob Blaustein Institute for the Advancement of Human Rights, 2015.

"Buddhist and State Power in Myanmar." International Crisis Group, September 2017.

Çaksu, A. "Islamophobia, Chinese Style: Total Internment of Uyghur Muslims by the People's Republic of China." *Islamophobia Studies Journal*, 2020.

Callimachi, Rukmini. "ISIS and the Lonely Young American." *The New York Times*, June 2015.

Carswell, Andrew J. "Unblocking the UN Security Council: The Uniting for Peace Resolution." *Journal of Conflict and Security Law*, Volume 18, Issue 3, August 2013. https://doi.org/10.1093/jcsl/krt016

Cavanaugh, William T. *The Myth of Religious Violence: Secular Ideology and the Roots of Modern Conflict*. Oxford University Press, 2009.

Chan, Aye. "The Development of a Muslim Enclave in Arakan (Rakhine) State of Burma (Myanmar)." SOAS Bulletin of Burma Research, Volume 3, No. 2, 2005.

Charleston, Steven. *Ladder to the Light: An Indigenous Elder's Meditations on Hope and Courage*. Broadleaf Books, 2021.

Chernow, Ron. *Grant*. Penguin Press, 2017.

Chiu, Yvonne. "Non-Violence, Asceticism, and the Problem of Buddhist Nationalism." Genealogy, 2020.

Tanenbaum Center for Interreligious Understanding. *Religion, Law, and the Role of Force*. Edited by Joseph Coffey and Charles Matthews. Transnational Publishers, 2002.

Coleman, Michelle. "The Applicability of 'Grievous Religious Persecution' in International Criminal Law: Response to Werner Nicolaas Nel." BYU Law, April 2021.

Committee on Foreign Affairs House of Representatives. "Women Under ISIS Rule: From Brutality to Recruitment." U.S. Government Publishing Office, July 2015.

Conference on Jewish Material Claims Against Germany. "Descriptive Catalogue of Looted Judaica." New York, World Jewish Restitution Organization, Partially Updated Edition, 2016.

Congressional-Executive Commission on China. "Hearing on the Communist Party's Crackdown on Religion in China." 29 November 2018. Accessed at https://www.youtube.com/watch?v=1WOem1tgDMc.

Cooper, Joshua. "25 Years of ILO Convention 169." *Cultural Survival Quarterly Magazine*, March 2015.

Dakhil, Vian. "Yazidi MP's emotional appeal to save Iraq's hunted minority." *euronews*, 8 August 2014. Accessed at https://www.youtube.com/watch?v=YJKHBnQXyRI.

Dadrian, Vahakn N. "The Role of Turkish Physicians in the World War I Genocide of Ottoman Armenians." *Holocaust and Genocide Studies*, Volume 1, Issue 2, February 1986.

Dawut, Zumeret and Radio Free Asia. "Interview: 'As Soon as I Was Taken Inside, I Knew it Was a Prison." Radio Free Asia, September 24, 2019.

De Zavala, Golec, et al. "Collective Narcissism and Its Social Consequences." Journal of Personality and Social Psychology, December 2009.

Denyer, Simon. "Former Inmates of China's Muslim 'reeducation' camps tell of brainwashing, torture." *The Washington Post*, 2018.

Dinstein, Yoram. "The Right to Humanitarian Assistance." *Naval War College Review*, Volume 52, No. 4, 2000.

Dubensky, Joyce (ed). *Peacemakers in Action: Volume 2: Profiles in Religious Peacebuilding*. Cambridge University Press, 2016.

Dunbar-Ortiz, Roxanne. *An Indigenous Peoples' History of the United States*. Beacon Press, 2014.

Durkheim, Emile. "Anomie and the Moral Structure of Industry." *Emile Durkheim: Selected Writings*. Edited by Anthony Giddens. Cambridge University Press, August 2012.

Ehrenkranz, Joseph & David Coppola (eds.). *Religion and Violence, Religion and Peace*. Sacred Heart University Press, 2000.

Ellis, Clyde. "American Indians and Christianity." *The Encyclopedia of Oklahoma History and Culture*. Oklahoma Historical Society.

Ellis, Hannah. "Jesus statue smashed in spate of attacks on India's Christian community." *The Guardian*, 27 December 2021.

Ellis, Marc S. "The ICC's Role in Combatting the Destruction of Cultural Heritage." *Case Western Reserve Journal of International Law*, Volume 1, Issue 7, 2017.

Emmons, Robert A. "Factor analysis and construct validity of the Narcissistic Personality Inventory." *Journal of Personality Assessment*, June 1984.

"Entry #10553." Xinjiang Victims Database.

"Faith-Based Reservations." Native American Netroots, February 2010.

FBI National Press Office. "FBI Releases Updated 2020 Hate Crime Statistics." Federal Bureau of Investigation, October 2021.

Finley, Joanne Smith. *The Art of Symbolic Resistance: Uyghur Identities and Uyghur-Han Relations in Contemporary Xinjiang*. BRILL, 2013.

Frankl, Viktor E. *Man's Search for Meaning*. Beacon Press, 1959.

Fromm, Erich. *Escape from Freedom*. Farrar & Rinehart Inc, 1941.

Gagnon, Gregory Omer. *Culture and Customs of the Sioux Indians*. ABC-CLIO, 2011.

Gao, Charlotte. "Chinese Communist Party Vows to 'Sinicize Religions' in China." *The Diplomat*, October 2017.

George, Susannah. "Yazidi women welcomed back to the faith." UNHCR USA, June 2015.

Gerson, Mark. *The Telling: How Judaism's Essential Book Reveals the Meaning of Life*. St. Martin's Essentials, 2021.

Goldman, Russell. "Myanmar's Coup Explained." *The New York Times*, November 29, 2021.

Green, Penny, et al. "Genocide Achieved, Genocide Continues: Myanmar's Annihilation of the Rohingya." International State Crime Initiative, 2018.

Grinde, Donald and Bruce Elliott Johansen. *Ecocide of Native America: Environmental Destruction of Indian Lands and Peoples.* Clear Light Publishers, 1997.

Gumbel, Andrew. "Junipero Serra's brutal story in the spotlight as Pope prepares for canonization." *The Guardian*, September 2015.

Hammer, Joshua. "The Hidden City of Myanmar." *Smithsonian Magazine*, December 2019.

Hashemite Kingdom of Jordan. "UNSC Resolution of 'Religicide.'" Unpublished, 2015.

Helderman, Rosalind S., et al. "'Trump said to do so': Accounts of rioters who say the president spurred them to rush the Capitol could be pivotal testimony." *The Washington Post*, January 2021.

Herscher, Rebecca. "Key Moments in the Dakota Access Pipeline Fight." *NPR*, February 2017.

Hill, Mary. "The Migration to the West of the Muskogee." April 1937. Published by American Native Press Archives and Sequoyah Research Center.

Holden, Kevin. "Amid US-China Tensions, Tibetans Seize the Moment." *The Diplomat*, December 2020.

Hoffer, Eric. *The True Believer: Thoughts on the Nature of Mass Movements.* Harper & Brothers, 1951.

Hosseini, Behnaz. "Yazidis' Illegitimate Children and a Crisis of Identity." *Iran International*, 2019.

Human Rights Watch. "Burma: New Satellite images Confirm Mass Destruction." Human Rights Watch, October 2017.

Human Rights Watch. "Genocide in Iraq: The Anfal Campaign Against the Kurds." Human Rights Watch, 1993.

Human Rights Watch. "I Saw It with My Own Eyes: Abuses by Chinese Security Forces in Tibet." Human Rights Watch, July 2010.

Human Rights Watch. "Myanmar: Imagery Shows 200 Buildings Burned." Human Rights Watch, May 2020.

Hume, Robert E. "Hinduism and War." The American Journal of Theology, Volume 20, No. 1, 1916.

Ibrahim, Azeem, The Rohingyas: Inside Myanmar's Hidden Genocide. Hurst, 2016.

Ihrig, Stefan. Justifying Genocide: Germany and the Armenians from Bismarck to Hitler. Harvard University Press, 2016.

International Campaign for Tibet. "60 Years of Chinese Misrule: Arguing Cultural Genocide in Tibet." International Campaign for Tibet, April 2012.

Jangiz, Khazan. "US launches million-dollar program to invest in Kurdistan Region agriculture." Rudaw, September 2021.

Jayson, Sharon and Kaiser Health News. "What Makes People Join Hate Groups?" US News, August 2017.

Jenkins, Stephen. "Making Merit through Warfare and Torture." Oxford University Press, 2010.

Jensen, Steven L. B. The Making of International Human Rights: The 1960s, Decolonization, and the Reconstruction of Global Values. Cambridge University Press, 2016.

Jewish Virtual Library. "Adolf Hitler: Political Testament" Published by American-Israeli Cooperative Enterprise, April 29, 1945.

Kaltman, Blaine. *Under the Heel of the Dragon: Islam, Racism, Crime and the Uighur in China.* Ohio University Press, 2007.

Kang, Dake. "Terror & Terrorism: Xinjiang eases its grip, but fear remains." *AP News,* October 2021.

Klug, Foster. "Rohingya say Myanmar targeted the educated in the genocide." *AP News,* June 5, 2018.

Konrath, Sara, et al. "Attenuating the Link Between Threatened Egotism and Aggression." *Psychological Science,* Volume 17, 2006.

Kristof, Nicholas. "One Woman's Journey Through Chinese Atrocities." *The New York Times,* June 2021.

Kurdistan 24. "Yezidi spiritual council revokes statement, will not accept children of ISIS rape victims." Kurdistan24, April 2019.

Kurspahic, Kemal. "Bosnia: Words Translated into Genocide: Speech, Power, Violence: Balkans experiences of 1990s." Media in Democracy Institute and United States Holocaust Memorial Museum, April 2010.

LaDuke, Winona. "Who Owns America? Minority Land and Community Security." *The Winona LaDuke Reader: A Collection of Essential Writings.* Voyageur Press, 2022.

Lee, Ronan. *Myanmar's Rohingya Genocide: Identity, History and Hate Speech.* I.B. Tauris, 2021.

Leider, Jaques. "Rohingya: The History of a Muslim Identity in Myanmar Summary and Keywords." *Oxford Research Encyclopedia of Asian History,* January 2018.

Lifton, Robert Jay. *The Nazi Doctors: Medical Killing and the Psychology of Genocide.* Basic Books, 1986.

Lipka, Michael and David McClendon. "Why people with no religion are projected to decline as a share of the world's population." Pew Research Center, April 7, 2017.

Lipset, Seymour Martin. *Political Man: The Social Bases of Politics*. Doubleday, 1960.

Lipset, Seymour Martin and Earl Raab. *Politics of Unreason: Right-Wing Extremism in America, 1790-1970*. HarperCollins, 1970.

Little, David (ed.). *Peacemakers in Action: Profiles of Religion in Conflict Resolution*. Cambridge University Press, 2007.

Longman, Timothy. "Church Politics and the Genocide in Rwanda." *Journal of Religion in Africa*, Volume 31, No. 2, 2001.

Maisel, Sebastian. "Sectarian-Based Violence: The Case of the Yezidis in Iraq and Syria." MEI, July 2014.

Mako, Shamiran. "Negotiating Peace in Iraq's Disputed Territories: Modifying the Sinjar Agreement." Lawfare, January 2021.

McBride, James. "How Does the U.S. Spend Its Foreign Aid?" Council on Foreign Relations, October 2018.

McNeill, Brandon. "Comparing Horror: The Irreducible Steps of the Nazi Holocaust and ISIS Genocide Against the Yazidis." National Catholic Center of Holocaust Education at Seton Hill University, 2020.

Miles, Tom. "U.N. investigators cite Facebook role in Myanmar crisis." *Reuters*, 2018.

Miles-Yepez, Netanel (ed.). *The Common Heart: An Experience of Interreligious Dialogue*. Lantern Publishing & Media, 2006.

Milmo, Dan. "Rohingya sue Facebook for £150bn over Myanmar Genocide." *The Guardian*, December 2021.

Mizban, Hadi and Qassim Abdul-Zahara. "France's Macron visits Iraq's Mosul destroyed by IS war." *AP News*, August 2021.

Mozur, P. "A Genocide Incited on Facebook, With Posts from Myanmar's Military." *The New York Times*, October 2018.

Murad, Nadia. *The Last Girl: My Story of Captivity and My Fight Against the Islamic State*. Tim Duggan Books, 2017.

Nasa, Rahima. "A Survivor of the War in Bosnia Recounts His 'Most Unsettling' Memory." *Frontline*, March 2019.

National Park Service. "President Ulysses S. Grant and Federal Indian Policy." U.S. Department of the Interior.

Ndahiro, Kennedy. "In Rwanda, We Know All About Dehumanizing Language." *The Atlantic*, April 2019.

Nel, Werner Nicolaas. *Grievous Religious Persecution: A Conceptualisation of Crimes Against Humanity of Religious Persecution.* Wipf and Stock, 2020.

Nelson, Melissa K. "Time to Indigenize Conservation." *Sierra Club Magazine*, 2021.

Nelson, Melissa K. and Maya Harjo. "From Soil to Sky: Mending the Circle of Our Native Food Systems." Cultural Survival, September 2020.

Open Letter to Dr. Ibrahim Awwad Al-Badri, alias 'Abu Bakr Al-Baghdadi' and to the Fighters and Followers of the Self-Declared 'Islamic State.' The Royal Islamic Strategic Studies Center, 2014.

Oxfam. "Voices Rising: Rohingya Women's Priorities and Leadership in Myanmar and Bangladesh." Oxfam International, April 2020.

Packer, George. *Our Man: Richard Holbrooke and the End of the American Century.* Alfred A. Knopf Inc., 2019.

Parvaneh, Danush and Sigal Samuel. "China's secret internment camps." Vox, May 2019.

Pew Research Center. "Global Restrictions on Religion." Pew Research Center, December 2009.

Polastron, Lucien X. *Books on Fire: The Destruction of Libraries Throughout History.* Inner Traditions, 2007.

Power, Samantha. *A Problem from Hell: America and the Age of Genocide.* Basic Books, 2013.

Qiao Collective. "Xinjiang: A Report and Resource Compilation." Qiao Collective, September 2021.

Qin, Amy. "China targets Muslim Women in Push to Suppress Births in Xinjiang." *The New York Times*, May 2020.

Radu, Sintia, "China Expands Media Influence Abroad," *US News*, June 2019.

Ramzy, Austin and Chris Buckley. "'Absolutely No Mercy': Leaked Files Expose How China Organized Mass Detentions of Muslims." *The New York Times*, 2019.

Rashid International, Yazda, and EAMENA Project. "Destroying the Soul of the Yazidis: Cultural Heritage Destruction During the Islamic State's Genocide Against the Yazidis." 2019.

Reiff, David. *In Praise of Forgetting.* Yale University Press, 2016.

Religions for Peace. "Rejecting Violent Religious Extremism and Advancing Shared Well-being." The Forum for Peace in Muslim Societies, December 2014.

"The Revival of Slavery Before the Final Hour." *Dabiq*, Issue 4 (15).

Rhodewalt, Frederick and Benjamin Peterson. "The Self and Intergroup Attitudes: Connecting 'Fragile' Personal and Collective Self-Concepts." Psychology Press, November 2010.

Roberts, Sean R. *The War on the Uyghurs: China's Internal Campaign against a Muslim Minority.* Princeton University Press, 2020.

Roscigno, Saverio. "Ethnic Division, Music and Violence: The Case of the 1994 Rwandan Genocide." Ohio State University, April 2021.

Rothschild, Mike. "Why Does the QAnon Conspiracy Thrive Despite All its Unfulfilled Prophecies." *TIME*, June 2021.

Russer, Nathan, et al. "Cultural Erasure." Australian Strategic Policy Institute, 2020.

Sacks, Jonathan. *The Dignity of Difference: How to Avoid the Clash of Civilizations*. Bloomsbury Continuum, 2002.

Sacks, Jonathan. *Not in God's Name: Confronting Religious Violence*. Schocken, 2015.

Sands, Philippe. *East West Street: On the Origins of "Genocide" and "Crimes Against Humanity."* Vintage, 2016.

Swanson, Ana et al. "U.S. Effort to Combat Forced Labor Targets Corporate China Ties." *The New York Times*, December 23, 2021.

Saydo, Said. "Geraubte Kindheit." Stapelfeld, Germany, Meeting translation by Sister Makrina Finlay, February 12, 2020.

Sengupta, Somini et al. "There's a Global Plan to Conserve Nature. Indigenous People Could Lead the Way." *The New York Times*, 2021.

Schneider, Gerald, Patrick M. Weber. "Punishing Putin: EU Sanctions Are More than Paper Tigers." stars for Leaders of the Next Generation, February 2018.

Schreiber, Mordecai. *Explaining the Holocaust: How and Why It Happened*. Cascade Books, 2015.

Security Council Report. "Security Council Deadlocks and Uniting for Peace: An Abridged History." Whatsinblue.org, October 2013.

Serlin, Ilene A. et al (eds.). *Integrated Care for the Traumatized: A Whole-Person Approach*. Rowman and Littlefield Publishers, 2019.

Shamdasani, Ravina. "Press briefing notes on Iraq and Bahrain." United Nations Human Rights Office of the High Commissioner, September 2014.

Sherwood, Harriet. "Religion in the US 'worth more than Google and Apple combined.'" *The Guardian*, September 2016.

Sidik, Qelbinur. "Full Statement." Accessed at https://uyghurtribunal.com/wp-content/uploads/2021/06/04-0930-JUN-21-UT-FW-005-Qelbinur-Sidik-English-1.pdf.

Singh, Anurag. "Madhya Pradesh Freedom of Religion Bill, 2021 passed in Assembly." *The New Indian Express*, March 8, 2021.

Snyder, Julia and Daniel Weiss. *Scripture and Violence*. Routledge, 2020.

Southwick, Steven M. and Dennis S. Charney. *Resilience: The Science of Mastering Life's Greatest Challenges*. Cambridge University Press, 2012.

Staub, Ervin. "Genocide and Mass Killing: Origins, Prevention, Healing and Reconciliation." *Political Psychology*, Volume 21, No. 2, June 2000.

Stowasser, Barbara Freyer. "The End is Near: Minor and Major Signs of the Hour in Islamic Texts and Contexts." Georgetown University.

Southerland, Dan. "After 50 years, Tibetans Recall the Cultural Revolution." Radio Free Asia, August 9, 2016.

Swart, Mia. "'Music to kill to': Rwandan genocide survivors remember RTLM." *Al-Jazeera*, June 7, 2020.

Tanenbaum Center for Interreligious Understanding. *Religion, Law, and the Role of Force*. Edited by Joseph Coffey and Charles Matthews. Transnational Publishers, 2002.

Taylor, Adam. "The Battle Over the World 'Rohingya.'" *The Washington Post*, April 26, 2019.

Tillman, Zoe. "Trump Gave Capitol Rioters The Language To Defend The Insurrection And Deny Reality." *BuzzFeed News*, July 17, 2021.

Treuer, David. "Return the National Parks to the Tribes." *The Atlantic*, May 2021.

Tucker, Patrick. "Why Do People Join ISIS? Here's What They Say When You Ask Them." Defense One, December 2015.

Uddin, Nasir. "Who are the Rohingya? Life through Roshang, Arakan, and Rakhine State." In *The Rohingya: An Ethnography of Subhuman Life.* Oxford University Press, 2021.

UK Parliament. "Written evidence from the Humanitarian Intervention Centre." November 2013.

Ullah, Akm Ahsan. "Rohingya Refugees to Bangladesh: Historical Exclusions and Contemporary Marginalization." *Journal of Immigrant & Refugee Studies* 9, June 2011.

United States Department of Justice. "Federal Bias Categories Included by State Laws." Updated 2 August 2021.

United States Holocaust Memorial Museum. "Burma's Path to Genocide."

United Nations. "United Nations Strategy and Plan of Action on Hate Speech." May 2019.

United Nations. "Universal Declaration of Human Rights." December 1948.

United Nations. *World Economic and Social Survey,* 2017.

United Nations Human Rights Office of the High Commissioner. "Statement of the UN High Commissioner for Human Rights, Zeid Ra'ad Al Hussein, at the 31st session of the Human Rights Council in Geneva, February 29, 2016."

United Nations Office on Genocide Prevention and the Responsibility to Protect. "Definitions."

United Nations Office on Genocide Prevention and the Responsibility to Protect. "Plan of Action for Religious Leaders and Actors to Prevent Incitement to Violence that Could Lead to Atrocity Crimes." July 2017.

United Nations Educational Scientific and Cultural Organization. "Lalish Temple." UNESCO World Heritage Centre, April 2020.

United Nations Human Rights Council. "Report of the detailed findings of the Independent International Fact-Finding Mission on Myanmar." 2018.

United Nations Human Rights Council. "'They came to destroy': ISIS Crimes Against the Yazidis." Independent International Commission on Inquiry of the Syrian Arab Republic, 2016.

University of Oxford. "Conspiracy beliefs reduce the following of government coronavirus guidance." May 2020.

USAID. "Shared Interest: How USAID Enhances U.S. Economic Growth." US Agency for International Development, May 2018.

USAID. "Where We Work: Iraq." 2021.

Uyghur Human Rights Project. "No Space Left to Run: China's Transnational Repression of Uyghurs." UHRP, June 2021.

Volkan, Vamik D. *Killing in the Name of Identity: A Study of Bloody Conflicts.* Pitchstone Publishing, 2006.

Vrdoljak, Ana Filipa. "The Criminalisation of the International Destruction of Cultural Heritage." SSRN, October 2015.

Wade, Francis. *Myanmar's Enemy Within: Buddhist Violence and the Making of a Muslim 'Other'.* Zed Books, 2017.

Walters, James. *Loving Your Neighbor in An Age of Religious Conflict.* Jessica Kingsley Publishers, 2019.

Walton, Johnny. "Improving Mental Health in Iraq." The Borgen Project, December 2020.

Walsh, Declan. "How Local Guerrilla Fighters Routed Ethiopia's Powerful Army." *The New York Times,* July 11, 2021.

Wang, Christoph Nedopil. "China Belt and Road Initiative (BRI) Investment Report 2020." Green Finance & Development Center, January 2021.

Wang, Qunyong and Xinyu Lin. "Does religious beliefs affect economic growth? Evidence from provincial-level panel data in China." *China Economic Review*, Volume 31 (pp. 277-287) December 2014.

"War, the UN and humanitarian intervention according to Pope John Paul II." *La Stampa*, August 2014.

Ware, Anthony and Costas Laoutides. *Myanmar's 'Rohingya' Conflict*. Oxford University Press, 2018.

Westcott, Tom. "Uptick in suicides signals deepening mental health crisis for Iraq's Yazidis." *The New Humanitarian*, July 2019.

White, Eric M. "Interior vs. war: The development of the Bureau of Indian Affairs and The Transfer Debates, 1849-1880." James Madison University, 2012.

Whitt, Laurelyn and Alan Clarke. *North American Genocides: Indigenous Nations, Settler Colonialism, and International Law.* Cambridge University Press, 2019.

Wilkerson, Isabel. *Caste: The Origins of Our Discontents*. Random House, 2020.

Woodward, Aylin. "European colonizers killed so many indigenous Americans that the planet cooled down, a group of researchers concluded." *Insider*, February 2019.

The World Bank. "Breaking Out of Fragility: A Country Economic Memorandum for Diversification and Growth in Iraq." World Bank Group, September 2020.

The World Bank. "Getting to Know the World Bank." World Bank Group, July 2012.

World Conference against Racism, Racial Discrimination, Xenophobia and Related Intolerance. "Declaration." The United Nations, 2001.

Yale Macmillan Center Genocide Studies Program. "Before It's Too Late - A Report Concerning the Ongoing Genocide and Persecution Endured by the Yazidis in Iraq, and Their Need for Immediate Protection." Persecution Prevention Project, June 2019.

Zambelich, Ariel and Cassi Alexandra. "In Their Own Words: The 'Water Protectors' of Standing Rock." *NPR*, December 2016.

Zenz, Adrian. "Sterilizations, IUDs, and Mandatory Birth Control." The Jamestown Foundation, June 2020.

ENDNOTES

1   Klug, Foster, "Rohingya say Myanmar targeted the educated in the genocide." *AP News*, 5 June 2018.

2   Lee, Ronan, *Myanmar's Rohingya Genocide: Identity, History and Hate Speech*. I.B. Tauris, 2021, p.1.

3   Committee on Foreign Affairs House of Representatives, "Iraq and Syria Genocide Emergency Relief and Accountability." 3 October 2017.

4   Ramzy, Austin and Chris Buckley, "Absolutely No Mercy: Leaked Files Expose How China Organized Mass Detentions of Muslims." *The New York Times*, 2019.

5   Human Rights Watch, "I Saw It with My Own Eyes." 2010.

6   Charleston, Steven, *Ladder to the Light: An Indigenous Elder's Meditations on Hope and Courage*. 2021, p. 15.

7   Final draft, as of September 2014, for a UN Resolution on Religicide, written by the Hashemite Kingdom of Jordan but never published or submitted for vote.

8   Ibid.

9   Lipka, Michael and David McClendon, "Why people with no religion are projected to decline as a share of the world's population." Pew Research Center, 7 April 2017.

[10]   Armstrong, Karen, *Fields of Blood: Religion and the History of Violence.* Alfred A. Knopf Inc., 2014, pp. 317-18.

[11]   Dadrian, Vahakn, "The Role of Turkish Physicians in the World War I Genocide of Ottoman Armenians." *Holocaust and Genocide Studies*, Vol.1, No. 2, 1986.

[12]   Ibid.

[13]   Ihrig, Stefan. *Justifying Genocide: Germany and the Armenians from Bismarck to Hitler.* Harvard University Press, 2016, p. 95.

[14]   Ibid., p. 103.

[15]   Ibid.

[16]   Wilkerson, Isabel, *Caste: The Origins of Our Discontents.* Random House, 2020, p. 80.

[17]   Ibid., p. 81.

[18]   Ibid., p. 88.

[19]   Schreiber, Mordecai, *Explaining the Holocaust.* Cascade Books, 2015, p. 10; Barnett, Victoria, "A Prelude to the Nazi Genocide of the Jews: The Rise of Religious Ethno-nationalism in Interwar Europe." United States Holocaust Memorial Museum, March 2019, p.3.

[20]   Schreiber, Mordecai, *Explaining the Holocaust.* Cascade Books, 2015, p. 12.

[21]   Ovenden, Richard. *Burning the Books: A History of the Deliberate Destruction of Knowledge.* The Belknap Press of Harvard University Press, 2020, p. 154.

[22]   Sands, Phillipe. *East West Street: On the Origins of "Genocide" and "Crimes Against Humanity."* Alfred A. Knopf Inc., 2016, p. 336.

[23]   Ibid., p. 361.

[24]   Ibid., p. 364.

[25] Ndahiro, Kenneth, "In Rwanda, We Know All About Dehumanizing Language," *The Atlantic*, April 2019.

[26] Swart, Mia, "'Music to kill to': Rwandan genocide survivors remember RTLM," *Al-Jazeera*, 7 June 2020.

[27] Roscigno, Saverio, "Ethnic Division, Music and Violence: The Case of the 1994 Rwandan Genocide." Ohio State University, April 2021.

[28] Longman, Timothy, "Church Politics and the Genocide in Rwanda." *Journal of Religion in Africa*, 2001, p. 167.

[29] Ibid., p. 164.

[30] Andreopoulos, George J., "ethnic cleansing," *Encyclopædia Britannica*.

[31] Kurspahic, Kemal, "Speech, Power, Violence: Balkans experiences of 1990s." United States Holocaust Memorial Museum, April 2010, p. 6.

[32] Ibid., p. 6.

[33] Packer, George, *Our Man: Richard Holbrooke and the End of the American Century*, Alfred A. Knopf Inc., 2019, p. 225.

[34] Kurspahic, Kemal, "Speech, Power, Violence: Balkans experiences of 1990s." United States Holocaust Memorial Museum, April 2010, p. 7.

[35] Nasa, Rahima, "A Survivor of the War in Bosnia Recounts His 'Most Unsettling' Memory." *Frontline*, March 2019.

[36] Bennett, Georgette F., *Thou Shalt Not Stand Idly By: How One Woman Confronted the Greatest Humanitarian Crisis of Our Time*. Wicked Son/Post Hill Press, 2021, p. 210.

[37] Zelalem, Zecharias, "'They Started Burning the Homes: Ethiopians Say Their Towns are Being Razed in Ethnic Cleansing Campaign." *Vice World News*, 27 February 2021.

38 Ibid.

39 Walsh, Declan, "How Local Guerrilla Fighters Routed Ethiopia's Powerful Army." *The New York Times*, 11 July 2021.

40 Abu Bakr Naji, *The Management of Savagery: The Most Critical Stage Through Which the Umma Will Pass*. Joseph M. Olin Institute for Strategic Studies at Harvard University, May 2006.

41 Armstrong, Karen, *Fields of Blood: Religion and the History of Violence*. Albert A. Knopf Inc., 2014, p. 294.

42 Polastron, Lucien, *Books on Fire: The Destruction of Libraries Throughout History*. Inner Traditions, 2004, p. 212.

43 Ibid., p. 180.

44 Ibid., p. 217.

45 Ovenden, Richard. *Burning the Books: A History of the Deliberate Destruction of Knowledge*. The Belknap Press of Harvard University Press, 2020, p. 154.

46 Polastron, Lucien, *Books on Fire: The Destruction of Libraries Throughout History*. Inner Traditions, 2004, p. 225.

47 Ibid., pp. 229-231.

48 Beech, Hannah, Saw Nang and Marlise Simons, "'Kill All you See': In a First, Myanmar Soldiers Tell of Rohingya Slaughter." *The New York Times*, September 2020.

49 Ehrenkranz, Joseph and David Coppola (eds.). *Religion and Violence and Peace*. Sacred Heart University Press, 2000, p. 22.

50 Stowasser, Barbara Freyer, "The End is Near: Minor and Major Signs of the Hour in Islamic Texts and Contexts." Georgetown University, p. 1.

51 Ibid., p. 5.

52   Sacks, Jonathan, *Not in God's Name*. Schocken Books, 2015.

53   United Nations, "Plan of Action for Religious Leaders
      and Actors to Prevent Incitement to Violence that
      Could Lead to Atrocity Crimes." July 2017, p. 2.

54   University of Oxford, "Conspiracy beliefs reduce the
      following of government coronavirus guidance." May 2020.

55   Armstrong, Karen, *Fields of Blood: Religion and
      the History of Violence*, Knopf, 2014, p. 11.

56   Ehrenkranz, Joseph and David Coppola
      eds., *Religion and Violence and Peace*. Sacred
      Heart University Press, 2000, p. 32.

57   Fromm, Erich, *Escape from Freedom*. Farrar
      & Rhinehart Inc, 1941, p. 270.

58   Greene, David and Masha Gessen, "The Brothers'
      Examines Motivation Behind Boston Marathon
      Bombing." NPR Morning Edition, April 2015.

59   Armstrong, Karen, *Fields of Blood: Religion and the
      History of Violence*. Albert A. Knopf Inc., 2014, p. 301.

60   Arendt, Hanna, *The Origins of Totalitarianism*.
      Meridian Books, 1958, p. 437.

61   Rothschild, Mike, "Why Does the QAnon Conspiracy
      Thrive Despite All its Unfulfilled Prophecies." *TIME*, 2021.

62   Hoffer, Eric, *The True Believer: Thoughts on the Nature
      of Mass Movements*. Harper & Brothers, 1951, p. 96.

63   Jayson, Sharon and Kaiser Health News, "What
      Makes People Join Hate Groups?" 2017.

64   WHAS11 Staff, "Here are all of the Kentucky residents
      charged in Capitol riots." 18 January 2021.

[65] Sacks, Jonathan, *Not in God's Name.*
Schocken Books, 2015, p. 3.

[66] Lifton, Robert Jay, *The Nazi Doctors: Medical Killing and the Psychology of Genocide.* Basic Books, Inc., 1986, pp. 15-16.

[67] FBI National Press Office, "FBI Releases Updated 2020 Hate Crime Statistics." October 2021.

[68] Ibid.

[69] Anti-Defamation League, "The ADL Global 100: An Index of Antisemitism." 2021.

[70] United States Department of Justice, "Federal Bias Categories Included by State Laws." Updated 2 August 2021.

[71] NJPS translation. Quoted in: Weiss, Daniel H. and Julia Snyder, *Scripture and Violence.* Taylor & Francis, 2020.

[72] English Standard Version.

[73] Abdul Haleem Version.

[74] Pew Research Center, "Global Restrictions on Religion." 2009.

[75] Sahih International Translation.

[76] Royal Aal al-Bayt Institute for Islamic Thought.

[77] *Open Letter to Dr. Ibrahim Awwad Al-Badri, alias 'Abu Bakr Al-Baghdadi' and to the Fighters and Followers of the Self-Declared 'Islamic State.'* The Royal Islamic Strategic Studies Center, 2014.

[78] Ibid.

[79] Ibid.

[80] Coffey, Joseph and Charles Matthews (eds), *Religion, Law, and the Role of Force.* Transnational Publishers, 2002, p. 22.

[81] New International Version.

[82] New American Bible Revised Addition.

83 Ricardo Esquiva Ballestas in Tanenbaum Center for Interreligious Understanding. *Peacemakers in Action: Profiles of Religion in Conflict Resolution.* 2007.

84 English Standard Version.

85 King James Bible.

86 English Standard Version.

87 New American Bible Revised Addition.

88 Banki, Judy Email to Jerry White, 30 September 2020.

89 Hume, Robert E., "Hinduism and War," *The American Journal of Theology,* 1916, p. 33.

90 Quoted in: Penny, D. H., *Ministers of Vengeance: God's Rules of Engagement.* Westbow Press, 2018.

91 Translated by Ralph T.H. Griffith.

92 Chiu, Yvonne, "Non-Violence, Asceticism, and the Problem of Buddhist Nationalism." Genealogy, 2020, p. 2.

93 Arnold, Dan and Alicia Turner, "Why Are We Surprised When Buddhists Are Violent." *The New York Times,* 5 March 2018.

94 Ibid., p. 8.

95 Ibid., p. 4.

96 Ibid., p. 4.

97 Jenkins, Stephen, "Making Merit through Warfare and Torture." Oxford University Press, 2010, p. 67.

98 Ehrenkranz, Joseph and David Coppola (eds.). *Religion and Violence and Peace,* Sacred Heart University Press, 2000, p. 32.

99 Sacks, Jonathan, *Not in God's Name.* Schocken Books, 2015, p. 241.

100 Common English Bible with Apocrypha.

[101] Snyder, Julia and Daniel Weiss, *Scripture and Violence*. Routledge, 2020, p. 40.

[102] Ford, David, Unpublished Paper.

[103] Gottlieb, Roger S., *Liberating Faith: Religious Voices for Justice, Peace, & Ecological Wisdom.* Rowman & Littlefield Publishers, 2003.

[104] "Yogyakarta Statement: Shared Values and Commitments," 2015.

[105] Ibid.

[106] Ehrenkranz, Joseph & David Coppola eds., *Religion and Violence and Peace*. Sacred Heart University Press, 2000, p. 37.

[107] Sacks, Jonathan, *Not in God's Name*. Schocken Books, 2015, p. 179.

[108] Rashid International, Yazda and EAMENA Project, "Destroying the Soul of the Yazidis: Cultural Heritage Destruction During the Islamic State's Genocide Against the Yazidis." 2019.

[109] United Nations Human Rights Council, "'They came to destroy': ISIS Crimes Against the Yazidis." 2016, p. 6.

[110] Ibid., p. 8.

[111] Ibid., p. 6.

[112] Ibid.

[113] Human Rights Watch, "Genocide in Iraq: The Anafal Campaign Against the Kurds." 1993.

[114] Durkheim, Emile. "Introduction: Durkheim's writings in sociology and social psychology," *Emile Durkheim: Selected Writings*. Cambridge University Press, August 2012.

115 Durkheim, Emile, "Anomie and the Moral Structure of Industry," *Emile Durkheim: Selected Writings*. Cambridge University Press, August 2012.

116 "The Revival of slavery before the final hour." *Dabiq*, Issue 4.

117 Ibid.

118 Ibid.

119 Interview with Mahmoud Khero from Sister Makrina Finlay.

120 Interview with Mahmoud Khero from Sister Makrina Finlay.

121 Saydo, Said, "Geraubte Kindheit." Stapelfeld, Germany, 12 February 2020.

122 "The Revival of slavery before the final hour." *Dabiq*, Issue 4.

123 Ibid.

124 Murad, Nadia, *The Last Girl: My Story of Captivity and My Fight Against the Islamic State*. Tim Duggan Books, 2017.

125 Committee on Foreign Affairs House of Representatives, "Women Under ISIS Rule: From Brutality to Recruitment." U.S. Government Publishing Office, 2015.

126 Interviews from 2018 with Sr. Makrina and Yazidi survivor from Tal Qasab, Shingal.

127 George, Susannah, "Yazidi women welcomed back to the faith." UNHCR USA, 2015.

128 Ibid.

129 Hosseini, Behnaz, "Yazidis' Illegitimate Children and a Crisis of Identity." July 2019.

130 Twitter @murad_isamael, April 2019.

[131] Arraf, Jane, "ISIS Forced Them Into Sexual Slavery. Finally, They've Reunited With Their Children." *The New York Times*, 12 March 2021.

[132] Westcott, Tom, "Uptick in suicides signals deepening mental health crisis for Iraq's Yazidis." *The New Humanitarian*, July 2019.

[133] Yale Macmillan Center Genocide Studies Program, "Before It's Too Late—A Report Concerning the Ongoing Genocide and Persecution Endured by the Yazidis in Iraq, and Their Need for Immediate Protection." 2019.

[134] Dakhil, Vian, "Yazidi MP's emotional appeal to save Iraq's hunted minority." *euronews*, 8 August 2014, Accessed at https://www.youtube.com/watch?v=YJKHBnQXyRI.

[135] The Borgen Project, "Improving Mental Health in Iraq." 2020.

[136] Amnesty International, "Dead Land Islamic State's Deliberate Destruction of Iraq's Farmland."

[137] Iraq Food Security Cluster Partners, "Sinjar Assessment: FSC Partners Report." August 2017, p. 56.

[138] Amnesty International, "Dead Land Islamic State's Deliberate Destruction of Iraq's Farmland."

[139] Ibid.

[140] Kurdistan 24, "Yezidi spiritual council revokes statement, will not accept children of ISIS rape victims." 2019.

[141] Amnesty International, "Dead Land Islamic State's Deliberate Destruction of Iraq's Farmland."

[142] Ibid.

[143] Ibid., p. 18.

[144] Ibid.

145 Ibid.

146 Ibid., p. 22.

147 Rashid International, Yazda and EAMENA Project. "Destroying the Soul of the Yazidis: Cultural Heritage Destruction During the Islamic State's Genocide Against the Yazidis." 2019.

148 United Nations Human Rights Office of the High Commissioner, "Press briefing notes on Iraq and Bahrain." 5 September 2014.

149 Yale Macmillan Center Genocide Studies Program, "Before It's Too Late—A Report Concerning the Ongoing Genocide and Persecution Endured by the Yazidis in Iraq, and Their Need for Immediate Protection." 2019.

150 Sister Makrina Finlay.

151 Arab News, "Amal Clooney brings to justice Daesh woman who oversaw rape, enslavement of Yazidis." June 2021.

152 Mako, Shamiran, "Negotiating Peace in Iraq's Disputed Territories: Modifying the Sinjar Agreement," Lawfare, January 2021; Yezidi Organization for Documentation, "Statement of Yazidi Elites, Leaders, and Institutions Regarding the Sinjar Agreement between Baghdad and Erbil." 2020.

153 Mizban, Hadi and Qassim Abdul-Zahara, "France's Macron visits Iraq's Mosul destroyed by IS war." *AP News*, 2021.

154 Sengupta, Somini et al., "There's a Global Plan to Conserve Nature. Indigenous People Could Lead the Way." *The New York Times*, 2021.

155 Jangiz, Khazan, "US launches million-dollar program to invest in Kurdistan Region agriculture." Rudaw, 2021.

156 World Bank, "Breaking Out of Fragility." IMF, Article IV, 2019.

157 Conversation between Sister Makrina Finlay and Ahmed Shammo in 2021.

158 ShareAmerica, "A Uighur Survivor Story: Mihrigul Tursun." December 12, 2018, Accessed at https://www.youtube.com/watch?v=WsHEIhbUR9Q.

159 Ibid.

160 Albert, Eleanor and Lindsay Maizland, "Religion in China." The Council on Foreign Relations, September 2020.

161 "Chinese Ethnic Groups: Overview Statistics." Albert & Maizland, 2020.

162 Kang, Dake, "Terror and Terrorism: Xinjiang eases its grip, but fear remains." *AP News*, October 2021.

163 Sidik, Qelbinur, "Full Statement." Accessed at https://uyghurtribunal.com/wp-content/uploads/2021/06/04-0930-JUN-21-UTFW-005-Qelbinur-Sidik-English-1.pdf.

164 Çaksu, A., "Islamophobia, Chinese Style: Total Internment of Uyghur Muslims by the People's Republic of China." *Islamophobia Studies Journal*, 2020.

165 Testimony from Zumret Dawut, Accessed at: https://shahit.biz/eng/viewentry.php?entryno=5524.

166 Bovingdon, Gardner, *The Uyghurs: Strangers in Their Own Land*. Columbia University Press, 2010.

167 Finley, Joanne N. Smith, *The Art of Symbolic Resistance*. 2013, pp. 19-20.

168 Human Rights Watch, "Eradicating Ideological Viruses." 2018.

169 Roberts, Sean, *The War on the Uighurs: China's Internal Campaign against a Muslim Minority.* Princeton UP, 2020.

170 Kaltman, Blaine, *Under the Heel of the Dragon: Islam, Racism, Crime, and the Uighur in China.* Ohio UP, 2007, pp. 130-3.

171 Roberts, Sean, *The War on the Uighurs: China's Internal Campaign against a Muslim Minority.* Princeton UP, 2020, pp. 69-70.

172 Ibid., p. 70.

173 Ibid., p. 77.

174 Human Rights Watch, "Eradicating Ideological Viruses." 2018.

175 Amnesty International USA, "Xinjiang Uighur Autonomous Region."

176 Zenz, A., "Sterilizations, IUDs, and Mandatory Birth Control: The CCP's Campaign to Suppress Uyghur Birthrates in Xinjiang." The Jamestown Foundation, 2020.

177 Testimony from Zumret Dawut, Accessed at: https://shahit.biz/eng/viewentry.php?entryno=5524.

178 Amnesty International USA, "Xinjiang Uighur Autonomous Region."

179 Çaksu, A., "Islamophobia, Chinese Style: Total Internment of Uyghur Muslims by the People's Republic of China." *Islamophobia Studies Journal*, 2020.

180 Ibid.

181 Qin, A., "China Targets Muslim Women in Push to Suppress Births in Xinjaing." *The New York Times*, 2021.

182 Ruser, Nathan, et al., *Cultural Erasure.* Australian Strategic Policy Institute, 2020.

[183] Buckley, C. and Ramzy, A., "Leaked China Files Show Internment Camps Are Ruled by Secrecy and Spying." *The New York Times*, 2019.

[184] "Entry # 10553." Accessed at https://shahit.biz/eng/#view.

[185] Abudu, Shalamu, et. al, "A Karez System's Dilemma: A Cultural Heritage on a Shelf or Still a Viable Technique for Water Resiliency in Arid Regions." 2019.

[186] Uyghur Human Rights Project, "No Space Left to Run: China's Transnational Repression." 2021.

[187] Ibid.

[188] Scull, Erika, "Environmental Health Challenges in Xinjiang." Wilson Center, 2008.

[189] Ibid.

[190] Denyer, Simon, "China's war on terror becomes all-out attack on Islam in Xinjiang." *The Washington Post*, September 2014.

[191] Denyer, Simon, "Former Inmates of China's Muslim 'reeducation' camps tell of brainwashing, torture." *The Washington Post*, May 2018.

[192] Trombert, É., "The Karez Concept in Ancient Chinese Sources Myth or Reality?" pp. 115-150.

[193] Zenz, A., "'Thoroughly reforming them towards a healthy heart attitude': China's political re-education campaign in Xinjiang." Central Asian Survey, 2019.

[194] Ibid.

[195] Qiao Collective, "Xinjiang: A Report and Resource Compilation."

196 Qin, Amy, and Edward Wong, "Why Calls to Boycott Mulan Over Concerns About China Are Growing." *The New York Times*, September 2020.

197 Instagram @qiaocollective, 2020.

198 Kao, Jeff et al., "'We Are Very Free Here.'" *The New York Times*, 22 June 2021.

199 Testimony from Zumret Dawut, Accessed at: https://shahit.biz/eng/viewentry.php?entryno=5524.

200 Nichols, Michelle, "U.S., UK, Germany clash with China at U.N. over Xinjiang." *Reuters*, 21 May 2018.

201 Wang, C. N., "China Belt and Road Initiative (BRI) Investment Report 2020." January 2021.

202 Sawnson, Ana, Catie Edmondson and Edward Wong, "U.S. Effort to Combat Forced Labor Targets Corporate China Ties." *The New York Times*, 23 December 2021.

203 Denyer, Simon, "Jesus won't save you—President Xi Jinping will, Chinese Christians told." *The Washington Post*, November 2017.

204 Biden, Joseph, "Remarks by President Biden on America's Place in the World." 4 February 2021.

205 Human Rights Watch, "Illegal Organizations." July 2018.

206 Arya, T.G., "China was only a part of the Mongol Yuan Dynasty, it was neither the authority nor the inheritor of the dynasty." November 2019.

207 Gruber, Elmar R., *From the Heart of Tibet*. Shambhala, 2010, p. 119.

208 Sutherland, Dan, "After 50 years, Tibetans Recall the Cultural Revolution." *Radio Free Asia*, 9 August 2016.

209 Keliher, Macabe and Hsinchao Wu, "How to Discipline 90 Million People." *The Atlantic*, 7 April 2015.

210 "Xi Calls for Improved Religious Work." 24 April 2016.

211 Gao, Charlotte, "Chinese Communist Party Vows to 'Sinicize Religions' in China." *The Diplomat*, 2017. (This dynamic is also described by the campaign to save Tibet at https://savetibet.org/party-above-buddhism/.)

212 Human Rights Watch, "Decision Ends Long-Standing Policy Allowing Nominal Self-Rule of Monasteries." March 2012.

213 "Party Above Buddhism." International Campaign for Tibet.

214 "2014 Report on International Religious Freedom: China (Includes Tibet, Hong Kong, and Macau)—Tibet." U.S. Department of State, October 2015.

215 "Party Above Buddhism." International Campaign for Tibet.

216 "Monks, Nuns Abandon Monasteries." Radio Free Asia.

217 "Our District Holds a Mobilization and Deployment Meeting for the Educational Practice Activities of 'Complying with the Four Standards and Striving to Be Advanced Monks and Nuns.'" Sohu, April 2020.

218 Tsultrim, Tenzin, "A Boiling Pot: The CCP's Increasingly Intrusive Surveillance in Tibet." *The Diplomat*, September 2018.

219 "Monks at Sera Monastery Lectured on Patriotism and Separatism." Tibet Watch, 29 March 2019.

220 "Party Above Buddhism." International Campaign for Tibet.

221 "The Region's 'Follow the Four Standards and Strive to Be Advanced Monks and Nuns' Educational Practice Activities Learning Exchange Symposium Was Held in Lhasa." December 2019.

222 "China: New Political Requirements for Tibetan Monastics." Human Rights Watch, 30 October 2018.

223 Shannan Municipal Party Committee United Front Work Department, "Shannan City Holds a Meeting on the Arrangement and Deployment of the Educational Practice Activities of 'Complying with the Four Standards and Striving to Be Advanced Monks and Nuns' in 2020." 14 April 2020.

224 "New Measures on reincarnation reveal Party's objectives of political control." International Campaign for Tibet, 15 August 2007.

225 "Dalai Lama Should Reincarnate Following Traditional Tibetan Practices, Tibetan Religious Leaders Say." International Campaign for Tibet, 27 November 2019.

226 "A Tibetan Nun in Gutsa Prison." 16 July 2009.

227 "Destruction, commercialization, fake replicas: UNESCO must protect Tibetan cultural heritage."

228 Save Tibet, "Party Above Buddhism."

229 "Tibetan Monk Dies After Living Two Years With Torture Injuries Sustained in Custody." Radio Free Asia, 24 April 2020.

230 "China detained two Tibetan monks for sharing illegal contents on social media." Tibet Express, 18 April 2018.

[231] "Monk from Tibet's Amdo Ngaba Arrested over
Social Media Posts on Tibetan Language." Central
Tibetan Administration, 5 October 2019.

[232] "Tibetan Monk Held Incommunicado for over One Year."
International Campaign for Tibet, 2 December 2020.

[233] "Party Above Buddhism." International
Campaign for Tibet.

[234] United Nations, Committee Against Torture,
"Concluding observations on the fifth periodic report
of China." 3 February 2016, CAT/C/CHN/CO/5.

[235] "Tibet: A Glossary of Repression." Human
Rights Watch, 19 June 2017.

[236] His Holiness the 14th Dalai Lama of Tibet, "Statement of
His Holiness the Dalai Lama on the Fiftieth Anniversary
of the Tibetan National Uprising Day." 2009.

[237] "60 Years of Chinese Misrul: Arguing Cultural Genocide
in Tibet." International Campaign for Tibet, 2012.

[238] Ibid.

[239] Central Tibetan Administration, "Tibet:
Proving Truth From Facts." 1996, p. 25.

[240] "COP21: His Holiness the Dalai Lama's message (Short
version)." *Tibet TV*, 2015, Accessed at https://www.
youtube.com/watch?v=u-4xJYowURw&t=12s.

[241] Hsu, Iris, "How many journalists are jailed
in China? Censorship means we don't know."
Committee to Protect Journalists, March 2019.

[242] Radu, Sintia, "China Expands Media
Influence Abroad." *US News*, June 2019.

[243] Ibid.

[244] Malho Tibetan Autonomous Prefecture Advanced Nationality Unity Prefecture Leading Unit Office, "It Must Be Made Clear that Involvement in an Incident of Instability is a Crime." 27 February 2014.

[245] Video at https://www.youtube.com/watch?v=RvBrulUVs44, minutes 4:28 and 6:50.

[246] "Developing technological totalitarianism in Tibet: Huawei and Hikvision." International Campaign for Tibet, 17 December 2018.

[247] Mozur, Paul, "One Month, 500,000 Face Scans: How China Is Using A.I. to Profile a Minority." *The New York Times*, 14 April 2019.

[248] Asher-Schapiro, Avi, "China found using surveillance firms to help write ethnic-tracking specs." *Reuters*, March 2021.

[249] Borak, Masha, "Chinese surveillance giant expanding in the US attracts scrutiny over possible targeting of Uyghurs." South China Morning Post, November 2020.

[250] Holden, Kevin, "Amid US-China Tensions, Tibetans Seize the Moment." The Diplomat, December 2020.

[251] Find additional resources at at https://www.umass.edu/rso/fretibet/do.html.

[252] Blinken, Antony, "New Frameworks for Countering Terrorism and Violent Extremism." 6 February 2016.

[253] United Nations Human Rights Office of the High Commissioner, "Statement of the UN High Commissioner for Human Rights, Zeid Ra'ad Al Hussein, at the 31st session of the Human Rights Council in Geneva, 29 February 2016."

254 Bielefeldt, Heiner, et al., *Freedom of Religion Or Belief: An International Law Commentary*. Oxford University, 2016, p. 11.

255 "This is what true leaders look like," High Commissioner Zeid Ra'ad Al Hussein's parting message. Office of the High Commissioner for Human Rights, 30 August 2018.

256 Lee, Ronan, *Myanmar's Rohingya Genocide: Identity, History and Hate Speech*. I.B. Tauris, 2021.

257 Blakemore, Erin, "Who are the Rohingya people?" *National Geographic*, 8 February 2019.

258 Ullah, Akm Ahsan, "Rohingya Refugees to Bangladesh: Historical Exclusions and Contemporary Marginalization." *Journal of Immigrant & Refugee Studies* 9, 2011.

259 Chan, Aye, "The Development of an Enclave in Arakan State of Burma." SOAS Bulletin of Burma Research, 2011.

260 Leider, Jaques, "Rohingya: The History of a Muslim Identity in Myanmar Summary and Keywords." *Oxford Research Encyclopedia of Asian History*, 2018.

261 Buchanan, Francis, "A Comparative Vocabulary of Some of the Languages Spoken in the Burma Empire." *Asiatic Researches* 5 (1799): 219-240. Reprinted in *SOAS Bulletin of Burma Research* 1, no. 1, (2003): 40-57. ISSN 1479-8484.

262 Ware, Anthony, and Costas Laoutides, *Myanmar's 'Rohingya' Conflict*. Oxford University Press, 2019.

263 Uddin, Nasir, "Who Are the Rohingya?: Life through Roshang, Arakan, and Rakhine State," *The Rohingya: An Ethnography of 'Subhuman' Life*. Oxford University Press, 2021.

264 Adam Taylor, "The Battle Over the World 'Rohingya.'" *The Washington Post*, 29 April 2016.

265 Blakemore, Erin, "Who are the Rohingya people?" *National Geographic*, 8 February 2019.

266 Ali, Mayyu, *Exodus: Between Genocide and Me.* Black Raven Publishers, 2019, p. 5.

267 Lee, Ronan, *Myanmar's Rohingya Genocide: Identity, History and Hate Speech.* I.B. Tauris, 2021, pp. 57-72.

268 Ibid., pp. 66-70.

269 Ibid., p. 72.

270 United States Holocaust Memorial Museum, "Burma's Path to Genocide."

271 Lee, Ronan, *Myanmar's Rohingya Genocide: Identity, History and Hate Speech.* I.B. Tauris, 2021, p. 80.

272 Wade, Francis, *Myanmar's Enemy Within: Buddhist Violence and the Making of a Muslim 'Other.'* Zed Books, 2017.

273 Lee, Ronan, "Heritage destruction in Myanmar's Rakhine state: legal and illegal iconoclasm." International Journal of Heritage Studies, 2020.

274 Wade, Francis, *Myanmar's Enemy Within: Buddhist Violence and the Making of a Muslim 'Other.'* Zed Books, 2017.

275 United Nations Human Rights Council, "Report of the detailed findings of the Independent International Fact-Finding Mission on Myanmar." September 2018.

276 Green, MacManus, and de la Cour Venning, "Genocide Achieved, Genocide Continues: Myanmar's Annihilation of the Rohingya." 2018, p. 16.

277 Ali, Mayyu, *Exodus: Between Genocide and Me.* Black Raven Publishers, 2019, p. 16.

[278] Green, MacManus, and de la Cour Venning, "Genocide Achieved, Genocide Continues: Myanmar's Annihilation of the Rohingya." 2018, p. 15.

[279] Ali, Mayyu, *Exodus: Between Genocide and Me.* Black Raven Publishers, 2019, p. 25.

[280] United Nations Human Rights Council, "Report of the detailed findings of the Independent International Fact-Finding Mission on Myanmar," September 2018.

[281] Justice Matters, "The Politics of Documentation: Narrative and the Rohingya Crisis."

[282] United Nations Human Rights Council, "Report of the detailed findings of the Independent International Fact-Finding Mission on Myanmar." September 2018.

[283] Beech, Hannah, Saw Nang and Marlise Simons, "'Kill All you See': In a First, Myanmar Soldiers Tell of Rohingya Slaughter." *The New York Times*, September 2020.

[284] United Nations Human Rights Council, "Report of the detailed findings of the Independent International Fact-Finding Mission on Myanmar." September 2018.

[285] Klug, F., "Rohingya say Myanmar targeted the educated in genocide." *AP News*, June 2018.

[286] Ibrahim, Azeem, *Rohingyas: Inside Myanmar's Hidden Genocide.* C. Hurst and Company Limited, 2016, p. 8.

[287] Lee, Ronan, *Myanmar's Rohingya Genocide: Identity, History and Hate Speech.* I.B. Tauris, 2021, p. 129.

[288] Amnesty International, "Myanmar: New Landmine Blasts Point to Deliberate Targeting of the Rohingya." 2017.

[289] Human Rights Watch, "Burma: New Satellite Images Confirm Mass Destruction." 2017.

[290] US State Department, "Documentation of Atrocities in Northern Rakhine State." 2019, pp. 9-10.

[291] Amnesty International, "Remaking Rakhine State." March 2018, p. 6.

[292] Amnesty International, "Myanmar: Scorched-earth campaign fuels ethnic cleansing of Rohingya from Rakhine State." 14 September 2017.

[293] Amnesty International, "Remaking Rakhine State." March 2018, pp. 7-9.

[294] Ibid., p. 13.

[295] Human Rights Watch, "Let Kar Satellite Imagery." 2020.

[296] Myanmar Now, "More than 190 homes set ablaze in Rakhine village." 2020.

[297] Chiu, Yvonne, "Non-Violence, Asceticism, and the Problem of Buddhist Nationalism." Genealogy, 2020.

[298] Wade, Francis, *Myanmar's Enemy Within: Buddhist Violence and the Making of a Muslim 'Other.'* Zed Books, 2017.

[299] Lee, Ronan, *Myanmar's Rohingya Genocide: Identity, History and Hate Speech.* I.B. Tauris, 2021, pp. 40-45.

[300] United Nations Human Rights Council, "Report of the detailed findings of the Independent International Fact-Finding Mission on Myanmar." September 2018.

[301] Crisis Group, "Buddhism and State Power in Myanmar." 2017.

[302] United Nations Human Rights Council, "Report of the detailed findings of the Independent International Fact-Finding Mission on Myanmar." September 2018.

[303] Wade, Francis, *Myanmar's Enemy Within: Buddhist Violence and the Making of a Muslim 'Other.'* Zed Books, 2017.

304 Miles, T., "U.N. investigators cite Facebook role in Myanmar crisis." *Reuters*, 2018.

305 Ibid.

306 Lee, Ronan, *Myanmar's Rohingya Genocide: Identity, History and Hate Speech.* I.B. Tauris, 2021, p. 193.

307 Mozur, P., "A Genocide Incited on Facebook, With Posts from Myanmar's Military." *The New York Times*, October 2018.

308 Milmo, Dan, "Rohingya sue Facebook for £150bn over Myanmar genocide." *The Guardian*, December 2021.

309 Advisory Commission on Rakhine State, "Towards a Peaceful, Fair and Prosperous Future for the People of Rakhine." August 2017.

310 United Nations High Commissioner for Refugees, "Rohingya Emergency." July 2019.

311 Goldman, Russell, "Myanmar's Coup, Explained." *The New York Times*, 29 November 2021.

312 Oxfam, "Voices rising: Rohingya Women's Priorities and Leadership in Myanmar and Bangladesh." July 2020.

313 Hammer, Joshua, "The Hidden City of Myanmar." *Smithsonian Magazine*, December 2019.

314 Grinde, Donald A. and Bruce E. Johanson. *Ecocide of Native America: Environmental Destruction of Indian Lands and Peoples.* Clear Light Publishers, 1994, p. 247.

315 The term "Indians" is a misnomer when applied to Indigenous Americans. The label was based on Christopher Columbus's mistaken assumption that, in his voyage of discovery, he had sailed to south Asia (and found natives of the Indus Valley) when he had

actually made landfall in the Bahamas. The authors use terms they hope are more accurate and respectful—i.e. Native Americans and Indigenous Americans.

[316] Woodward, Aylin, "European colonizers killed so many indigenous Americans that the planet cooled down, a group of researchers concluded." *Insider*, February 2019.

[317] Gagnon, Gregory Omer, *Culture and Customs of the Sioux Indians*. 2011.

[318] National Park Service, "President Ulysses S. Grant and Federal Indian Policy." p. 3.

[319] Chernow, Ron, *Grant*. Penguin Press, 2017, p. 657.

[320] White, Eric M., "Interior vs. war: The development of the Bureau of Indian Affairs and The Transfer Debates. 1849-1880," James Madison University, 2012, p. 10.

[321] Ibid., p. 2.

[322] Chernow, Ron, *Grant*. Penguin Press, 2017, p. 659.

[323] "Faith-Based Reservations," Accessed at http://nativeamericannetroots.net/diary/378.

[324] Chernow, Ron, *Grant*. Penguin Press, 2017, p. 659.

[325] Ibid., p. 830.

[326] Ibid., p. 834.

[327] Ibid., p. 835.

[328] History.com, "This Day in History: December 29."

[329] Herscher, Rebecca, "Key Moments in the Dakota Access Pipeline Fight." *NPR*, February 2017.

[330] Zambelich, Ariel and Cassi Alexandra, "In Their Own Words: The 'Water Protectors' of Standing Rock." *NPR*, December 2016.

331 Alvarez, Alex, *Native America and the Question of Genocide*. Rowman & Littlefield Publishers, 2014, p. 9.

332 Ibid., p. 14.

333 Dunbar-Ortiz, Roxanne, *An Indigenous People's History of the United States*. p. 9.

334 Whitt, L., and Clarke, A., *North American Genocides: Indigenous Nations, Settler Colonialism, and International Law*. p. 66.

335 Grinde, Donald A. and Bruce E. Johanson, *Ecocide of Native America: Environmental Destruction of Indian Lands and Peoples*, p. 10.

336 Ibid.

337 Gumbel, Andrew, "Junípero Serra's brutal story in spotlight as pope prepares for canonization." *The Guardian*, September 2015.

338 Smith, Andrea for the Secretariat of the United Nations Permanent Forum on Indigenous Issues, "Indigenous Peoples and Boarding Schools: A comparative study."

339 Ibid.

340 Grinde, Donald A. and Bruce E. Johanson, *Ecocide of Native America: Environmental Destruction of Indian Lands and Peoples*. "Native American Environmental Testimonies: The Last Frontiers of Ecocide." 1994.

341 Ibid.

342 Phippen, J. Weston, "'Kill Every Buffalo You Can! Every Buffalo Dead is an Indian Gone.'" *The Atlantic*, May 2016.

343 Dunbar-Ortiz, Roxanne, *An Indigenous Peoples' History of the United States*. Beacon Press, 2014, p.143.

[344] Treuer, David, "Return the National Parks to the Tribes." *The Atlantic*, May 2021.

[345] Grinde, Donald A. and Bruce E. Johanson, *Ecocide of Native America: Environmental Destruction of Indian Lands and Peoples.*

[346] Cassady, J, "A Tundra of Sickness: The Uneasy Relationship between Toxic Waste, TEK, and Cultural Survival." *Arctic Anthropology*, 2007, pp. 87-98.

[347] Carelton College, "Impacts of Resource Development on American Indian Lands."

[348] Grinde, Donald A. and Bruce E. Johanson, *Ecocide of Native America: Environmental Destruction of Indian Lands and Peoples.*

[349] Kirkpatrick, Nick, et al. "Climate change fuels a water rights conflict built over a century of broken promises." *The Washington Post*, 22 November 2021.

[350] Grinde, Donald A. and Bruce E. Johanson, *Ecocide of Native America: Environmental Destruction of Indian Lands and Peoples.*

[351] United Nations Human Rights Council, "Report of the Special Rapporteur on the rights of indigenous peoples." November 2017, p. 3.

[352] Grinde, Donald A. and Bruce E. Johanson, *Ecocide of Native America: Environmental Destruction of Indian Lands and Peoples.* p. 238.

[353] Whitt, L., and Clarke, A, *North American Genocides: Indigenous Nations, Settler Colonialism, and International Law.* 2019, p. 57.

354 Carman, Diane, "Colorado should remove its monuments to genocide." *The Denver Post*, 26 May 2017.

355 Colorado Public Radio, "Colorado Civil War Soldier Statue Torn Down At The Capitol." June 2020.

356 Dunbar-Ortiz, Roxanne, *An Indigenous Peoples' History of the United States*, p. 156.

357 Ibid.

358 Ibid., p. 196.

359 Kimmerer, Robin Wall, *Braiding Sweetgrass: Indigenous Wisdom, Scientific Knowledge and the Teachings of Plants*. Milkweed Editions, 2015.

360 The Organization of American States, "American Declaration on the Rights of Indigenous Peoples."

361 IWGIA, "ILO Convention No. 169."

362 International Labour Organization, "About the ILO."

363 International Labour Organization, "Ratifications of C169."

364 Cooper, Joshua, "25 Years of ILO Convention 169." *Cultural Survival Quarterly Magazine*, March 2015.

365 International Labour Organization, "C169— Indigenous and Tribal Peoples Convention, 1989."

366 United Nations Human Rights Council, "Report of the Special Rapporteur on the rights of indigenous peoples." November 2017, p. 6.

367 LaDuke, Winona, "Who Owns America? Minority Land and Community Security." p 145.

368 Treuer, David, "Return the National Parks to the Tribes." *The Atlantic*, May 2021.

369 Nelson, Melissa K., "Time to Indigenize Conservation."

370 The Cultural Conservancy, "Native Foodways."

371 Treuer, David, "Return the National Parks to the Tribes." *The Atlantic*, May 2021.

372 Nelson, Melissa K. and Maya Harjo, "From Soil to Sky: Mending the Circle of Our Native Food Systems."

373 Robin Wall Kimmer, *Braiding Sweetgrass*. 2013.

374 United Nations Department of Economic and Social Affairs, "United Nations Declaration on the Rights of Indigenous Peoples."

375 The World Bank, "Operational Manual: OP 4.10—Indigenous Peoples."

376 OHCHR, "Special Rapporteur on the rights of indigenous peoples."

377 OHCHR, "Expert Mechanism on the Rights of Indigenous Peoples."

378 United Nations Department of Economic and Social Affairs, "Permanent Forum."

379 Universal Declaration of Human Rights, Article 2.

380 Universal Declaration of Human Rights, "Introduction," p. vi.

381 United Nations Human Rights, "About the Universal Declaration of Human Rights Translation Project."

382 Jensen, Steven L. B., *The Making of International Human Rights: The 1960s, Decolonization, and the Reconstruction of Global Values*. Cambridge University Press, 2016, p. 139.

383 Ibid.

384 Ibid., p. 154.

385 Jensen, Steven L. B. *The Making of International Human Rights: The 1960s, Decolonization, and the Reconstruction of Global Values*. New York, NY: Cambridge University

Press, 2016, p. 157-58. Citing U.N. testimony by Mr.
Richardson (Jamaica), Commission on Human Rights,
21st session, 820th meeting, March 24, 1965, p. 10.

386 Jensen, Steven L. B. *The Making of International
Human Rights: The 1960s, Decolonization, and the
Reconstruction of Global Values.* New York, NY:
Cambridge University Press, 2016, p. 154.

387 Ibid., p. 145.

388 Ibid., pp. 147-8.

389 Ibid., p. 170.

390 United Nations General Assembly, "Promotion
and protection of the right to freedom of
opinion and expression." October 2016, p. 6.

391 Ibid., p. 12.

392 International Criminal Court, "The States
Parties to the Rome Statute."

393 International Criminal Court, "Defendants."

394 Coleman, Michelle, "The Applicability of "Grievous
Religious Persecution" in International Criminal Law:
Response to Werner Nicolaas Nel." BYU Law, April 2021.

395 Ellis, Marc S., "The ICC's Role in Combatting
the Destruction of Cultural Heritage." 2017.

396 Carnegie Council for Ethics in International
Affairs, "Rethinking Cultural Genocide
Under International Law." April 2005.

397 UNESCO, "1954 Convention for the Protection of
Cultural Property in the Event of Armed Conflict."

398 Vrdoljak, Ana Filipa, "The Criminalization of the
International Destruction of Cultural Heritage." 2016.

399 United Nations Educational, Scientific, and Cultural Organization, "Text of the Convention for the Safeguarding of the Intangible Cultural Heritage."

400 Ellis, Marc S., "The ICC's Role in Combatting the Destruction of Cultural Heritage." 2017.

401 Ibid.

402 ICRC, "The Geneva Conventions of 12 August 1949," p. 31.

403 Ibid., p. 32.

404 Dinstein, Yoram, "The Right to Humanitarian Assistance." 2000, p. 1.

405 Ibid., p. 84.

406 Ibid., p. 86.

407 "Convention relating to the Status of Refugees," Article 1.

408 UNHCR, "The 1951 Convention Relating to the Status of Refugees and Its 1967 Protocol," p. 5.

409 Nel, Werner Nicolaas, *Grievous Religious Persecution: A Conceptualization of Crimes Against Humanity of Religious Persecution.* Wipf and Stock, December 2020, p. 19.

410 Gregory, Julie and Aditi Gorur, "Violence Based on Religion or Belief." Stimson Center, January 2021, p. 5.

411 Maucec, Gregor, "Law Development by the International Criminal Court as a Way to Enhance the Protection of Minorities—the Case for Intersectional Consideration of Mass Atrocities." March 2021, pp. 42-83.

412 Gregory, Julie and Aditi Gorur, "Violence Based on Religion or Belief." Stimson, January 2021, pp. 2-3.

413 Ibid., pp. 12-14.

414 Carnegie Commission on the Preventing Deadly Conflict, p. xxxv.

415 United Kingdom Parliament, "Intervention: When, Why, and How?" 2013.

416 General Assembly of the United Nations, "Emergency special sessions."

417 Staub, Ervin, "Genocide and Mass Killing: Origins, Prevention, Healing and Reconciliation." *Political Psychology*, June 2000.

418 Carnegie Commission on Preventing Deadly Conflict and David A. Hamburg, *Preventing Deadly Conflict*. DIANE Publishing, 1997.

419 "Full Speech of Shaykh Abdallah Bin Bayyah Delivered at the UN on Friday 14th July."

420 *La Stampa*, "War, the UN and humanitarian intervention according to Pope John Paul II." 26 August 2014.

421 Ibid.

422 Coffey, Joseph and Charles Matthews (eds), *Religion, Law, and the Role of Force in Conflict Resolution*. Transnational Publishers, 2002, pp. 96-97.

423 Ibid.

424 Mojzes, Paul, "Religion and Armed Humanitarian Intervention in the Former Yugoslavia." p. 142.

425 Ochs, Peter, *Religion without Violence: The Practice and Philosophy of Scriptural Reasoning*. 2020.

426 Cure Violence Global, "What We Do."

427 Ibid.

428 Ibid.

429 Cure Violence Global.

430 Little, David (ed), *Peacemakers in Action: Profiles of Religion in Conflict Resolution*. Cambridge University Press, 2007, p. 84.

431 Ibid., p. 68.

432 Carnegie Commission on Preventing Deadly Conflict and David A. Hamburg, *Preventing Deadly Conflict*. DIANE Publishing, 1997, p. 114.

433 Carnegie Commission on the Preventing Deadly Conflict, p. xxxviii.

434 Little, David (ed), *Peacemakers in Action: Profiles of Religion in Conflict Resolution*. Cambridge University Press, 2007.

435 Ibid., p, 106.

436 Pierpoint, Mary, "Was Frank Baum a racist or just the creator of Oz?" *Indian Country Today*, 12 September 2018.

437 Volkan, Vamik, *Killing in the Name of Identity*. p. 152.

438 Armstrong, Karen., *Fields of Blood: Religion and the History of Violence*. Albert A. Knopf Inc., 2014, p. 303.

439 Dubensky, Joyce (ed), *Peacemakers in Action: Profiles of Religion in Conflict Resolution*. Cambridge University Press, 2016, p. 500.

440 Ibid.

441 Reiff, David, *In Praise of Forgetting*. Yale University Press, 2016, p. 118.

442 Ibid., p. 117.

443 Ibid., p. 64.

444 Volkan, Vamik, *Killing in the Name of Identity*. p. 144.

445 Shaukat, Omar, "Reading and Debating the Qur'an with ISIS." pp. 30-31.

446 Hoffer, Eric, *The True Believer: Thoughts on the Nature of Mass Movements*. Harper & Brothers, 1951.

447 Shaukat, Omar, "Reading and Debating the Qur'an with ISIS." p. 26.

[448] Miles-Yepez, Netanel, et al. *The Common Heart: An Experience of Interreligious Dialogue.* Lantern Books, 2006.

[449] Ibid., p. 59.

[450] Charleston, Steven, *Ladder to the Light: An Indigenous Elder's Meditations on Hope and Courage.* 2021.

[451] Ibid., p. 76.

[452] Serlin, Illene A. et al., *Integrated Care for the Traumatized: A Whole-Person Approach.* 2019

[453] Sherwood, Harriet, "Religion in the US 'worth more than Google and Apple combined.'" *The Guardian*, September 2016.

[454] Ibid.

[455] Ellis, Hannah, "Jesus statue smashed in spate of attacks on India's Christian community." *The Guardian*, 27 December 2021.

[456] Ibid.

[457] Wang, Qunyong and Xinyu Lin, "Does religious beliefs affect economic growth? Evidence from provincial-level panel data in China." China Economic Review, December 2014.

[458] Ibid.

[459] Pew Research Center, "The Global Religious Landscape." 2012.

[460] Southwick, Steven M. and Dennis S. Charney, *Resilience: The Science of Mastering Life's Greatest Challenges.* Cambridge University Press, 2018.

[461] Gandhi, Mahatma. *Peace: The Words and Inspiration of Mahatma Gandhi.* Blue Mountain Press, 2007, pp.34.

462 Gettleman, Jeffery, and Suhasini Raj, "India's Christians Attacked Under Anti-Conversion Laws." *The New York Times*, 23 December 2021.

463 Ibid.

464 Ellis, Hannah, "Jesus statue smashed in spate of attacks on India's Christian community." *The Guardian*, 27 December 2021.

465 Mufti Taqi Usmani.

466 Interview with Ahmed Hamo by Sister Makrina Finlay and co-author Jerry White, January 2022.

ACKNOWLEDGMENTS

This book would not have been written if not for David Ford, OBE, Regius Professor of Divinity Emeritus at the University of Cambridge, and Peter Ochs, the Edgar M. Bronfman Professor of Modern Judaic Studies at the University of Virginia. David introduced us (the coauthors) in London. He and Peter cofounded the Scriptural Reasoning movement, one of our inspirations for the concept for a Global Covenant of religions. We are also grateful for the encouragement of our mutual covenantal friends: Aref Nayed, Chinmay Pandya, William Vendley, and Sister Makrina Finlay, among others.

Direct descendants of the Prophet Muhammad, the Hashemite Royal Family of Jordan, also deserve our gratitude. H.M. King Abdullah II and H.R.H. Prince Ghazi bin Muhammad invited us to join faith leaders and other subject experts at the Dead Sea to address the roots of religion-related violence. They helped us move from theory to action, putting together the first draft of a UN resolution to mention religicide in the context of international law. Jordan has been a leader in the promotion of interreligious understanding, including the introduction of the UN World Interfaith Harmony Week, an event observed annually during the first week of February.

We are indebted to the University of Virginia (UVA). Ian Baucom, former dean of arts and sciences and now UVA provost, together with Francesca Fiorani, former associate dean of arts and sciences, created space for transdisciplinary research on religion, politics, and conflict in Charlottesville. They appointed coauthor Jerry White in 2015 as a professor of practice, inviting him to deliver the James W. Richard Lectures, an opportunity to synthesize his research to assess the positive role religion can play in strategic peace-building.

It took a village of dedicated researchers and fact-checkers to deliver this complicated book. Our gratitude extends to UVA research coordinator Jordan Crivella and her teammate Emily Engebretson, who were with us from the beginning. They helped coordinate support from their fellow students: Kat Descamp-Renner, Fiona Moriarty, Jule Voss, Catherine McHugh, Rebecca Shiloff, Stephen Luckoff, and Mohammed Muslim.

We were tutored by Benedictine Sister Makrina Finlay from St. Scholastika Abbey in Dinklage, Germany, an expert champion for Yazidi rights and asylum in Germany and internationally. We are grateful for covenantal insight from Robbie Leigh and support from Leah Salzman. We were blessed and schooled firsthand from Yazidi religicide survivors Hamo and Ahmed Shammo and their extended family in Iraq, supporting our initiative to regenerate their community and land in Nineveh Province.

UVA graduate Reuben Shank offered a critique of our preliminary draft manuscript, as did Dr. Sohail Nakhooda, with decades of interfaith experience. We are grateful and offer a shout-out for the encouragement from Monica Sharma, Jay Hughes, Ambassador Rick Barton, Myron Eshowsky, Sheetal Vaidya, Erica Taylor, Christiana Gammon Richardson, James Hodge, and Chris Googoo. Another bow goes to Tony Sorci and his mother Viki Blackgoat, who shared with us the ancestral wisdom of the late Navajo dissenter and role model, Roberta Blackgoat. Thank you all.

Every good book welcomes talented editors. We were fortunate to have American University Professor Kelly Gammon White and Adam Bellow, executive editor at Bombardier Books, imprint of Post Hill Press. We have tried, however imperfectly, to present our vision for a more peaceful and just world that protects the vital importance of religion and celebrates the wisdom of biodiversity and polyculture—creation itself.